ALL FIRED UP!

All Fired Up!

OUTDOOR AND INDOOR GRILLING

MARGARET HOWARD

FIREFLY BOOKS

A Firefly Book

Published by Firefly Books 1998

Cataloguing in Publication Data

Howard, Margaret
      All fired up: outdoor and indoor grilling

Includes index
ISBN 1-55209-217-8

1. Barbecue cookery.   I. Title

TX840.B3H68 1998   641.7'6   C97-932807-1

Design: Counterpunch/Linda Gustafson
Editor: Ruth Pincoe
Production: Denise Schon Books Inc.
Front cover photograph, barbecued chicken: Skip Dean

Published in Canada in 1998
by Firefly Books Ltd.
3680 Victoria Park Avenue
Willowdale, Ontario
Canada M2H 3K1

Published in the United States in 1998
by Firefly Books (U.S.) Inc.
P.O. Box 1338, Ellicott Station
Buffalo, New York
U S A 14205

Printed and bound in Canada by Friesens, Altona, Manitoba

Printed on acid-free paper

Contents

Introduction to Grilling

THIS BOOK IS DESIGNED to get people "fired up" about grilling. It tells all you really need to know to get fun and satisfaction from your barbecue grill, whether it's charcoal or gas-fired, outdoors on your deck or indoors on your kitchen range. The book deals with meats, poultry, fish and vegetables and the different methods of grilling them – direct, indirect, spit roasting and kebabs. It also covers all the elements that complete the meal – appetizers and other starters, side dishes, marinades, bastes, rubs, pastes, sauces and desserts. In this book, you will find all the ingredients for a complete grilled meal, including suggested menus.

What is grilling, and how does it differ from barbecuing? Although often used interchangeably, these two terms are quite opposite. Grilling uses high temperatures for fast cooking. Barbecuing uses low temperatures for slow cooking. True barbecuing is done with a fire of various kinds of wood in the same enclosure but a distance away from the food. The fire imparts a rich, smoky flavor to the food. Barbecuing is a much slower process than grilling, and requires greater patience. Few of us have the time in our busy lives to wait out the long cooking times of a true barbecue. Nor do we possess the necessary equipment.

This book is about grilling, and the terms grilling and grill are used throughout. However, many recipes do use indirect grilling – a method that removes the food from close contact with the heat source for a longer cooking period. It's not barbecue, but it's a delicious compromise.

Why do we grill? Perhaps we are led by some primeval instinct. No one knows exactly when people first started cooking food over a fire, but it was certainly several millennia ahead of the microwave oven. Some scholars date the practice back 100,000 years, when our ancestors first discovered that meat placed over hot embers became tender and released its natural juices. A more likely answer is that grilling is a lot of fun. It moves meal preparation out of the sometimes humdrum drudgery of the kitchen to a more festive outdoor setting of the backyard with family and friends. Grilling often shifts the cooking responsibility from mom to dad to the delight of both parties. Grilling implies a more casual approach to both meal preparation and dining. And of course, food cooked on an outdoor grill tastes good anytime of the year. The grill imparts a taste to food that no other cooking method quite duplicates. That's why many of us grill all year round.

Equipment

Grilling can be enjoyed on the simplest of grills, but the "bells and whistles" do add a lot of convenience. Purists tend to stay with their charcoal grills and would never even consider using any other medium. Others, taken with the convenience of gas, feel that it is the only way to go. Some people choose the indoor grilling option available with a few kitchen ranges. This allows comfortable grilling in inclement weather and makes grilling available to apartment dwellers who may not have access to an outdoor setting. The choice is yours, the ultimate pleasure is the same.

In addition to a grill, you will need long handled tongs, spatulas and basting brushes, fire-proof oven mitts, a meat thermometer for roasts and a wire brush for cleaning grill racks. You really do not need a fork; piercing the meat allows loss of precious juices. Perforated cooking trays and baskets are useful for cooking foods that would otherwise fall through the grill racks. Heavy-duty aluminum foil helps to maintain neat and tidy grilling. Metal or wooden skewers are necessary for kebab grilling. And finally, charcoal grillers need a starter chimney or an electric starter to get everything going.

There are two ways to grill – direct and indirect. Kebab grilling is a variation of direct grilling, while spit grilling is a variation of indirect grilling. The grilling method to be used is specified in each recipe.

Direct Grilling

Direct grilling, or fast grilling, is used primarily for foods that take less than 25 minutes to cook. Steaks, burgers, chops, chicken breasts, halved broiler-fryer chickens and fish fillets are examples. In direct grilling, food is placed directly above the heat source and is usually only turned once. The grill lid may be open or closed. I prefer direct grilling with the lid down because it is more efficient and it keeps the grilled side of the meat warm after it is turned, particularly in cold and windy weather. Direct grilling produces foods with more browning than is the case with indirect grilling.

Indirect Grilling

Indirect grilling, or slow grilling, is used for roasts, whole poultry, thick meats, game, ham and some vegetables. In indirect grilling, food is not cooked directly over the heat source and the grill is always covered so that heat circulates evenly – much like an oven. No turning or basting is required, and drippings are caught in a pan below the food being cooked. Often water or another liquid such as beer, wine, broth or juice is placed in the pan. The liquid and the drippings vaporize, basting the food automatically. There are no flare-ups which could ruin food. Because covered indirect grilling resembles oven roasting, it is essential to keep temperatures stable. Thus it is a "no-peek" cooking method. I have found that indirect grilling guarantees the slow, even heat needed to produce moist, tender meat with a pleasantly crisp exterior.

Indirect grilling on a gas grill: Place a shallow metal pan of water (or other liquid) under the grill rack on which the food is to be placed. Preheat the covered grill for 5 to 10 minutes. Open the lid, place food on a lightly oiled rack over the pan of water, turn off the burner under the pan, but leave remaining burner(s) on. Cover the grill, and cook for the length of time specified in the recipe. The pan of water catches juices from the cooking food that can later be used to add a smoky flavor to sauces and gravies.

Indirect grilling on a charcoal grill: When the coals are covered with a light gray ash and no longer flaming, bank them around the edges of the grill. Place a shallow metal pan of water between coals, under the rack. Place meat on the lightly oiled rack over the pan of water. Cover the grill and cook for the length of time specified in the recipe. To keep heat stable, preheat new coals at the edge of the fire before adding them to hot coals.

Here are a few tips to keep you from having too hot a time at your next outdoor grill-fest.

Grilling Tips

Check your fuel supply before starting. It is embarrassing and inconvenient to run out.

For charcoal grills, build briquettes into a pyramid or place in a charcoal chimney for easy lighting. Use only enough charcoal to form a single layer under the grill rack. Coals are ready when a gray ash forms and the residue of any fire starter used is burned off. You may wish to keep an area with fewer coals to provide a spot for food that is cooking too quickly.

Preheat gas grills for 5 to 10 minutes.

If you need to estimate the temperature of your grill, place your hand about 4 inches (10 cm) above the coals, lava rocks or sear pan, and calculate the temperature by how long you can keep it there – 5 seconds is low, 4 seconds is medium, 3 seconds is medium-high, 2 seconds is high.

Since grilling is a dry-heat cooking technique,

it is best to choose better quality, more tender cuts of marbled meats. However, if you have chosen less tender cuts with less marbling, marinating techniques come to the rescue.

To marinate food prior to cooking, place the food in a resealable plastic bag, pour the marinade over the food, seal the bag, and turn it to cover the food evenly. This method keeps the marinade flowing around and over the food and minimizes the mess. Refrigerate until just before cooking starts. Remove food from the marinade for grilling. You can bring the remaining marinade to a boil for 5 minutes, then pour it over the cooked food or brush it on during the cooking. (See safety tip below.)

Choose cuts that are at least ¾-inch (2 cm) thick. Thicker cuts grill better than thinner cuts.

Trim excess fat from meat and discard. If some fat remains on steaks or chops, be sure to nick the outside edges at 2-inch (5 cm) intervals to help prevent meat from curling during grilling. Be careful to avoid cutting into the meat.

Lightly oil the grill rack or spray with a non-stick vegetable coating before placing food on rack to prevent foods sticking and to facilitate cleanup.

Apply bastes and sauces part way through cooking; excessive amounts will fall into the heat source causing flare-ups that often scorch the food above. Excess sugar-based sauces caramelize on the grill creating a clean-up chore.

As a general rule, turn steaks and hamburgers only once during cooking, because each turning causes loss of juices.

Salt meat only after it is turned or when cooking is complete to retain tasty juices.

Check doneness of food earlier than indicated in a recipe; cooking times will be affected by the type of grill, the temperature and wind.

Safety Tips

Store gas cylinders or starter fluids outdoors and away from heat sources. Be sure gas cylinder connectors and regulators are in good condition and hooked up according to manufacturer's instructions.

Open the gas grill lid before lighting.

Use only fire starters that are certified for use on outdoor grills. Never use gasoline or other flammable liquids to start charcoal. Never spray fire starter on hot coals.

Do not line the bottom of either a gas or charcoal grill with aluminum foil. It will obstruct airflow.

Never use a grill in an enclosed area. Do not grill too close to trees, deck railings or roof overhangs.

Children should never be allowed to operate a grill. Don't leave a lit grill unattended.

Use appropriate tools for the job-long handled tongs, spatulas and basting brushes, and fireproof oven mitts.

Keep a water-filled spray bottle to extinguish minor flare-ups and baking soda for grease flare-ups. Also, make sure a fire extinguisher is readily available.

Trim excess fat from meat to prevent flare-ups. If a fire occurs, cover the grill tightly until the flames subside.

Marinades can be brushed on food during grilling or used as a serving sauce. Be sure to bring the marinade to a boil, and keep boiling for 5 minutes to prevent bacteria growth. Discard any unused marinade.

Remove cooked food from grill to a clean plate to reduce risk of cross-contamination and food poisoning.

Health Concerns

Provided a few precautions are taken, grilling does not present any more health risks than other types of high temperature cooking, such as broiling and pan frying. Furthermore, grilling is a low-fat method of cooking since fat within the meat drains off during grilling. According to cancer authorities, any dangers from grilled food stem from cancer-causing chemicals produced in the smoke from burning fat that drifts over the cooking food and in charring that may occur on the food. To minimize these risks, use lean meats and trim excess fat before cooking to help reduce smoke. Keep the grill rack as far from the heat source as possible, and watch cooking times and temperatures to reduce the danger of charring. Any charring that does occur should be removed from food before eating.

Chicken Satay with Mexican
Cranberry Salsa, page 18

CHAPTER 1

Appetizers and Other Starters

APPETIZERS, LIKE THE PROLOGUE to a play, prepare us for further, even greater delights to come from the grill. The recipes in this section are chosen to excite palates. Most are grilled; the others, such as the soups and salsas, match well with grilled main courses.

Appetizers fit the logistics of the typical outdoor dinner party. Everyone gathers around the grill in anticipation of good things to come. This is your opportunity to build that anticipation with well-chosen appetizers. If you have time, and room on the grill, it's good theatre to grill the appetizers while the main meal cooks. Failing this, appetizers can be grilled beforehand and kept warm in the kitchen oven. Or you might choose an appetizer that doesn't even see the grill, for example, Broccoli Pesto (page 12) or Tapenade (page 13). And then there is soup – a cold soup such as Cucumber Vichyssoise with Dill (page 25) for a hot and steamy summer evening or a hot soup such as Sweet Potato Soup with Portabello Mushrooms (page 22) for brisker spring or fall occasions.

Dips and other clever little appetizers make perfect light preludes to memorable outdoor feasting. The imaginative snacks and inspired breads and soups found in this chapter will satisfy appetites sharpened in the great outdoors. Also, some of the recipes can be used as main courses by simply doubling the quantities or serving larger amounts. Try this with the pork or chicken satays (pages 17 and 18), Italian Provolone and Red Pepper Pizza (page 15), and Dilled Scallops, Bruschetta-style (page 20).

The Versatile Salsas (page 23) are not grilled, but their fresh flavors will really enliven plain grilled meats. Serve them as appetizer dips, and have extra on hand to perk up a grilled chicken leg or a steak. The lively combinations of fresh tastes, colors and textures are magnificent.

Appetizers and starters are also a good basis for tasty luncheon menus. Try Chunky Gazpacho (page 24), Grilled Polenta with Basil and Tomatoes (page 14), and Herbed Italian Loaf (page 27) for your next patio luncheon.

Broccoli Pesto

Pesto sauce need not always be the classic basil variety – broccoli pesto is just as delicious. With its longer growing season, broccoli is available over a longer period of time. This pesto can serve as the basis of a host of different dishes, a few of which are given below.

Broccoli Pesto

3 cups	cut-up broccoli florets and stems	750 mL
2	cloves garlic	2
3 tbsp	extra virgin olive oil	45 mL
⅓ cup	slivered almonds or pine nuts	75 mL
¼ cup	chopped fresh basil or 4 tsp (20 mL) dried	50 mL
⅓ cup	grated Parmesan cheese	75 mL

1 Cook broccoli in boiling water for 4 to 5 minutes or until crisp-tender; drain and cool.
2 In food processor or blender, purée broccoli, garlic, oil, almonds and basil until coarsely chopped. Add cheese; process until well mixed. *Makes 2½ cups (625 mL).*

Uses for Broccoli Pesto

1 *Bruschetta:* Spread Broccoli Pesto over thick slices of Italian bread. Grill for 2 to 3 minutes or until just bubbling and starting to brown. For extra color, add diced tomatoes.
2 *Cream Cheese and Broccoli Pesto Appetizer:* Cream 1 package (125 g) light cream cheese and ½ cup (125 mL) butter or margarine until smooth. In plastic lined bowl, alternately layer one-third cream cheese mixture and one-half Broccoli Pesto, beginning and ending with cheese. Cover and refrigerate until firm. Unmold and serve at room temperature with assorted crackers. Mold smaller amounts in small custard cups and freeze for future use.
3 *Broccoli Vinaigrette:* Prepare a vinaigrette dressing with ⅓ cup (75 mL) extra virgin olive oil, 2 tbsp (25 mL) white wine vinegar and 1 tbsp (15 mL) Broccoli Pesto.
4 *Broccoli Dip:* Stir a small amount of Broccoli Pesto into sour cream or plain yogurt. Serve with vegetable crudités.
5 *Pasta:* Toss Broccoli Pesto with hot cooked pasta. Sprinkle with extra Parmesan cheese, if desired.
6 *Pesto Tomatoes:* Spread Broccoli Pesto on thickly sliced tomatoes. Grill until tomatoes are heated.

Tapenade and Broccoli Pesto

Tapenade

Tapenade, a traditional hors d'oeuvre of Provence, is the most wonderful appetizer. Its name comes from *Tapeno*, the Provençal word for caper, one of the ingredients. Any flavorful black olives can be used, but be sure to buy them in bulk, preferably still sitting in their brine. Serve tapenade spooned over chèvre cheese spread on thin slices of baguette or just on a cracker.

½ lb	kalamata olives, pitted (about ¾ cup/175 mL)	250 g
¼ cup	capers, rinsed and drained	50 mL
¼ cup	anchovy paste	50 mL
2	large cloves garlic	2
2 tbsp	each: olive oil and Cognac or brandy	25 mL
1 tbsp	lemon juice	15 mL
⅛ tsp	each: freshly ground pepper and dry mustard	0.5 mL
1	long baguette, thinly sliced and toasted	1
½ cup	chèvre cheese, softened	125 mL
	Lemon slices	

1 In food processor, process olives, capers, anchovy paste, garlic, olive oil, Cognac and lemon juice with on/off turns until mixture is finely chopped but not smooth. Season to taste with pepper and mustard. Remove to serving bowl and garnish with lemon slices.

2 Arrange toast and cheese on a platter with tapenade bowl in center.
Makes 1½ cups (375 mL).

Grilled Red Pepper and Herb Dip

The smoky-sweet taste of grilled red peppers is incredible in this yogurt-based dip. Enjoy dipping raw vegetables, corn tortillas or baked chips.

1	large sweet red pepper	1
1	clove garlic	1
¼ cup	plain yogurt or sour cream	50 mL
3 tbsp	light mayonnaise	45 mL
2 tsp	red wine vinegar	10 mL
1 tbsp	chopped fresh oregano or 1 tsp (5 mL) dried	15 mL
⅛ tsp	granulated sugar	0.5 mL
	Salt and freshly ground pepper	

1 Preheat grill on medium. Place red pepper on oiled grill rack. Close lid and cook (use Direct Grilling, page 7) for 8 to 10 minutes or until pepper is streaked with brown and tender when pierced; turn frequently. Place in paper bag until cool enough to handle. Remove any blackened skin, stem and seeds and discard.

2 In blender or food processor, purée red pepper, garlic, yogurt and mayonnaise until smooth. Stir in vinegar, oregano and sugar. Season to taste with salt and pepper. Cover and refrigerate for up to one week.
Makes about 1 cup (250 mL).

Tip: Baguette slices can be toasted quickly on the grill rack while other foods are grilling. Tapenade is a great appetizer to keep on hand, and it can also serve as a sauce for full-flavored grilled fish. It freezes well.

Grilled Polenta with Basil and Tomatoes

Thin slices of cornmeal polenta grilled until golden, then topped with tomato bits and basil, make a tasty nibble.

4 cups	chicken broth	1 L
1⅓ cups	yellow cornmeal	325 mL
3	large tomatoes, finely diced	3
½ cup	chopped fresh basil leaves	125 mL
½ cup	grated Parmesan cheese	125 mL
	Salt and freshly ground pepper	

1 In large saucepan, bring broth to a boil over high heat. Gradually stir in cornmeal until thickened. Reduce heat to low and cook, stirring constantly, for about 10 minutes. Spoon into lightly greased 9-x 5-inch (2 L) loaf pan; cool until firm.

2 Remove polenta from pan onto a cutting board. Slice crosswise into 10 thin slices.

3 Preheat grill on medium-high. Place polenta slices on oiled grill rack. Cook (use Direct Grilling, page 7) until golden brown and crisp; turn once. Remove from grill and cut each slice into 4 squares. Top with tomato, basil and cheese; sprinkle lightly with salt and pepper. Serve warm.

Makes 40 pieces.

Onion, Nut and Cheese Bites

Create these delicious small appetizer bites from ingredients usually found in your kitchen.

They can be prepared beforehand to the end of Step 1, covered with a damp tea towel, then grilled at serving time.

1	large onion, halved and thinly sliced (Vidalia or Spanish preferred)	1
1 tbsp	olive oil	15 mL
¼ cup	chopped pecans, almonds or walnuts	50 mL
1 tsp	granulated sugar	5 mL
1 tbsp	Dijon mustard	15 mL
16	slices (½-inch/1 cm thick) French bread stick	16
¾ cup	shredded Cheddar cheese	175 mL

1 In nonstick skillet, cook onion in oil on medium-high heat for about 5 minutes; stir often. Reduce heat, add nuts and sugar; cover and cook for 5 minutes longer or until onion has caramelized and is tender. Stir in mustard. Spoon onion mixture on bread slices and sprinkle with cheese.

2 Preheat grill on medium-high. Place bread on oiled grill rack. Cook, uncovered (use Direct Grilling, page 7), for 3 to 4 minutes or until bread is warm and toasted and cheese has started to melt. Watch carefully to avoid overcooking.

Makes 16 slices.

Italian Provolone and Red Pepper Pizza

For a backyard gathering, prepare lots of vegetables, shredded cheese and seasonings and invite guests to add their own toppings to an Italian-style gourmet flatbread base.

1	round Italian-style gourmet flatbread (14 oz/400 g)	1
1 tbsp	olive oil	15 mL
2 cups	shredded Provolone cheese	500 mL
1 cup	roasted sweet red peppers, cut into long, thin slices*	250 mL
1 cup	broccoli florets, blanched	250 mL
1/3 cup	chopped red onion	75 mL
1/4 cup	grated Parmesan cheese	50 mL
2 tbsp	pine nuts	25 mL
1 tsp	dried oregano or 1 tbsp (15 mL) chopped fresh	5 mL
1/8 tsp	freshly ground pepper	0.5 mL

1 Brush flatbread with oil. Sprinkle with Provolone cheese. Top with red pepper, broccoli, onion, Parmesan cheese, pine nuts, oregano and pepper.

2 Preheat grill on medium-high. Place pizza directly on oiled grill rack. Close lid and cook (use Indirect Grilling, page 7) for about 20 minutes or until cheese starts to melt and vegetables are hot. Remove flatbread from grill and cut into thin wedges.

Makes 16 servings.

* See grilling instructions for peppers on page 169.

Roasted Garlic

This recipe is so good you may want to do more than one garlic head. Out of the grill season, roast garlic in a moderate oven (375°F/190°C).

1	large head garlic	1
1 tbsp	olive oil	15 mL
	Sliced sourdough bread	

1 Cut the top off the garlic head and place root side down in a small aluminum foil pan. Sprinkle with oil and cover pan with foil.

2 Preheat grill on medium-high. Place pan on grill rack. Close lid and cook (use Direct Grilling, page 7) for about 30 minutes or until garlic is soft. Remove from grill. Cut a thin slice from the top so that the garlic cloves can be scooped out and spread on sliced sourdough bread.

Makes enough roasted garlic to spread on 8 bread slices.

Pork Satay with Spicy Peanut Sauce,
page 17

Pork Satay with Spicy Peanut Sauce

Satay – marinated cubes of meat, fish or poultry threaded on skewers and grilled – is a traditional Indonesian snack, usually served with a spicy peanut sauce. You can serve this satay as an appetizer or a main course, and the peanut sauce is also delicious on a noodle salad with vegetables.

Marinade

1 lb	pork tenderloin	500 g
½ tsp	grated lime peel	2 mL
1 tbsp	each: lime juice, water and liquid honey	15 mL
1 tsp	curry powder	5 mL
1	clove garlic, crushed	1

Peanut Sauce

3 tbsp	smooth peanut butter	45 mL
2 tbsp	each: liquid honey, light soy sauce and water	25 mL
1 tbsp	rice vinegar	15 mL
1 tbsp	minced gingerroot	15 mL
⅛ tsp	hot red pepper sauce	0.5 mL

1 Trim visible fat from meat and discard. Cut meat into 4 x ½-inch (10 x 1 cm) strips. (You should have about 16 pieces.)

2 *For marinade:* In small bowl, combine lime peel and juice, water, honey, curry powder and garlic; add pork and toss to coat. Cover and marinate in refrigerator for 1 to 3 hours.

3 *For sauce:* In small bowl, whisk or blend together peanut butter, honey, soy sauce, water, vinegar, gingerroot and hot sauce until smooth. Taste and adjust seasonings if desired.

4 Remove meat from marinade; reserve marinade. Place marinade in small saucepan, bring to a boil, reduce heat and cook for 5 minutes; keep warm. Thread pork on 16 soaked wooden skewers.

5 Preheat grill on medium-high. Place skewers on lightly oiled grill rack. Close lid and cook (use Direct Grilling, page 7) for about 6 minutes per side or until pork is cooked through. Remove pork from skewers and serve with peanut sauce for dipping or drizzled over.

Makes 16 appetizers.

Suggested Menu: Serve the satay as an appetizer with raw vegetables or as a main course with rice pilaf.

Tip: For appetizers, it is best to use wooden or bamboo skewers. Be sure to soak them in water for at least 30 minutes before using to prevent skewers burning. Metal skewers are also good; they are reusable and possibly preferred when the satay is a main course.

Chicken Satay with Mexican Cranberry Salsa

This marriage of Mexican and Asian brings an exciting world of flavors to your backyard cook-out. Although we suggest using the salsa with a chicken satay, try it wherever you would use cranberry sauce.

Mexican Cranberry Salsa

2 cups	fresh or frozen cranberries	500 mL
¾ cup	orange juice	175 mL
1	sweet yellow or red pepper, seeded and finely chopped	1
1	hot yellow pepper, seeded and finely chopped	1
1 cup	finely chopped onion (1 large)	250 mL
1	clove garlic, finely chopped	1
¼ cup	each: red wine vinegar and packed brown sugar	50 mL
½ tsp	each: ground cumin and pickling salt	2 mL
½ cup	loosely packed fresh cilantro leaves, coarsely chopped	125 mL

Chicken

½ lb	boneless, skinless chicken breasts	250 g

1 *For salsa:* In medium saucepan, combine cranberries, orange juice, sweet pepper, hot pepper, onion, garlic, vinegar, sugar, cumin and salt. Bring to a boil, reduce heat and cook, uncovered, for 15 minutes or until mixture thickens and vegetables are tender. Cool, then stir in cilantro. Pour salsa into sealed container and store in refrigerator.

2 *For chicken:* Cut chicken breasts into thin strips. Preheat grill on high. Thread chicken strips on 6 metal or soaked wooden skewers. Place skewers on oiled grill rack. Close lid and cook (use Direct Grilling, page 7) for about 7 minutes or until chicken is golden brown and no longer pink inside; turn often. Serve satays with salsa.
Makes 6 appetizer servings and about 2 cups (500 mL) salsa.

Tips:

1 Refrigerate unused salsa for another use (see page 75). Salsa will keep, refrigerated, for up to one month.

2 Use fresh and frozen cranberries interchangeably. Beef strips may be a replacement for the chicken with this salsa.

Seafood Chowder

This recipe utilizes a technique of famous chefs. Instead of thickening the soup with a butter-flour roux, garden-fresh cooked vegetables are puréed and added back into the soup providing extra flavor as well as thickness.

2 tbsp	butter or margarine, divided	25 mL
1	large stalk celery, chopped, divided	1
1	large onion, chopped, divided	1
2	cloves garlic, minced, divided	2
3 cups	tomato juice	750 mL
½ tsp	each: salt, dried oregano, basil and thyme	2 mL
¼ tsp	freshly ground pepper	1 mL
12	jumbo shrimp, deveined	12
12	sea scallops	12
2	green onions, sliced	2
1 tbsp	rice vinegar	15 mL
	Chopped fresh cilantro	

1 In large saucepan, melt 1 tbsp (15 mL) butter. Add half of the chopped celery, onion and garlic; cook for 5 minutes, stirring occasionally. Stir in tomato juice and seasonings; cover and cook for 10 minutes. Cool slightly. Purée in small batches in blender or food processor until smooth; reserve.

2 In same saucepan, cook remaining celery, onion and garlic in 1 tbsp (15 mL) butter for 5 minutes. Add reserved purée, and cook for 5 minutes. Add shrimp and scallops and cook for 5 minutes longer or until seafood is opaque and vegetables are cooked. Stir in green onions and vinegar; heat slowly. Sprinkle each serving with chopped cilantro.

Makes 6 servings.

Seafood Chowder

Dilled Scallops, Bruschetta-style

Traditional bruschetta are made by rubbing slices of toasted bread with garlic and drizzling with olive oil. Often a tomato-garlic mixture is served on the toasted bread. This recipe adds grilled scallops with fantastic results. A light Italian red wine, slightly chilled, goes well with this rather flavorful appetizer.

8	large scallops, cut in half	8
1 tbsp	each: olive oil and lime juice	15 mL
1	green onion, finely chopped	1
1	clove garlic, minced	1
2 tbsp	chopped fresh dill	25 mL
	Lemon pepper	
1 cup	diced tomatoes	250 mL
	Salt and freshly ground pepper	
4	thick slices Italian bread	4
	Chopped fresh dill and lemon wedges	

1 In small bowl, toss scallop halves with oil, lime juice, onion, garlic, dill and lemon pepper; set aside for 15 minutes.

2 In second bowl, combine tomatoes, salt and pepper.

3 Preheat grill on medium. Toast bread on grill rack on both sides until golden brown; keep warm.

4 Remove scallops from lime mixture and place on grill rack. Close lid and cook (use Direct Grilling, page 7) for about 5 minutes or just until opaque; turn once. Remove from grill. Top each toast slice with some tomato mixture and 4 scallop halves. Cut each slice into 4 squares and serve with chopped dill and lemon wedges.

Makes 16 squares.

Dilled Scallops, Bruschetta-style, page 20

Sweet Potato Soup with Portobello Mushrooms

This wonderful soup is a sweet potato version of the more familiar pumpkin soup. While similar, it has a distinctly sweet potato taste. Sautéed mushrooms add visual and flavor impact.

6 cups	chicken broth, divided	1.5 L
1 cup	sliced leeks (white part only)	250 mL
1	piece gingerroot, (1 inch/2.5 cm), minced	1
3	cloves garlic, minced	3
2	large sweet potatoes, peeled and cubed	2
1 tsp	curry powder	5 mL
	Salt and freshly ground pepper	
1 tbsp	canola oil	15 mL
6	large portobello mushrooms, cleaned and sliced	6
	Chopped fresh parsley	

1 In large saucepan, heat ½ cup (125 mL) chicken broth. Add leeks, gingerroot and garlic; cook, covered until tender. Add remaining stock and sweet potatoes. Bring to a boil, reduce heat and simmer covered for about 20 minutes or until potatoes are tender.

2 Remove from heat, cool slightly. In food processor or blender, purée in small batches until smooth. Season with curry powder, salt and pepper to taste. Return soup to saucepan and heat to serving temperature.

3 Meanwhile, heat oil in nonstick skillet; sauté mushrooms until golden brown. Garnish each bowl of soup with mushrooms and parsley. *Makes 8 servings.*

DIRECT GRILLING

Warmed Chèvre with Pine Nut and Tomato Salsa

Warming brings out the lively tart flavor of chèvre cheese and the toasty pungency of pine nuts. Serve this simple elegant appetizer with your favorite summer wine as you wait for dinner to finish grilling.

Tomato Salsa

1 ½ cups	finely chopped tomato (2 medium)	375 mL
½	jalapeño pepper, seeded and finely chopped	½
¼ cup	fresh basil leaves, chopped	50 mL
2 tbsp	finely chopped onion	25 mL
1 tbsp	red wine vinegar	15 mL
1	clove garlic, minced	1
¼ tsp	freshly ground pepper	1 mL
5 oz.	chèvre cheese	150 g
3 tbsp	pine nuts	45 mL
1	small baguette, thinly sliced	1

1 *For salsa:* In bowl, combine tomato, jalapeño pepper, basil, onion, vinegar, garlic and pepper. Cover and refrigerate for at least 30 minutes or up to 1 day.

2 Place cheese in shallow oven-proof casserole. Press pine nuts into surface. Preheat grill on medium-high. Place casserole on grill rack (use Direct Grilling, page 7) and heat for 5 to 8 minutes or until cheese is warm and softened.

3 Place cheese dish in center of serving plate surrounded by baguette slices and a bowl of salsa. To serve, spread bread with warm cheese and pine nuts; top with a spoonful of salsa.

Makes about 1½ cups (375 mL) salsa and 24 appetizers.

Versatile Salsas

No kitchen should be without several salsas for very long. They are so versatile, serving as appetizer dips or as accompaniments to grilled meats, fish and poultry. These two salsas, one vegetable, the other fruit, are fresh and quickly made.

Fresh Multi-Vegetable Salsa

1 cup	finely chopped tomatoes	250 mL
½ cup	finely chopped seedless cucumber	125 mL
¼ cup	finely chopped sweet green pepper	50 mL
2 tbsp	finely chopped red onion	25 mL
1 to 2 tbsp	chopped fresh cilantro	15 to 25 mL
1	small jalapeño pepper, seeded and minced	1
1	clove garlic, minced	1
1 tsp	each: lemon or lime juice and tomato paste	5 mL
¼ tsp	salt	1 mL
¼ tsp	each: dried basil and oregano or 1 tsp (5 mL) fresh	1 mL
⅛ tsp	freshly ground pepper	0.5 mL

In medium bowl, combine tomatoes, cucumber, green pepper, onion, cilantro, jalapeño, garlic, lemon juice and tomato paste. Stir in seasonings; cover and let stand at room temperature until serving time.

Makes 1½ cups (375 mL).

Mint Variation: Replace cilantro with chopped fresh mint.

Island Salsa

1 cup	diced mango	250 mL
½ cup	diced papaya	125 mL
½ cup	crushed pineapple	125 mL
½ cup	finely chopped sweet red pepper	125 mL
½ cup	finely chopped onion	125 mL
¼ cup	chopped fresh cilantro	50 mL
1 to 2	small jalapeño peppers, seeded and finely chopped	1 to 2
2 tbsp	lime juice	25 mL
	Salt and freshly ground pepper	

In bowl, combine mango, papaya, pineapple, red pepper, onion, cilantro and jalapeño.
Stir in lime juice, salt and pepper to taste. Cover and refrigerate for 3 hours before serving to develop the flavors. Stir before serving.

Makes about 3 cups (750 mL).

Chunky Gazpacho

Were the Spanish thinking of gazpacho when they wrote the proverb "Of soup and love, the first is best"? The fresh taste and bright color of tomatoes highlight this famous cold soup.

1½ cups	tomato juice	375 mL
4	tomatoes, chopped	4
1	seedless cucumber, diced	1
¼ cup	chopped sweet green pepper	50 mL
¼ cup	minced green onion	50 mL
2 tbsp	olive oil	25 mL
1 to 2	cloves garlic, crushed	1 to 2
1 tbsp	red wine vinegar	15 mL
½ tsp	hot pepper sauce	2 mL
	Chopped fresh chives	

1 In large bowl, combine tomato juice, tomatoes, cucumber, green pepper and green onion. Stir in oil, garlic, vinegar and hot pepper sauce.

2 Remove one-half of mixture to food processor bowl and process until smooth. Return to remaining vegetables.

3 Cover and refrigerate for several hours until chilled. To serve, garnish each bowl with chopped chives.

Makes 4 to 6 servings.

> **Variation:** For a summer weekend lunch, my good friend, home economist Shirley Ann Holmes turned gazpacho into a main course soup by adding jumbo shrimp and a topping of creamed mayonnaise and feta cheese. What delicious additions!

Beet Borscht

Beet Borscht

Borscht is the most famous of the Slav soups. Some cooks add horseradish and so do I, as it definitely adds that extra "zing." Borscht is always served with a sour cream garnish and has a most wonderful flavor.

4 cups	beef broth	1 L
3	large beets, peeled and diced	3
1	small onion, finely chopped	1
1 tbsp	each: lemon juice and horseradish	15 mL

½ tsp	salt	2 mL
¼ tsp	freshly ground pepper	1 mL
	Sour cream or plain yogurt	
	Chopped fresh dill	

1 In large saucepan, bring broth to a boil. Add beets, onion, lemon juice, horseradish, salt and pepper. Cook for 20 minutes or until vegetables are tender. Remove from stove and allow to cool for a short time.

2 In food processor, process half of soup until smooth. Return to remaining soup and heat to serving temperature. Taste and adjust seasonings if needed.

3 Garnish each bowl with a large dollop of sour cream or yogurt and sprinkle with chopped fresh dill.

Makes 7 cups (1.75 L), about 6 servings.

Tip: Although borscht is usually served hot, chilled borscht is also very refreshing on a warm summer day.

Cucumber Vichyssoise with Dill

Cucumber Vichyssoise with Dill

Fresh cucumber and dill replace leeks and chives in this version of vichyssoise. It makes a cool introduction to a hot summer grill.

¼ cup	butter or margarine	50 mL
½ cup	chopped onion	125 mL
3 cups	chicken broth	750 mL
2	medium potatoes, peeled and chopped	2
1	large seedless cucumber, coarsely chopped	1
	Salt and freshly ground pepper	
½ cup	buttermilk	125 mL
	Chopped fresh dill or fresh flowers	

1 In large saucepan, melt butter; add onion and cook for about 5 minutes or until softened. Add chicken broth and potatoes. Cover and cook for 15 minutes or until potato is tender. Remove from heat and cool slightly.

2 In food processor or blender, purée soup with cucumber in several small batches until smooth. Season to taste with salt and pepper, add buttermilk and chill. Sprinkle each serving with dill.

Makes eight ¾-cup (175 mL) servings.

Variation: *Cream of Cucumber Soup:* Reheat soup to serving temperature.

Crostini with Grilled Vegetables and Mozzarella

Crostini are like thin bruschetta. Grill crostini on one rack and serve them as appetizers while the main course is cooking on the other rack. If your grill does not have a lid, place foil over the baking pan so that the vegetables stew rather than sauté.

2 tbsp	each: butter or margarine and olive oil	25 mL
2	medium carrots, thinly sliced	2
1	medium onion, thinly sliced	1
1	sweet green pepper, seeded and thinly sliced lengthwise	1
2	large cloves garlic, minced	2
2	yellow squash, thinly sliced on the diagonal	2
4	plum tomatoes, diced	4
½ cup	fresh basil or parsley, minced	125 mL
	Salt and freshly ground pepper	
1 cup	shredded mozzarella cheese	250 mL
1	clove garlic, halved	1
1	loaf French bread, cut into sixteen ½-inch (1 cm) slices	1

1 Preheat grill on medium-high. In oblong baking pan, heat butter and oil on grill rack. Add carrots and onion. Close lid and cook (use Direct Grilling, page 7) for about 5 minutes or until onions are softened; stir well. Add green pepper and garlic; close lid and cook for about 3 minutes; stir. Add squash and tomatoes; close lid and cook for about 4 minutes or until all vegetables are just tender.

2 Stir in basil, salt and pepper to taste. Sprinkle with cheese; cover and cook for about 3 minutes or until cheese melts. Remove pan from grill, cover and keep warm.

3 Rub cut sides of garlic over 1 side of each bread slice. Place bread slices around outer edge of grill rack; toast for 1 minute or until bread is golden; turn once. Transfer bread to serving platter. Top each slice with a portion of grilled vegetables and serve immediately.
Makes 6 to 8 servings.

Gourmet Mushroom Bruschetta

Bruschetta, also known as grilled bread, has become very popular. The outdoor grill is a perfect way to cook bruschetta for either a luncheon picnic on the deck or an appetizer before dinner. Use different breads such as the commercial and readily available gourmet-style flatbreads or a crusty Italian loaf.

1 tbsp	olive oil	15 mL
½	small onion, finely chopped	½
2	cloves garlic, minced	2
¾ lb	button, shiitake, oyster or portobello mushrooms, sliced	375 g
1 tbsp	each: chopped fresh basil and tarragon or 1 tsp (5 mL) dried	15 mL
½ tsp	freshly ground pepper	2 mL
⅛ tsp	salt	0.5 mL

2 tbsp	chopped fresh cilantro	25 mL
½ cup	chèvre cheese, softened	125 mL
3 tbsp	light cream cheese, softened	45 mL
1	plain gourmet Italian-style flatbread	1
	(14 oz/400 g)	
	Fresh basil leaves	

1 In nonstick skillet, heat oil over medium-high heat. Cook onion and garlic for about 2 minutes. Add mushrooms, basil, tarragon and pepper. Cook for about 8 minutes or until mushroom liquid evaporates. Add salt to taste; stir in cilantro and reserve.

2 In bowl, blend together cheeses. (You may need to add a small amount of milk to have a consistency soft enough for spreading.) Spread one side of flatbread with cheese mixture. Top with mushroom mixture.

3 Preheat grill on medium. Place bread on grill rack and cook (use Direct Grilling, page 7) for about 10 minutes or until golden and cheese has started to melt. Remove from grill, cut into 10 to 12 thin wedges. Top each with fresh basil leaf and serve.

Makes 10 to 12 servings.

DIRECT GRILLING

Herbed Italian Loaf

Herbed bread toasted on the grill makes a wonderful appetizer. Cooking appetizers and the main meal on the grill allows you to remain outside with your guests throughout most of the meal preparation.

2 tbsp	each: butter and olive oil	25 mL
¼ cup	finely minced green onion	50 mL
2 tbsp	each: finely minced fresh dill	25 mL
	and parsley	
1	clove garlic, crushed	1
⅛ tsp	crushed red pepper flakes	0.5 mL
1	large crusty Italian loaf	1
⅓ cup	grated Parmesan cheese	75 mL

1 In nonstick skillet, heat butter and oil over medium heat. Cook onion for 2 minutes; add dill, parsley and garlic and cook for 2 minutes or until wilted. Stir in pepper flakes; let cool.

2 Preheat grill on medium. Cut bread in half lengthwise. Toast bread, cut side down, on grill for about 2 minutes or until golden brown. Remove from grill and spread each half with herbed mixture. Sprinkle with cheese, return to grill and heat (use Direct Grilling, page 7) for 3 to 4 minutes or until underside is toasted. Remove and cut crosswise into slices.

Makes 8 to 10 servings.

Other International Breads:

1 *Garlicky Bread:* Thickly slice crusty Italian bread and rub with cut garlic clove; spread lightly with either butter or olive oil. Heat on grill rack until toasted.

2 *Focaccia:* Grill a gourmet flatbread or focaccia until golden brown; place in basket for guests to pull chunks apart for munching and dipping. To add an extra touch, provide a dish of a fruity olive oil mixed with a small amount of balsamic vinegar for dipping. The focaccia can also be split in half and sandwiched with Grilled Sweet Peppers (page 169).

3 *Bruschetta:* Top one of the above breads with a commercial bruschetta mixture or make your own; warm briefly on the grill.

Crab-stuffed Quesadillas

Crabmeat is an interesting departure from the usual meat or refried bean quesadilla filling. Because quesadillas cook so quickly, check the underside frequently. Light grill marks are your clue to doneness. Serve with a fruity white wine.

¼ cup	sun-dried tomatoes (not oil-packed)	50 mL
1	pkg (125 g) light cream cheese, softened	1
½ cup	shredded Monterey Jack or Cheddar cheese	125 mL
1 tbsp	snipped fresh thyme or 1 tsp (5 mL) dried	15 mL
1 tbsp	milk	15 mL
6	7-inch (18-cm) flour tortillas	6
2 tbsp	canola oil	25 mL
½ cup	flaked crabmeat	125 mL
1	green onion, thinly sliced	1

1 In small saucepan, place tomatoes and just enough water to cover; bring to a boil. Reduce heat and simmer for about 2 minutes or until tender; drain and finely chop. Stir together tomatoes, cream cheese, Monterey Jack or Cheddar cheese, thyme and milk in small mixing bowl.

2 Brush one side of three tortillas with some oil. Place tortillas, oil side down, on large baking sheet. Spread cream cheese mixture over each tortilla on baking sheet. Sprinkle each with ⅓ of crab and green onion; top with remaining tortillas. Lightly brush the top tortillas with remaining oil.

3 Preheat grill on medium. Place quesadillas on lightly oiled grill rack. Close lid and cook (use Direct Grilling, page 7) for about 3 minutes or until cream cheese mixture is heated through and tortillas start to brown; turn once halfway through grilling.

4 To serve, cut each tortilla into 6 wedges.
Makes 4 to 6 servings.

Roquefort Appetizer Bread

The pungent, somewhat salty taste of Roquefort combines with the rich sharp flavor of Parmesan in this simple, easy-to-make appetizer.

½ cup	Roquefort or blue cheese salad dressing	125 mL
¼ cup	grated Parmesan cheese	50 mL
4	slices sourdough French bread, cut 1-inch (2.5 cm) thick	4
2 tbsp	diced green chilis or sweet green pepper	25 mL
2 tbsp	grated Parmesan cheese	25 mL

1 In small bowl, combine Roquefort dressing and ¼ cup (50 mL) Parmesan cheese; mix well. Grill one side of each bread slice; spread about 2 tbsp (25 mL) of mixture on grilled side; top with green chilis. Sprinkle each slice with additional Parmesan cheese.

2 Preheat grill on high. Place slices on lightly oiled grill rack, cheese side up. Cook, covered (use Direct Grilling, page 7), for 3 to 5 minutes or until lightly browned on under side. Remove from grill and cut into finger-size pieces; serve hot. (To serve as a lunch entrée, leave whole.)

Makes about 2 dozen.

> **Tip:** Assemble ahead of time, cover with a damp cloth and aluminum foil. Grill just before serving.

DIRECT GRILLING

Grilled Soffrito Bread

Soffrito is an Italian sauce made by sautéing onions, green peppers, garlic and sometimes celery in olive oil with herbs until all ingredients are tender and the mixture is thick. This recipe uses the sauce as an appetizer topping on toasted bread. *Soffrito* can also be used to flavor soups, sauces and meat dishes.

1 cup	chopped sweet red pepper	250 mL
1	small onion, chopped	1
¼ cup	tightly packed fresh cilantro sprigs	50 mL
2	cloves garlic, crushed	2
1 tsp	dried oregano or 1 tbsp (15 mL) fresh	5 mL
½ tsp	cumin seeds or ground cumin	2 mL
1 tbsp	olive oil	15 mL
	Salt and freshly ground pepper	
12	slices Italian bread, ¼-inch (3 mm) thick and halved	12

1 In blender or food processor, purée red pepper, onion, cilantro, garlic, oregano and cumin until coarsely chopped.

2 In small nonstick skillet, heat oil. Add puréed ingredients and cook, stirring frequently for 3 to 5 minutes or until mixture is softened and moisture has evaporated. Season with salt and pepper to taste. (*Soffrito* may be made 2 days ahead, covered and chilled.)

3 Preheat grill on medium. Spread some *soffrito* on one side of each bread slice (reserve any remaining sauce for another use). Place on lightly oiled grill rack. Cook, uncovered (use Direct Grilling, page 7), for about 2 minutes or until golden brown.

4 Transfer *soffrito* bread with tongs to a bread basket and serve warm.

Makes 6 servings.

Moroccan Lamb Chops, page 57

CHAPTER 2

Meats on the Grill

RED MEAT IS A MOST important part of a grill chef's repertoire – after all, it's what many people think of when they consider grilling. This chapter presents a variety of beef, veal, pork and lamb recipes that are sure to enhance your grilling reputation, ranging from Spicy Peppered Sirloin Steak (page 37), through Barbecued Leg of Lamb Persillade (page 60) and Ham Steak with Citrus Salsas (page 39) to Pecan Veal with Armagnac Mushroom Sauce (page 68).

DIRECT GRILLING

All cooking times assume using closed lid grilling. If grilling with the lid open, allow extra time.

Cut and Thickness	Minutes per side			Grill Temperature
	Rare	Medium	Well-Done	
Beef *				
Tender steaks (T-bone, sirloin, etc.)				
1/2–3/4-inch (1 to 2 cm)	3–5	5–7	7–9	medium-high
1-inch (2.5 cm)	5–7	7–9	9–11	medium-high
Less tender (flank, round, etc.)		4–5		medium-high
Burgers**				
1/2-inch (2 cm)			5	medium
Pork				
Loin chops				
1-inch (2.5 cm)			3–6	medium-low to medium
1 1/2-inch (3.5 cm)			6–8	medium-low to medium
Tenderloin			10–12	medium-low to medium
Lamb				
Chops: loin 1-inch (2.5 cm)	5–7	7–8		medium-high
Veal				
Chops: 1-inch (2.5 cm)		7–9		medium-high

*Cook tender steaks such as rib, rib eye, sirloin, tenderloin, T-bone and strip loin to rare, medium or well-done according to individual preference. For maximum tenderness, marinate less tender steaks (such as flank, round, sirloin tip, blade, and cross rib) and do not cook past medium.

**Cook burgers to well-done or until no longer pink inside.

There are also two meat alternatives: Mexican Bean Burgers (page 45) and Indian-style Lentil Vegetable Burger (page 44). These burgers, along with two tofu kebab recipes (pages 134 and 135) in the Kebab Grilling Chapter, provide a modest vegetarian selection.

Meat is not tricky to grill, but it is important to understand why it toughens. Red meats, like poultry and fish, are high protein foods. As proteins cook, the protein molecules draw together, squeezing out any water they hold. So, the longer a once-juicy steak is cooked, the dryer and tougher it becomes. Longer cooking also causes shrinkage and weight loss. With quick grilling of tender meats over high heat, the internal temperature remains low enough during the brief cooking time to prevent the meat from drying out and toughening. Less tender steaks need a tenderizing marinade, but they are still most tender when not cooked past medium. Thus a steak cooked medium-rare will always be more tender and juicy than one that is well-done.

The aspiring grill chef must also understand direct grilling and indirect grilling methods. (Both are discussed on page 7.) Finally, there is the signature of the master grill chef – cross sear markings on meat cuts off the grill. To produce them, move the cut a quarter turn halfway through each side of the cooking process.

Each recipe in this chapter includes details about the individual cooking needs of the particular cut of meat specified. However, let's briefly discuss cooking methods for the major meat categories.

INDIRECT GRILLING

All cooking times assume using closed lid grilling. If grilling with the lid open, allow extra time.

	Rare	Medium	Well-Done	Grill Temperature
Beef *				
Roasts				
minutes per lb/500 g	15–20	25–30	35	medium
internal temperature	140°F (60°C)	160°F (70°C)	170°F (75°C)	
Pork				
Boneless Roasts				
minutes per lb/500 g	—	—	20–30	low
internal temperature			160°F (70°C)	
Bone-in				
minutes per lb/500 g	—	—	15–25	low
internal temperature			160°F (70°C)	
Lamb				
Butterflied Roast				
minutes per lb/500 g	10	12	15–18	medium-high
internal temperature	140°F (60°C)	150°F (65°C)	160°F (70°C)	
Veal				
Roast				
minutes per lb/500 g	—	25–30	35	medium
internal temperature		160°F (70°C)	170°F (75°C)	

Beef

Steaks are generally cooked rare, medium or well-done according to individual preference. To check for doneness, use your finger, rather than a knife. If the steak is soft through to the center, it is rare; if it feels slightly firm but spongy and bouncy, it is medium; if it is firm to the touch, it is well-done.

Tender steaks, such as rib, rib eye, sirloin, tenderloin, T-bone, and strip loin, are more tender cuts that do not require marinating except for flavour addition. Grill these steaks using medium-high heat, turning only once or twice with tongs.

Less tender steaks, such as round, sirloin tip, blade, cross rib, and flank, require tenderizing by marinating for 12 to 24 hours in the refrigerator. (See Chapter 9 for marinade recipes.) For maximum tenderness, do not cook a less tender steak past medium, and let it stand for 5 to 10 minutes before serving. The standing time allows the meat to reabsorb some of its juices, making it more succulent. When serving, slice across the grain.

Lamb and Veal

Treat lamb and veal in much the same way as beef; be careful to not cook it past medium.

Pork

Tender cuts such as chops, boneless loin and tenderloin, give fabulous results, but they should never be overcooked. Today's pork is a very lean meat that becomes tough and dry when overcooked. Tougher cuts such as spareribs need long slow cooking to tenderize the meat.

Steak with Horseradish Marinade,
page 35

Steak with Horseradish Marinade

T-Bone, porterhouse, rib or strip loin steaks may be used in this recipe. The spiciness of the marinade adds a subtle flavour to the meat.

4	steaks (1 inch/2.5 cm thick)	4

Marinade

2 tbsp	red wine vinegar	25 mL
4 tsp	each: horseradish and canola oil	20 mL
1	clove garlic, crushed	1
½ tsp	each: dried thyme and hot pepper sauce	2 mL

1 *For marinade:* In small bowl, combine vinegar, horseradish, oil, garlic, thyme and hot sauce. Trim excess fat from steak and discard. Place in resealable plastic bag; pour marinade over steak and turn to coat. Refrigerate for 12 hours or up to 24; turn steak occasionally.

2 Remove steak from marinade; discard marinade. Preheat grill on medium-high. Place steak on oiled grill rack. Close lid and cook (use Direct Grilling, page 7) for 3 to 5 minutes per side for rare, 5 to 7 for medium and 7 to 9 for well-done. *Makes 4 servings.*

Suggested Menu: For a fabulous backyard grill steak feast, serve with Potatoes and Onions in a Pouch (page 155) and Warm Spinach and Radicchio Salad (page 190).

Greek Grilled Steak

Taste the Mediterranean! Whenever possible, grill other items while the barbecue is hot.

1 lb	flank, blade or inside round steak	500 g
2 tbsp	each: red wine vinegar and olive oil	25 mL
2	small cloves garlic, crushed	2
1 tsp	each: dried oregano and mint or 1 tbsp (15 mL) fresh	5 mL
¼ tsp	freshly ground pepper	1 mL

1 Place steak in resealable plastic bag or shallow nonreactive dish.

2 In bowl, combine vinegar, oil, garlic, oregano, mint and pepper. Pour over steak and marinate in refrigerator for 12 hours or overnight; turn meat occasionally. Remove from marinade; discard marinade.

3 Preheat grill on medium-high. Place steak on oiled grill rack. Close lid and cook (use Direct Grilling, page 7) for 8 to 10 minutes, or until desired stage of doneness (see chart on page 31); turn once. (For maximum tenderness, do not cook less tender cuts, such as flank steak, past medium.)

4 Remove meat and cover with foil for 5 minutes. Slice steak in thin strips across the grain and serve. *Makes 3 to 4 servings.*

Suggested Menu: Accompany this steak with Grilled Mediterranean Vegetables (page 160), mashed potatoes beaten with feta cheese, Artichoke Salad (page 176), and a Greek red wine.

Tip: Give heavy-duty plastic milk bags a second life by using them (once only) to marinate meats. Use twist ties or clothes pins to seal the top.

Spice-crusted Steak with Cilantro Sauce

Be sure to use whole spices in this recipe. Pre-ground spices are too fine to form a crust, and they'll turn bitter during cooking. Crush whole spices by pulsing in a coffee grinder or food processor. The mixture should have a sandy texture – be careful to not turn it into a powder. You can use T-bone, rib, rib eye, strip loin or sirloin steaks in this recipe.

Spice Crust and Steak

1 tbsp	each: coriander seeds, cumin seeds and fennel seeds	15 mL
1 tsp	coarse salt	5 mL
¼ tsp	freshly ground pepper	1 mL
1 to 2 lb	steak (1 inch/2.5 cm thick)	500 g to 1 kg

Cilantro Sauce

1¼ cups	plain yogurt	300 mL
3 tbsp	lime juice	45 mL
2	cloves garlic, crushed	2
1 tsp	liquid honey	5 mL
¼ cup	olive oil	50 mL
1 cup	loosely packed fresh cilantro leaves, coarsely chopped	250 mL
⅛ tsp	each: salt and freshly ground pepper	0.5 mL

1 *For crust:* Pulse coriander, cumin and fennel seeds to a sandy texture. Combine with coarse salt and pepper. Trim excess fat from steak and discard. Press the spices over steak, coating the surface thoroughly to make a crust. Cover with plastic wrap and refrigerate until ready to grill.

2 *For sauce:* Place yogurt in very fine strainer or coffee filter and suspend it over a bowl. Let stand for 20 minutes; discard liquid. In small bowl, combine lime juice, garlic and honey. Beat in olive oil and then mix in drained yogurt until just blended; stir in cilantro. Season to taste with salt and pepper; cover and chill.

3 Preheat grill on medium-high. Place steak on oiled grill rack. Close lid and cook (use Direct Grilling, page 7) to desired stage of doneness (see chart on page 31); turn once. Cover steak with foil for 5 minutes. Slice in serving-size pieces and serve with sauce.

Makes 4 to 6 servings.

Suggested Menu: If using sirloin steak, slice the steak thinly and nestle it on a bed of crisp lettuce, along with Grilled Red and White Onions (page 156) and Grilled Sweet Potatoes (page 169). Cook the vegetables alongside the steak.

Tip: Well-trimmed steak with not more than 1/4 inch (5 mm) exterior fat reduces smoking and flare-ups.

Spicy Peppered Sirloin Steak

Rubs are an easy way to add flavour to tender beef cuts that do not need a tenderizing marinade.

Spice Rub

1 tbsp	chili powder	15 mL
1 tsp	each: ground cumin and freshly ground pepper	5 mL
¼ tsp	each: ground allspice and granulated sugar	1 mL
2	cloves garlic, crushed	2
1 tsp	Worcestershire sauce	5 mL
1½ lb	sirloin steak (1 inch/2.5 cm thick)	750 g
	Chopped cilantro	

1 *For rub:* In small bowl, combine chili powder, cumin, pepper, allspice, sugar, garlic and Worcestershire sauce. Trim excess fat from steak and discard. Press spice mixture evenly over both sides of meat. Cover and refrigerate for 2 to 24 hours.

2 Preheat grill on medium-high. Place steak on oiled grill rack. Close lid and cook (use Direct Grilling, page 7) for about 7 minutes per side for rare or 9 for medium. Remove steak to cutting board, cover with foil for 5 minutes before cutting into serving-size pieces. Sprinkle with cilantro.
Makes 4 servings.

Suggested Menu: Serve with Artichoke Kebabs with Thyme (page 152), Corn-stuffed Rainbow Peppers (page 160) and a simple green salad.

Steak with Chimichurri Rub

Traditional *chimichurri* is a sauce, but this version is a rub.

2	T-bone or porterhouse steaks (¾ inch/2 cm thick)	2
1 cup	loosely packed fresh parsley	250 mL
2 tbsp	each: red wine vinegar and canola oil	25 mL
2 tbsp	chopped fresh oregano or 2 tsp (10 mL) dried	25 mL
½ tsp	freshly ground pepper	2 mL
3 to 4	cloves garlic	3 to 4
½ tsp	salt	2 mL

1 Trim excess fat from steak and discard; place in shallow dish.

2 In food processor or blender, process parsley, vinegar, oil, oregano, pepper, garlic and salt until coarsely chopped. Press parsley mixture over both sides of steak. Cover steak with plastic wrap and refrigerate for up to 6 hours.

3 Preheat grill on medium-high. Place meat on oiled grill rack, retaining as much of the rub as possible. Close lid and cook (use Direct Grilling, page 7) to desired stage of doneness (see chart on page 31); turn once.
Makes 2 servings.

Suggested Menu: Bulgur Tabbouleh (page 188) is an excellent accompaniment to the steaks along with Grilled Tarragon Shiitake Mushrooms (page 159), and juicy sliced tomatoes.

Tropical Sirloin Steak

The sherry marinade with Caribbean spices turns this sirloin into a spicy meal to remember.

1½ lb	sirloin steak (1 inch/2.5 cm thick)	750 g

Sherry Marinade

2	cloves garlic, crushed	2
½ tsp	each: ground cinnamon, cloves, hot red pepper flakes	2 mL
¼ tsp	each: salt and pickling spice	1 mL
¼ cup	dry sherry	50 mL
	Thinly sliced green onions	

1 Trim excess fat from steak and discard. Place meat in shallow nonreactive dish or resealable plastic bag.

2 *For marinade:* In bowl, combine garlic, cinnamon, cloves, pepper flakes, salt and pickling spice. Stir in sherry, pour over steak, turn to coat, cover and refrigerate for 2 to 4 hours.

3 Remove steak from marinade. Place marinade in small saucepan, bring to a boil, reduce heat and cook for 5 minutes; keep warm.

4 Preheat grill on medium-high. Place steak on oiled grill rack, close lid and cook (use Direct Grilling, page 7) for about 7 minutes per side for rare and 9 for medium or until desired degree of doneness is reached (see chart on page 31). Turn steak once, brushing occasionally with warm marinade. Remove from grill, cover with foil for 5 minutes before cutting into serving-size pieces. Garnish with green onions.
Makes 4 servings.

> **Suggested Menu:** Accompany this steak with steamed green beans and broccoli and cellophane noodles garnished with slivers of green onions.

Tropical Sirloin Steak

Ham Steak with Citrus Salsa

Citrus Salsa with grilled ham is an interesting change from more traditional pineapple. The complementary collection of flavours is quite outstanding.

Citrus Salsa

2	oranges, peeled and diced	2
½	lemon, peeled and diced	½
½	pink grapefruit, peeled and diced	½
2 tbsp	each: chopped fresh cilantro and diced red onion	25 mL
1	jalapeño pepper, seeded and finely chopped	1
1 tsp	olive oil	5 mL
⅛ tsp	each: salt, freshly ground pepper and dried thyme	0.5 mL

Ham

4	ham steak slices (½ inch/1 cm thick)	4
1 tsp	Dijon mustard	5 mL

1 *For salsa:* In bowl, combine oranges, lemon, grapefruit, cilantro, onion, jalapeño pepper, oil and seasonings; stir to combine. Cover and refrigerate until ready to serve.

2 *For ham:* Preheat grill on medium-high. Place ham steaks on oiled grill. Close lid and cook (use Direct Grilling, page 7) for 4 minutes per side; just before turning, brush lightly with mustard. Serve ham with Citrus Salsa.

Makes 4 servings and 2 cups (500 mL) salsa.

Suggested Menu: Serve with Grilled Asparagus (page 168) and Black Olive, Rice and Spinach Salad (page 172). Ice cream with Decadent Chocolate Fondue Sauce (page 216) makes an easy dessert. You might also serve ham and salsa on 4 split and toasted Kaiser buns.

Tip: Since jalapeño peppers vary greatly in heat level, add them to taste.

Ham Steak with Citrus Salsa

Grilled Steak with Bok Choy

Bok choy provides an attractive and comfortable, tasty bed for grilled steak. It requires a very short cooking time and is also delicious added at the last moment to stir-fries and soups.

1½ lb	sirloin steak (1 inch/2.5 cm thick)	750 g
2 tsp	sesame oil	10 mL
½ tsp	each: garlic powder, salt and freshly ground pepper	2 mL
1 lb	bok choy, washed	500 g
1 tbsp	oyster or fish sauce	15 mL

1 Remove excess fat from beef and discard. Brush beef lightly on each side with oil; season to taste with garlic powder, salt and pepper.
2 Preheat grill on medium-high. Place beef on lightly oiled grill rack. Close lid and cook (use Direct Grilling, page 7) to desired stage of doneness (see chart on page 31); turn once.
3 Meanwhile, in large saucepan, blanch bok choy in boiling water for 2 minutes; drain well. Arrange bok choy on warm serving platter. Slice beef in 1-inch (2.5 cm) thick slices across the grain. Arrange beef on bok choy, drizzle with oyster sauce and serve.
Makes 4 servings.

Suggested Menu: Serve with basmati rice or cellophane noodles tossed with a small amount of sesame oil and soy sauce.

Steak au Poivre

Dramatic, particularly when prepared as dusk falls, this classic flamed dish can be done outside on the grill rack during good weather or on the stove top anytime.

2 lb	sirloin steak (2 inches/5 cm thick)	1 kg
1 tbsp	freshly ground pepper	15 mL
2 tsp	seasoned salt	10 mL
2 tbsp	each: butter or margarine and olive oil	25 mL
2 tbsp	beef broth	25 mL
⅓ cup	dry red wine	75 mL
¼ cup	brandy or Cognac	50 mL

1 Trim excess fat from steak and discard. Press pepper and seasoned salt into both sides of steak.
2 In large heavy skillet, heat butter and olive oil over medium-high heat on grill rack. Add steak and cook (use Direct Grilling, page 7) for 7 to 10 minutes on each side, depending on degree of doneness desired (see chart on page 31).
3 Remove meat from pan to carving board, cover with foil for 5 minutes. Slice meat in thin strips across the grain. Add broth and wine to skillet; heat gently until bubbling. Pour in brandy; set mixture aflame. Pour flaming sauce over steak and serve.
Makes 4 to 6 servings.

Suggested Menu: Serve with Summertime Pasta (page 179) and Zucchini Fingers (page 156).

Turkish Skewered Burgers

Mediterranean flavours predominate in these burgers wrapped in an oval shape around skewers. The oval shape fits a pita pocket better than the usual round shape. The skewers help to retain the oval shape during grilling and then serve as a handle. A light rather than firm touch when shaping patties will make the cooked burgers moister.

1 lb	lean ground beef	500 g
½ cup	rolled oats	125 mL
½ cup	finely chopped onion	125 mL
1	egg	1
¼ cup	plain yogurt	50 mL
½ tsp	each: dried thyme and oregano or 2 tsp (10 mL) chopped fresh	2 mL
¼ tsp	each: salt and freshly ground pepper	1 mL
⅛ tsp	hot pepper sauce	0.5 mL
3	cloves garlic, minced	3

Cucumber Sauce

½ cup	grated cucumber	125 mL
½ cup	plain yogurt	125 mL
¼ cup	light mayonnaise	50 mL
4	pita pockets, halved	4
	Salt and freshly ground pepper	

1 In bowl, combine beef, rolled oats, onion, egg, yogurt, seasonings, hot sauce and garlic. Divide into 8 portions. Shape each portion lightly around a short metal skewer making a 4-inch (10 cm) oval.

2 Preheat grill on medium. Place skewers on oiled grill rack. Close lid and cook (use Direct Grilling, page 7) for about 8 minutes or until meat is no longer pink inside; turn once.

3 *For sauce:* In small bowl, combine cucumber, yogurt and mayonnaise; season to taste with salt and pepper. Serve oval burgers in halved pita bread with a spoonful of sauce.

Makes 8 burgers, 4 servings of 2 burgers each.

Pick-a-Burger Variations

Forget fuss and formality. Summertime is Great Hamburger World Tour time. Nothing beats a juicy burger, and this basic recipe can be used to prepare a quantity of them. Start with the Basic Burger and take it from there with our international suggestions.

Basic Burger

1 lb	lean ground beef	500 g
1	small onion, finely minced	1
1	clove garlic, crushed (optional)	1
1	egg, beaten	1
1/3 cup	rolled oats	75 mL
2 tbsp	milk	25 mL
	Salt and freshly ground pepper	

1 In medium bowl, combine beef, onion, garlic (if using), egg, rolled oats, milk, salt and pepper. Shape mixture lightly into 4 to 6, evenly shaped, flat patties. Chill patties for at least 1 hour before grilling (see Tips).

2 Preheat grill on medium. Place patties on oiled grill rack. Close lid and cook (use Direct Grilling, page 7) for about 5 minutes per side or until patties are well-done (centers are no longer pink). Well-done burgers are brownish throughout with clear juices and no pink showing.

3 Serve with world tour fixings from the wide variety of pickles, relishes, sauces and extras suggested below.

Makes 4 to 6 patties.

Tips:

1 Double or triple the recipe, freeze the patties, and then turn them into the world tour burger of your choice. For freezing, place each patty in a single layer on plastic wrap on a tray, cover and freeze. When frozen, remove from the tray and pack in a resealable plastic bag. Since the patties are individually frozen, it will be easy to remove just the right number.

2 Medium ground beef makes a moister burger. Grilling is a low-fat cooking method because it allows fat to drip away.

3 Patties hold together best if covered and refrigerated for about 1 hour before cooking.

4 Never smash the burger with a spatula as it cooks – you'll chase away the juices.

Pick-a-Burger, Canadian style

PICK-A-BURGER VARIATIONS

Bread	Type of Pickle or Relish	Extras
Canadian hamburg buns	hamburger relish,	sliced tomatoes, cheese, sliced dill pickles, mustard, onion slices
Italian thick Italian bread slices	savory tomato relish	sprinkle with oregano and basil; top with shredded romaine lettuce and sliced Mozzarella cheese
German sliced rye or pumpernickel	sauerkraut, onion relish	sprinkle with caraway seed; top with shredded Muenster cheese
Asian sesame seed hamburg buns	sweet mixed pickles	drizzle patties with soy sauce before grilling; top with bean sprouts
Hawaiian cheese buns	sliced sweet pickles	add a pineapple slice while cooking second side and garnish with sprouts
Mexican flour tortillas	hot pepper rings, salsa	shredded lettuce, sliced avocado, grated Cheddar or Monterey Jack cheese
California thick whole wheat bread slices	baby dill pickles	alfalfa sprouts, tomato slices, light mayonnaise
Greek halved pita bread	sweet green relish	plain yogurt, Tzatziki, crumbled feta cheese, tomato, black olives

Indian-style Lentil Vegetable Burgers

This Indian-style lentil burger is chockablock with vegetables – carrots, broccoli and cauliflower. Great for you and great tasting too!

½ cup	dried green lentils	125 mL
2	medium potatoes, peeled and cubed	2
½ cup	each: chopped broccoli, cauliflower and carrots	125 mL
	Salt and freshly ground pepper	
2 tsp	canola oil	10 mL
1	small onion, chopped	1
1	clove garlic, minced	1
½ tsp	each: ground cumin, ginger, mustard seeds and hot red pepper flakes	2 mL
2 tbsp	chopped fresh cilantro	25 mL
1	egg, beaten	1
⅔ cup	dried bread crumbs, divided	150 mL
6	whole wheat pita pockets	6

Toppings

Cucumber Raita, sliced tomato, alfalfa sprouts

1 In medium saucepan, cover lentils and potatoes with water; bring to a boil and cook for 10 minutes. Add broccoli, cauliflower and carrots and return to boil; cook until tender; drain well. (Watch this mixture does not boil dry; lentils absorb water during cooking.) Combine lentil mixture with salt and pepper to taste.

2 In nonstick skillet, heat oil over medium heat until hot. Add onion and garlic; sauté for 5 minutes. Add cumin, ginger, mustard seeds and red pepper flakes. Remove from heat; stir in cilantro.

3 Stir onion mixture into lentil mixture along with egg and ½ cup (125 mL) bread crumbs; stir gently. With floured hands, divide mixture into 6 equal portions. Shape into 6 patties; dredge with remaining bread crumbs.

4 Preheat grill on medium. Carefully place patties on well-oiled grill rack. Close lid and cook (use Direct Grilling, page 7) for about 5 minutes per side. If desired, brush cooked side with a barbecue sauce. Heat pita pockets during last part of grilling.

5 Open pita and place one patty in each pocket. Garnish with choice of toppings as desired.
Makes 6 servings.

Cucumber Raita: In small bowl, combine 1 cup (250 mL) plain yogurt, 1 tbsp (15 mL) each of lime juice and chopped fresh mint, 1 tsp (5 mL) ground cumin, 1 medium seedless cucumber, peeled and diced, and salt and freshly ground pepper to taste. Makes about 1 1/2 cups (375 mL).
Use any leftover sauce as a dip.

Tip: Chilling the patties on foil makes them easier to remove to the grill.

Mexican Bean Burgers

Start with beans, an important part of Mexican cuisine. Add Mexican spice flavours – cumin, garlic and coriander. Top it all with avocado, sour cream and shredded cheese. You end up with the wonderful taste of Mexico in a vegetarian burger.

2	cans (14 oz/398 mL) pinto beans, drained	2
1 tbsp	canola oil	15 mL
¾ cup	finely chopped onion	175 mL
3	cloves garlic, minced	3
2 tbsp	ground coriander	25 mL
4 tsp	each: all purpose flour and ground cumin	20 mL
½ tsp	each: salt and freshly ground pepper	2 mL

Toppings

Sliced avocado, sour cream, shredded Monterey Jack cheese, mild or medium salsa

6	hamburg or sesame seed buns	6

1 In large bowl, mash pinto beans with a fork or a potato masher; set aside.

2 In nonstick skillet, heat oil over medium-high heat; cook onions and garlic for 5 minutes or until tender. Add coriander, flour, cumin, salt and pepper; cook, stirring constantly, for 1 minute. Add onion mixture to pinto beans; stir well.

3 Cut 6 squares of waxed paper. Divide bean mixture into 6 equal amounts; shape into patties on each waxed paper square.

4 Preheat grill on medium. Carefully place patties on well oiled grill rack. Close lid and cook (use Direct Grilling, page 7) for 4 minutes per side. Heat buns during last part of grilling.

5 Place a patty in each warmed bun and serve with a choice of toppings.

Makes 6 servings.

Suggested Menu: Serve with a tossed green salad with orange slices and a zesty vinaigrette dressing and finish off with one of the grilled desserts in Chapter 11 for a meat-alternative meal to remember.

Spicy Beef Fajitas

Back in the 1980s, fajitas took on new celebrity status. Today they continue their popularity through many variations on the original steak fajita. To make a fajita, wrap a warm flour tortilla around grilled strips of spicy meat; add grilled onions, sweet green peppers, Guacamole, shredded lettuce and you have a taste treat beyond description.

1 lb	flank or round steak	500 g

Marinade

2 tbsp	soy sauce	25 mL
1 tbsp	each: lime juice and liquid honey	15 mL
1	clove garlic, crushed	1
½	small jalapeño pepper, seeded and finely diced	½
1	medium onion, sliced	1
½	sweet red pepper, sliced	½
2 tsp	canola oil	10 mL
1 cup	shredded lettuce	250 mL
	Guacamole*	
8	12-inch (30 cm) flour tortillas	8

1 Trim excess fat from steak and discard. Place steak in resealable plastic bag or shallow nonreactive dish.

2 *For marinade:* In bowl, combine soy sauce, lime juice, honey, garlic and jalapeño pepper. Pour over steak, turn to coat. Refrigerate for 12 hours or overnight; turn steak occasionally. Remove steak from marinade; reserve marinade. Place marinade in small saucepan, bring to a boil, reduce heat and cook for 5 minutes; keep warm.

3 Preheat grill on medium-high. Place steak on oiled grill rack. Close lid and cook (use Direct Grilling, page 7) to desired stage of doneness (see chart on page 31), brushing often with warm marinade. (For maximum tenderness, do not cook less tender cuts, such as flank steak, past medium.) Remove from grill; cover with foil for 5 minutes before slicing. Slice steak across the grain into thin strips.

4 Meanwhile, sauté onion and red pepper in nonstick skillet in hot oil for 10 minutes or until tender.

5 Wrap tortillas in dampened paper towel; microwave on high (100%) for 3 minutes to soften. Place portions of the steak, cooked vegetable mixture and lettuce on each warm tortilla and top with Guacamole. Roll tortillas tightly around filling. *Makes 8 servings.*

Variation: Chicken strips may replace beef.

*Guacamole: In a bowl, mash 1 medium avocado, peeled. Stir in 1 tbsp (15 mL) lime juice, 1 medium tomato, peeled and finely chopped, 1/2 cup (125 mL) finely chopped onion, 1 tbsp (15 mL) chopped fresh cilantro and dash hot pepper sauce. Makes about 1 1/2 cups (375 mL).

Tip: Placing an avocado pit in the avocado mixture helps to prevent it from turning brown.

Spicy Beef Fajitas, page 46;
with Guacamole, page 46

Asian-marinated Steak

Use this Thai-inspired marinade for less tender beef cuts such as flank, blade and round steaks.

2 lb	inside round, blade, sirloin tip or flank steak (1 inch/2.5 cm thick)	1 kg

Asian Marinade

	Juice and peel of 1 lime	
¼ cup	chopped fresh mint	50 mL
¼ cup	light soy sauce	50 mL
1	piece gingerroot (1 inch/2.5 cm), minced	1
½	jalapeño pepper, seeded and finely chopped	½
2	cloves garlic, crushed	2
1 tsp	sesame oil	5 mL

1 Trim excess fat from steak and discard. Place steak in resealable plastic bag or shallow nonreactive dish.

2 *For marinade:* In bowl, combine lime juice and peel, mint, soy sauce, gingerroot, jalapeño pepper, garlic and oil. Pour over steak; turn to coat. Refrigerate for 12 to 24 hours; turn steak occasionally. Remove steak from marinade; reserve marinade. Place marinade in small saucepan, bring to a boil, reduce heat and cook for 5 minutes; keep warm.

3 Preheat grill on medium-high. Place steak on lightly oiled grill rack. Close lid and cook (use Indirect Grilling, page 7) to desired stage of doneness (see chart on page 32). Brush occasionally with warm marinade. (For maximum tenderness, do not cook less tender cuts, such as flank steak, past medium.)

4 Remove steak from grill; cover with foil for 10 minutes before carving. Cut steak into thin slices across the grain and serve.
Makes 4 to 5 servings.

Suggested Menu: Prepare Grilled Basil Tomatoes (page [129]) toward the end of the cooking time for the steak. Basmati rice, a green salad and crunchy rolls complete the meal.

Tip: Use steak leftovers in a salad the next day. Cut steak into slivers and toss with torn romaine lettuce, bean sprouts, strips of sweet red pepper and a zesty oil and vinegar dressing.

Peeling Gingerroot: Gently peel the thin beige skin from gingerroot. The flesh beneath the skin is the most flavorful. Unpeeled gingerroot may be kept in the refrigerator for two weeks. Peeled gingerroot can be placed in a jar of sherry and kept refrigerated for up to three months.

Bayou Steak

The zesty hot-pepper flavours of Louisiana come through in this marinade for less tender steaks. Use it to tenderize and flavour any of the more economical beef cuts.

2 lb	inside round, sirloin tip or blade steak (2 inches/5 cm thick)	1 kg

Zesty Marinade

½ cup	beef broth	125 mL
3 tbsp	Worcestershire sauce	45 mL
3 tbsp	cider vinegar	45 mL
1 tbsp	canola oil	15 mL
½ tsp	each: dry mustard, chili powder and paprika	2 mL
½ to 1 tsp	hot pepper sauce	2 to 5 mL
1	bay leaf	1
2	cloves garlic, minced	2
Dash	freshly ground pepper	Dash

1 Trim excess fat from meat and discard. Pierce meat several times with a fork. Place in a resealable plastic bag or shallow nonreactive dish.

2 In small saucepan, combine broth, Worcestershire sauce, vinegar, oil, mustard, chili powder, paprika, pepper sauce, bay leaf, garlic and pepper. Bring to a boil over high heat; reduce heat and simmer for 10 minutes, stirring occasionally. Cool before pouring over meat. Refrigerate for 12 to 24 hours; turn meat occasionally.

3 Remove meat from marinade; discard bay leaf and reserve marinade. Place marinade in small saucepan, bring to a boil, reduce heat and cook for 5 minutes; keep warm.

4 Preheat grill on medium-high. Place meat on lightly oiled grill rack. Close lid and cook (use Indirect Grilling, page 7) to desired degree of doneness (see chart on page 32). Brush occasionally with warm marinade. (For maximum tenderness, do not cook less tender cuts past medium.)

5 Cover steak with foil for 10 minutes before carving. Slice steak in thin strips across the grain. *Makes 4 to 5 servings.*

Suggested Menu: Serve with cooked pasta tossed with a fruity olive oil and basil sauce and Zucchini Fingers (page 156).

Garlic Variation: Thread unpeeled garlic cloves on soaked wooden skewers. Before grilling the steak, cook garlic over medium heat on covered grill rack for about 10 minutes or until very soft. Allow to cool before handling. Squeeze garlic pulp from the cloves to top the cooked steak or burgers.

Steak Pinwheels with Mushroom
and Asparagus, page 51

Steak Pinwheels with Mushroom and Asparagus

Mushrooms and shallots along with fresh asparagus spears and carrots make a colorful filling for these steak pinwheels. You get your meat and vegetables in the same grilling.

1 ½ lb	flank steak	750 g
3	large shiitake mushrooms, chopped	3
½ cup	finely chopped shallots or onions	125 mL
2	cloves garlic, minced	2
1 tsp	canola oil	5 mL
2 tbsp	horseradish, drained	25 mL
½ tsp	salt	2 mL
¼ tsp	freshly ground pepper	1 mL
10	blanched asparagus spears, cut in lengths to fit across meat	10
10	blanched carrot sticks, cut in lengths to fit across meat	10

1 Score meat on both sides by making shallow cuts at 1-inch (2.5 cm) intervals in a diamond pattern. Place steak between 2 pieces of waxed paper. Pound meat evenly over entire surface with the flat side of a meat mallet to form a 12–x 8–inch (30 x 19 cm) rectangle.

2 Meanwhile, in nonstick skillet, over medium-high heat, sauté mushrooms, shallots and garlic in hot oil for about 10 minutes or until soft and all liquid has evaporated. Stir in horseradish, salt and pepper; allow to cool.

3 Spread cooled mushroom mixture evenly over the inside surface of the meat. Arrange asparagus and carrot pieces crosswise on meat. Roll meat tightly from short side around vegetables; secure with wooden toothpicks at 1-inch (2.5 cm) intervals. Cut between toothpicks into eight 1-inch (2.5 cm) slices. Thread 2 pinwheels onto each of 4 skewers.

4 Preheat grill on medium-high. Place pinwheels on oiled grill rack. Cook, uncovered (use Direct Grilling, page 7), for 12 to 14 minutes for medium; turn once halfway through grilling.
Makes 4 servings.

Suggested Menu: Serve with fluffy rice and Grilled Tarragon Shiitake Mushrooms (page 159).

Tip: Since flank steak is very lean, it becomes dry and tough if overcooked. It's best not to cook it beyond medium.

Deep South Beef Brisket BBQ

This recipe emulates barbecuing – a style of cooking found in the Southern United States that tends to be less known further north. In fact, a barbecue in the north is nothing like the traditional southern barbecue. Typically, in this style of barbecue, the beef is covered and cooked slowly in a pit or on a spit over hot hardwood coals. After a period of long slow cooking, the meat is cut or pulled apart into smaller pieces and cooked again in a rich tomato sauce. The pungent and complex flavours are the result of the combination of cooking techniques. In our version, the initial long slow cooking is done on an outdoor grill using indirect grilling. The second cooking in tomato sauce is done on the stove top, so as to free up the grill for other uses. We think the results are up to the real thing. In fact, it makes the best "beef on a bun" we have ever tasted!

4 to 5 lb	lean beef brisket	2 to 2.5 kg

Barbecue Sauce

1 tbsp	canola oil, divided	15 mL
1	large onion, coarsely chopped	1
1	bottle (375 mL) ketchup	1
1	bottle (285 mL) chili sauce	1
¼ cup	each: cider vinegar and dark molasses	50 mL
1 to 2 tbsp	each: hot pepper sauce, prepared mustard and Worcestershire sauce	15 to 25 mL
1½ tsp	black pepper	7 mL
1½ cups	water	375 mL
2 tbsp	lime or lemon juice	25 mL
12 to 16	Kaiser or hamburg buns, toasted	12 to 16

1 Preheat grill on high; brush lightly with oil. Place brisket on grill rack; sear on all sides until brown. Remove meat briefly and lower heat to medium-low; if your grill has a thermometer, this would be about 350°F/180°C. Return meat to grill rack. Close lid and cook (use Indirect Grilling, page 7) for 4 to 5 hours or until meat is fork tender and beef registers well-done on meat thermometer. (During this long cooking time, check water in pan below meat and replenish if necessary.)

2 *For sauce:* Meanwhile, heat remaining oil on medium-high in large heavy saucepan or Dutch oven; add onion and cook for 5 minutes or until softened. Add ketchup, chili sauce, vinegar, molasses, hot pepper sauce, mustard, Worcestershire sauce, black pepper and water. Bring to a boil, reduce heat and simmer for about 20 minutes, stirring occasionally. Remove from heat; stir in lime juice.

3 When meat is done and cool enough to handle, gently pull or slice into strands. Cut into 2-inch (5 cm) pieces and add to sauce. Cover and cook gently for about 1 hour, stirring occasionally. Add more water (or pan drippings) during cooking if needed. Serve meat on toasted buns.
Makes 12 to 16 servings.

> **Suggested Menu:** For a beef-on-a-bun meal, serve with potato and coleslaw salads, lots of pickles, raw celery and carrot sticks, sliced tomatoes and probably several fruit pies for dessert.

Beef Tenderloin Roast with Port Wine Marinade

Port Wine Marinade is especially versatile. While used to marinate beef in this recipe, it also works well with chicken and lamb and it also doubles as a salad vinaigrette. (See the recipe for Greens with Port Wine Vinaigrette.)

Port Wine Marinade

⅓ cup	port	75 mL
3 tbsp	extra virgin olive oil	45 mL
2 tbsp	balsamic vinegar	25 mL
1 tbsp	Dijon mustard	15 mL
1½ tsp	dried basil or 1 tbsp (15 mL) chopped fresh	7 mL
½ tsp	each: salt, freshly ground pepper and granulated sugar	2 mL
2 to 3 lb	beef tenderloin roast	1 to 1.5 kg

1 *For marinade:* In small bowl, combine port, oil, vinegar, mustard, basil, salt, pepper and sugar; set aside.

2 Trim excess fat from beef and discard. Place beef in shallow nonreactive dish large enough to hold it and pour marinade over. Cover and refrigerate for up to 6 hours or overnight; turn beef occasionally.

3 Remove beef from marinade; reserve marinade. Place marinade in small saucepan, bring to a boil, reduce heat and cook for 5 minutes; keep warm.

4 Preheat grill on medium. Place beef in center of oiled grill rack; sear all sides until grill marks appear. Close lid and cook (use Indirect Grilling, page 7) to desired stage of doneness (see chart on page 32); baste occasionally with reserved marinade.

5 Remove meat to cutting board and cover with foil; allow to stand for 10 minutes before carving. Cut strings and carve meat.
Makes 6 servings.

Suggested Menu: Cook Caramelized Leeks and Onions (page 163) in a foil package on the grill rack over the heat source during the last 30 minutes of roasting time. After the roast is removed, cook Grilled Mushrooms (page 169).

Greens with Port Wine Vinaigrette

8 cups	assorted salad greens – arugula, red leaf lettuce, romaine	2 L
⅓ cup	Port Wine Marinade (see above)	75 mL
2 cups	mesclun	500 mL
	Red onion slices, strips of sweet green and red pepper, and bean sprouts	

1 Place assorted greens in large salad bowl. Toss gently with vinaigrette.

2 Arrange dressed greens on 6 to 8 salad plates. Top each with mesclun, red onion, green and red pepper and bean sprouts.
Makes 6 to 8 servings.

Thick Sirloin with Creamy Mushroom Sauce

Steak needs no seasoning when served with this amazing mushroom and mustard sauce.

Mushroom Sauce

2	large shallots, minced	2
1 tbsp	canola oil	15 mL
8	medium mushrooms, thinly sliced	8
½ cup	vermouth or dry white wine	125 mL
½ cup	heavy cream	125 mL
1 tsp	dried thyme or 1 tbsp (15 mL) chopped fresh	5 mL
	Salt and freshly ground pepper	
1 tbsp	coarse-grained mustard	15 mL

Steak

1½ lb	sirloin steak (1-inch/2.5 cm thick)	750 g

1 *For sauce:* In nonstick skillet, sauté shallots in oil over medium-high heat until softened. Add mushrooms; cook until all mushroom liquid has evaporated; stir often. Add vermouth; cook until liquid is reduced to half. Stir in cream, thyme, salt and pepper to taste, and mustard; cook gently until sauce has thickened; keep warm.

2 Trim excess fat from steak and discard. Preheat grill on medium-high. Place steak on oiled grill rack. Close lid and cook (use Direct Grilling, page 7) until desired degree of doneness is reached (about 5 minutes per side for rare, 7 for medium, see chart on page 31). Turn steak once. Remove steak from grill; cover with foil for 5 minutes before serving.

3 Serve each portion with warm mushroom sauce. *Makes 4 servings.*

Suggested Menu: Potatoes and Onions in a Pouch (page 155), Grilled Zucchini (page 169) and a large green salad with Poppy Seed Vinaigrette (page 180) are the best companions for this steak.

Thick Sirloin with Creamy
Mushroom Sauce, page 54

Prime Rib of Beef with Herbes de Provence

Marinated in red wine and *herbes de Provence* and roasted on the grill, this most exotic beef cut becomes a mouth-watering experience. Any leftovers? Serve thin slices on croissants with tomato slices, arugula, mayonnaise and Dijon mustard.

| 6 lb | prime rib of beef | 3 kg |

Rub

2 tbsp	each: olive oil and red wine	25 mL
½ cup	*herbes de Provence**	125 mL
1 tsp	freshly ground pepper	5 mL
1	clove garlic, crushed	1

1 Trim excess fat from meat and discard.

2 *For rub:* In small bowl, stir together oil, wine, *herbes de Provence*, pepper and garlic. Rub over entire surface of roast. Cover meat with plastic wrap and refrigerate for 4 hours or overnight.

3 Preheat grill on medium. Unwrap meat, and place in center of oiled grill rack. Close lid and cook (use Indirect Grilling, page 7]) for about 2 ½ hours, depending on the degree of doneness desired (see chart on page 32). During the final 30 minutes of cooking, add flavoured wood chips to coals if desired.

4 Remove roast to cutting board when about 5°F (2°C) below desired degree of doneness. Cover with foil; allow to stand for 15 minutes before carving thinly across the grain.
Makes 8 servings.

Suggested Menu: Roasted Horseradish Beets are a marvelous accompaniment.

Roasted Horseradish Beets: While the beef is roasting, place a foil package of 4 medium beets on the rack beside the meat. They will require about 1 hour to become tender. When tender, remove from grill, unwrap and allow to cool; peel and dice. In nonstick skillet, sauté 1 cup (250 mL) chopped red onion in 3 tbsp (45 mL) olive oil; add 2 tbsp (25 mL) balsamic vinegar, 1 tsp (5 mL) coarse salt and 1/4 tsp (1 mL) freshly ground pepper. Stir in beets and 1/4 cup (50 mL) horseradish. Reheat to serving temperature.

**herbes de Provence* is a blend of herbs usually containing equal parts of basil, fennel, sage, summer savory and thyme. You can buy it at specialty or gourmet food shops or kitchen supply stores, or you can prepare your own mixture at home.

Moroccan Lamb Chops

Moroccan seasonings are a savoury blend of spices, garlic, orange or lemon juice and often their peel. These flavours are becoming increasingly popular in North American home cooking due to the growth of restaurants specializing in Moroccan cuisine.

Marinade

½ cup	plain yogurt	125 mL
3 tbsp	orange juice concentrate	45 mL
2	cloves garlic, minced	2
1 tsp	each: ground coriander and grated orange peel	5 mL
½ tsp	each: salt, ground cumin and cinnamon	2 mL
¼ tsp	each: ground cloves and ginger	1 mL

Meat

6	lamb steaks or chops (¾ inch/2 cm thick)	6

Cucumber Tomato Sauce

¾ cup	diced cucumber	175 mL
½ cup	chopped tomato	125 mL
⅓ cup	finely chopped onion	75 mL
½ cup	plain yogurt	125 mL
	Salt and freshly ground pepper	

1 *For marinade:* In small bowl, combine yogurt, juice, garlic and seasonings; stir well.

2 *For lamb chops:* Trim excess fat and discard. Place lamb in shallow nonreactive dish or resealable plastic bag. Pour marinade over lamb; turn to coat. Cover and refrigerate for at least 4 hours or overnight; turn chops occasionally.

3 Remove lamb from marinade; reserve marinade. Place marinade in small saucepan, bring to a boil, reduce heat and cook for 5 minutes; keep warm.

4 Preheat grill on medium-high. Place lamb on oiled grill rack. Close lid and cook (use Direct Grilling, page 7) for about 9 minutes for medium-rare; turn once. Baste often with warm marinade.

5 *For sauce:* Meanwhile, in small bowl, combine cucumber, tomato, onion and yogurt. Season to taste with salt and pepper. Serve sauce with lamb steaks.

Makes 6 servings.

Suggested Menu: Serve with grilled new potatoes and artichokes (see page 169) along with a green salad and a lighter red wine such as a Merlot.

Grilled Rosemary Lamb Chops

Rosemary is the herb most often associated with lamb. When you taste these lamb chops you'll know why! We found marinating the lamb no less than four hours developed the best herb flavours.

Marinade

⅓ cup	wine (white, rosé or red)	75 mL
2 tbsp	olive oil	25 mL
1 tbsp	lemon juice	15 mL
2	bay leaves, broken in half	2
1 tsp	each: dried thyme and rosemary or 1 tbsp (15 mL) chopped fresh	5 mL
½ tsp	freshly ground pepper	2 mL

Lamb

8 to 12	lean loin lamb chops (1 inch/2.5 cm thick)	8 to 12

1 *For marinade:* In nonreactive shallow dish or resealable plastic bag, combine wine, oil, lemon juice, bay leaves, thyme, rosemary and pepper.

2 *For lamb chops:* Trim excess fat and discard. Place lamb in marinade; turn to coat. Cover and refrigerate for at least 4 hours or overnight; turn chops occasionally.

3 Remove lamb chops from marinade; reserve marinade, discard bay leaves. Place marinade in small saucepan, bring to a boil, reduce heat and cook for 5 minutes; keep warm.

4 Preheat grill on medium-high. Place lamb chops on lightly oiled grill rack. Close lid and cook (use Direct Grilling, page 7) for about 10 minutes for medium-rare; turn once, basting often with warm marinade.

Makes 4 to 6 servings, 2 chops per person.

Suggested Menu: Add a few chopped kalamata olives to mashed potatoes and top with minced fresh parsley to complement the rosemary-lamb flavours. Complete the meal with crunchy multigrain dinner rolls and, in the springtime, tender asparagus spears and steamed carrot sticks.

Greek Lamb Burgers

Lamb, mint, feta cheese, olives and yogurt, all flavours of Greece, make these spicy grilled burgers a hit with lamb lovers.

1 lb	lean ground lamb	500 g
3	cloves garlic, crushed	3
½ cup	soft bread crumbs	125 mL
3 tbsp	minced fresh mint or	45 mL
	1 tbsp (15 mL) dried	
½ tsp	each: salt and ground cinnamon	2 mL
¼ tsp	each: freshly ground pepper and	1 mL
	hot red pepper flakes	
¾ cup	crumbled feta cheese	175 mL
3	pita breads, halved	3

Garnishes

sliced black olives, sliced tomatoes,
plain yogurt, chopped cucumber

1 In bowl, combine lamb, garlic, bread crumbs, mint, salt, cinnamon, pepper and pepper flakes. Shape mixture lightly into 6 evenly shaped flat patties.

2 Preheat grill on medium. Place patties on oiled grill rack. Close lid and cook (use Direct Grilling, page 7) for about 5 minutes per side or until patties are well-done (centers are no longer pink). During the final few minutes of cooking, warm pitas and top patties with cheese; cook until cheese softens and pitas are lightly brown.

3 Serve each patty in half an open pita pocket with your choice of garnishes.

Makes 6 pitas, 3 servings of two or 6 servings of one.

Suggested Menu: Serve with a traditional Greek salad: cucumbers, tomatoes, black olives, drizzled with olive oil and lemon juice and generously sprinkled with oregano and pepper.

Leg of Lamb Persillade

Persil is the French word for parsley, and the combination of parsley with chopped garlic is called *persillade* – a mixture that always gives a fabulous flavour to lamb.

Persillade

⅓ cup	packed parsley leaves, divided	75 mL
¼ cup	olive oil, divided	50 mL
4	cloves garlic, divided	4
1 tsp	grated lemon peel	5 mL
½ tsp	salt	2 mL
¼ tsp	freshly ground pepper	1 mL
4 to 6 lb	boneless rolled leg of lamb	2 to 3 kg
3 tbsp	lemon juice	45 mL

1 *For* Persillade: In blender or food processor, process 3 tbsp (45 mL) parsley, 2 tbsp (25 mL) oil, 2 cloves garlic, lemon peel, salt and pepper to a smooth paste; set aside.

2 Slice remaining 2 garlic cloves into thin slices and chop remaining parsley. Unroll lamb, sprinkle with garlic and parsley, reroll and tie with kitchen cord. Press *persillade* mixture over outside of lamb.

3 Preheat grill on medium-high. Place lamb in center of oiled grill rack. Close lid and cook (use Indirect Grilling, page 7) for about 1¼ hours or until well browned but still pink in the center and meat thermometer registers 150°F (65°C) for medium-rare. Combine lemon juice and remaining oil. Baste lamb occasionally during cooking with lemon-oil mixture.

4 Transfer meat to cutting board, cover with foil and let stand for 10 minutes before carving. Cut strings and carve meat.

Makes 8 servings.

Serving Suggestions: Grilled lemon slices and Tuscan Garlic Bread are an interesting addition to the roast. A medium-bodied red wine such as a Merlot is a good choice because its sweet tannins do not overpower the delicate lamb flavours and the meal is a "fait accompli."

Tuscan Garlic Bread: Lightly grill thick slices of French bread on both sides. Rub one side with a cut clove of garlic. Drizzle some fruity olive oil over the bread and season with salt and freshly ground pepper. Bon appétit!

Tip: Follow same procedure for a butterflied leg of lamb using Direct Grilling. Reduce cooking time to about 20 minutes per side for medium-rare and 25 for well-done.

Zesty Barbecued Pork Ribs

Everyone enjoys a good feed of ribs. This family recipe has been enjoyed for many years, either grilled on the barbecue or baked in the oven.

Barbecue Sauce

1 cup	ketchup or chili sauce	250 mL
⅓ cup	cider vinegar	75 mL
⅓ cup	brown sugar, lightly packed	75 mL
2 tsp	prepared mustard	10 mL
1	small onion, finely chopped	1
2 tbsp	Worcestershire sauce	25 mL
1 tbsp	vegetable oil	15 mL
2	cloves garlic, crushed	2
⅛ tsp	each: salt, hot pepper sauce and freshly ground pepper	0.5 mL
4 lb	pork spareribs (side or back)	2 kg

1 In medium saucepan, combine ketchup, vinegar, sugar, mustard, onion, Worcestershire sauce, oil, garlic, salt, hot pepper sauce and pepper. Simmer, uncovered, for 20 minutes; stir occasionally. Remove from heat and cool slightly.

2 *To precook ribs:* Meanwhile, place ribs in large saucepan. Add enough water to cover, bring to a boil, reduce heat and cook gently for about 45 minutes or until tender; drain and discard cooking liquid. Place ribs in shallow dish. Pour sauce over ribs, cover and refrigerate for several hours.

3 Preheat grill on medium. Remove ribs from sauce; reserve sauce. Place ribs on lightly oiled grill rack. Close lid and cook (use Direct Grilling, page 7) for about 20 minutes, turning and brushing with sauce once. (Watch closely to prevent burning.)

4 Remove ribs from grill; cover with foil for 10 minutes before serving.

Makes 6 servings and about 1½ cups (375 mL) sauce.

Suggested Menu: Ribs are often served with a potato salad or baked potatoes, cabbage or tossed green salad and apple pie for dessert. If you are looking for a change, serve these ribs with Braised Red Cabbage (page 161), Grilled Corn on the Cob with Herb Butter (page 164) and crusty Italian bread. The zesty glaze suggests a full-flavoured beer that won't get lost between bites.

Tips:

1 Any unused basting sauce can be covered and refrigerated for another use. It is excellent brushed on chicken during grilling. Be sure to boil sauce before using.

2 Have your butcher crack the ribs for easy serving. Precooking pork back and side ribs in liquid before grilling has a number of advantages: it helps the meat stay moist and tender, it shortens the grilling time, and it cooks out some of the excess fat.

Pungent Pork Tenderloin Medallions

This pungent sweet and sour apricot marinade adds moisture and great flavour to lean pork tenderloin.

1 lb	pork tenderloin	500 g

Apricot Marinade

⅓ cup	each: white wine and strained apricot preserves	75 mL
¼ cup	white wine vinegar	50 mL
1 tbsp	each: cornstarch and granulated sugar	15 mL
1 tbsp	each: dry sherry and light soy sauce	15 mL
1	clove garlic, minced	1
	Chopped fresh chives	

1 Cut pork tenderloin crosswise into 12 pieces, each approximately 1 inch (2.5 cm) thick. Place each piece, cut side down on flat surface, between 2 sheets of waxed paper. Pound meat evenly over all surfaces with the flat side of a meat mallet or large knife to ¼ inch (6 mm) thick.

2 *For marinade:* In small bowl, combine wine, preserves, vinegar, cornstarch, sugar, sherry, soy sauce and garlic. Place meat in shallow nonreactive dish or resealable plastic bag. Pour mixture over meat, turn to coat and refrigerate for 2 to 6 hours.

3 Remove pork from marinade; reserve marinade. Place marinade in small saucepan, bring to a boil, reduce heat and cook for 5 minutes; keep warm.

4 Preheat grill on medium. Place meat on oiled grill rack. Close lid and cook (use Direct Grilling, page 7) for about 10 minutes per side, brushing frequently with warm marinade. Remove to platter; pour remaining marinade over pork and serve sprinkled with chives.

Makes 4 servings.

Suggested Menu: Prepare Roasted Beets with Creamy Orange Sauce (page 161) beforehand and keep warm while the pork and Grilled Sweet Potatoes (page 169) are cooking. Add crusty rolls and a green salad.

Pungent Pork Tenderloin
Medallions, page 62

Maple Lemon Pork Tenderloin

Suggested Menu: Serve with Grilled Sweet Potatoes (page 169), a green vegetable, and a tossed salad with Creamy Buttermilk Dressing (page 180) to make an easy company meal.

The tang of lemon juice combined with the sweet flavour of maple syrup adds a marvelous taste and glaze to grilled pork.

1 lb	pork tenderloin	500 g
2 tbsp	maple syrup	25 mL
1 tbsp	each: Dijon mustard, oil and lemon juice	15 mL
1 tsp	grated lemon peel	5 mL
1	clove garlic, crushed	1
1 tsp	dried thyme	5 mL
¼ tsp	freshly ground pepper	1 mL

1 Trim excess fat from meat and discard. Score meat crosswise and place in shallow nonreactive dish or resealable plastic bag.

2 In small bowl, combine maple syrup, mustard, oil, lemon juice and peel, garlic and seasonings. Pour over meat, turn to coat and refrigerate for several hours.

3 Remove meat from marinade; reserve marinade. In small saucepan, bring marinade to a boil, reduce heat and cook for 5 minutes; keep warm.

4 Preheat grill on medium. Place meat on lightly oiled grill rack. Close lid and cook (use Direct Grilling, page 7) for about 20 minutes, turning once; brush occasionally with warm marinade. Remove meat from grill, cover with foil and let stand for 5 minutes before slicing.

Makes 3 to 4 servings.

Glazed Pork Loin Roast

This roast develops extra-special flavours from long exposure to the rub and slow grilling. The orange honey mustard glaze adds the final touch.

4 lb	boneless pork loin roast (center cut)	2 kg

Rub

2	cloves garlic, crushed	2
¼ cup	finely chopped onion	50 mL
2 tsp	dried thyme	10 mL
2 tsp	finely grated lemon peel	10 mL
1 tsp	each: dried oregano and paprika	5 mL
½ tsp	salt	2 mL
¼ tsp	freshly ground pepper	1 mL

Glaze

⅓ cup	orange juice	75 mL
2 tbsp	each: ketchup, herb vinegar and liquid honey	25 mL
½ tsp	dry mustard	2 mL

1 Trim excess fat from meat and discard.

2 *For rub:* In small bowl, combine garlic, onion, thyme, lemon peel and seasonings. Rub evenly over surface of meat. Wrap meat in plastic wrap and refrigerate for 12 to 24 hours.

3 *For glaze:* In small bowl, combine juice, ketchup. vinegar, honey and mustard.

4 Preheat grill on high. Place meat in center of oiled grill rack. Close lid and cook (use Indirect Grilling, page 7) for about 1¼ hours. Brush meat with glaze. Continue cooking, brushing frequently with glaze, for 30 minutes or until meat thermometer registers 160°C (70°C). (For total cooking time of a boneless roast, allow 20 to 30 minutes per lb/500 g.)

5 Remove meat to cutting board and cover with foil; allow to stand for 10 minutes before carving. Cut strings and carve meat.

Makes 8 servings.

Suggested Menu: Serve with Shredded Zucchini, Carrot and Parsnip (page 167), and Grilled Corn on the Cob with Herb Butter (page 164).

Orange-Spiced Pork Chops,
page 67

Orange-spiced Pork Chops

Use this excellent citrus orange marinade with any grilled pork – tenderloin, chops or steaks. Add a fresh Watercress and Bean Sprout Salad (page 182) and dinner is almost on the table.

| 4 | pork loin or rib chops (1 inch/2.5 cm thick) | 4 |

Marinade

1 tsp	grated orange peel	5 mL
½ cup	orange juice	125 mL
1 tbsp	liquid honey	15 mL
½ tsp	ground cinnamon	2 mL
¼ tsp	each: ground ginger and mace	1 mL
⅛ tsp	white pepper	0.5 mL
2	small cloves garlic, crushed	2

1 Trim excess fat from chops and discard.

2 *For marinade:* Combine orange peel and juice, honey, seasonings and garlic and pour into a resealable plastic bag. Place chops in bag; turn to coat meat. Refrigerate for 6 to 24 hours; turn bag occasionally.

3 Drain pork, reserving marinade. Place marinade in small saucepan, bring to a boil, reduce heat and cook for 5 minutes; keep warm.

4 Preheat grill on medium. Place pork on oiled grill rack. Close lid and cook (use Direct Grilling, page 7) for about 6 minutes per side or until juices run clear; brush occasionally with warm marinade.

Makes 4 servings.

Apricot-glazed Veal Cutlets

Served on a nest of thinly sliced green onions, these sweet and spicy veal cutlets are a treat to the eye and the palate. It's not a bad idea to cook extra. The leftovers make wonderful sandwiches and can also be cut in slivers to add to a spinach salad.

6	veal cutlets, ¾-inch (2 cm) thick	6
½ cup	apricot jam	125 mL
1 tbsp	Dijon mustard	15 mL
2 tsp	lemon juice	10 mL
1 tsp	dried thyme or 1 tbsp (15 mL) fresh	5 mL
1	bunch thinly sliced green onions	1

1 Trim excess fat from veal and discard.

2 In bowl, combine jam, mustard, lemon juice and thyme. Spread over each side of veal; cover with plastic wrap and refrigerate for several hours.

3 Preheat grill on medium. Place veal on oiled grill rack. Close lid and cook (use Direct Grilling, page 7) for 6 minutes per side or until veal is done to medium; the center will be slightly pink.

4 Serve veal over a nest of green onions.

Makes 6 servings.

Suggested Menu: Serve with Lemon Mashed Potatoes (page 164), steamed snow peas and julienne carrot strips for a colorful meal.

Pecan Veal with Armagnac Mushroom Sauce

The flavour of wild mushrooms in the sauce, with the "stuffed" marbling of the veal roast, creates an elegant meal for guests. To facilitate carving this roast, have your butcher crack between the rib bones.

Pecan Veal Roast

4 to 6 lb	veal rib roast	2 to 3 kg
3	cloves garlic, slivered	3
¼ cup	chopped pecans	50 mL
½ cup	Armagnac or brandy, divided	125 mL
	Salt and freshly ground pepper	
1 cup	dry white wine	250 mL

Armagnac Mushroom Sauce:

1 oz	dried wild mushrooms	30 g
¼ cup	butter or margarine, divided	50 mL
1	clove garlic, minced	1
1 lb	mushrooms, thinly sliced	500 g
1 tbsp	Armagnac or brandy	15 mL

1 *For roast:* Remove excess fat and discard. With a sharp knife, make many small evenly-spaced slits on surface of roast. Insert garlic slivers and pecans into slits. Brush roast with ¼ cup (50 mL) Armagnac; sprinkle lightly with salt and pepper and let stand for 30 minutes.

2 Preheat grill on medium. Place pan with wine and 2 cups (500 mL) water below where roast will be placed; place roast on oiled grill rack. Close lid and cook (use Indirect Grilling, page 7) for 2½ hours or until thermometer registers 160°F (70°C), about 25 minutes per pound (55 minutes per kg) and meat is medium. Baste roast occasionally with remaining Armagnac during last 30 minutes of cooking.

3 *For sauce:* Meanwhile, in bowl, soak dried mushrooms in ½ cup (125 mL) hot water for 15 minutes or until softened. Drain and discard liquid; set mushrooms aside.

4 Remove meat to cutting board and cover with foil; allow to stand for 10 minutes before carving. Reserve ½ cup (125 mL) pan juices.

5 In saucepan, over medium-high heat, melt 2 tbsp (25 mL) butter; add garlic and mushrooms and sauté for 10 minutes or until softened. Add Armagnac and reserved pan juices and bring to boil. Reduce heat and whisk in remaining butter, 1 tbsp (15 mL) at a time. Season to taste with salt and pepper. Cut strings and carve veal; serve with sauce.

Makes 8 servings.

Suggested Menu: Basil Ratatouille Kebabs (page 166) and Potatoes and Onions in a Pouch (page 155) are very appropriate with this roast. They can be grilled on the rack towards the end of the veal cooking time. An elegant red wine with some depth of flavour is a must to accompany the veal – possibly a Chianti Classico.

Farmer's Sausage with Fresh Tropical Fruit Salsa

The tropical mint flavours beautifully complement grilled sausages and the salsa pairs equally well with pork chops, pork tenderloin and chicken.

6	large farmer's sausages or Bratwurst	6

Tropical Fruit Salsa

1	kiwifruit, peeled and diced	1
½	mango, peeled and diced	½
½	papaya, peeled, seeded and chopped	½
½ cup	quartered strawberries	125 mL
½ cup	diced cantaloupe	125 mL
½	jalapeño pepper, seeded and finely chopped	½
2 tbsp	finely chopped fresh mint leaves	25 mL
1 tbsp	each: lime juice and granulated sugar	15 mL

1 Pierce sausages with fork in several places. In skillet, cover and precook sausages in boiling water for 20 minutes; drain and discard liquid. Reserve sausages.

2 In bowl, stir together kiwifruit, mango, papaya, strawberries, cantaloupe and jalapeño pepper. Add mint, lime juice and sugar; stir to blend. Refrigerate for about 30 minutes to allow flavours to develop.

3 Preheat grill on medium-high. Place sausage on oiled grill rack. Close lid and cook (use Direct Grilling, page 7) for 7 to 10 minutes or until browned and heated through; turn several times. *Makes 6 servings and 3 cups (750 mL) salsa.*

Suggested Menu: Serve with buttered egg noodles and Grilled Sweet Peppers (page 169).

Tips:

1 Precooking sausage helps to lower the fat content.

2 Extra salsa may be refrigerated for up to 3 days. Try it on a fruit or cottage cheese salad.

Quails with Lemon Marinade,
page 82

CHAPTER 3

Birds on the Grill

CHICKEN, TURKEY, DUCK and Rock Cornish hens are all wonderful cooked on the grill. The recipes in this chapter give some interesting approaches to grilling these tasty birds.

Boneless and bone-in chicken breasts, legs and thighs are all cooked on medium-high using direct grilling (page 7) until no longer pink inside. See chart below for grilling times. If using a marinade, keep marinating times short so as not to overpower the chicken's delicate taste. Maximum

DIRECT GRILLING

All cooking times assume using grill lid closed. If using open, allow extra time.

Cut	Total Cooking Time	Grill Temperature	Doneness
Turkey			
Leg 1 lb (500 g)	30–35 minutes	medium	tender, no pink remains
Wings 1/2 lb (250 g)	25–30 minutes	medium	tender, no pink remains
Half breast (boneless, skin on) 1 lb (500 g)	30–35 minutes	medium	tender, no pink remains
Burgers	10–14 minutes	medium-high	well done, no pink remains
Chicken			
Thigh	20 minutes	medium-high	tender, no pink remains
Drumstick	20 minutes	medium-high	tender, no pink remains
Leg	20 minutes	medium-high	tender, no pink remains
Breast	about 14 minutes	medium-high	tender, no pink remains
Broiler-fryer halves 3 lb (1.5 kg)	about 45 minutes	medium-high	tender, no pink remains
Burgers	12–14 minutes	medium-high	well-done, no pink remains
Whole chicken 3 lb (1.5 kg)	1–1 1/2 hours	medium-high	tender, no pink remains
Whole chicken 4 lb (2 kg)	1 3/4 hours	medium-high	tender, no pink remains
Whole chicken 5 lb (2.5 kg)	2 hours	medium-high	tender, no pink remains
Cornish hen			
	1 1/2 hours	medium-high	tender, no pink remains
Quail			
6 oz (180 g)	30 minutes	medium-high	tender, no pink remains
Duck			
breast	about 10 minutes	medium-high	tender, no pink remains

marinating times should be no more than 2 hours for a highly seasoned marinade and 4 hours for a mild one.

Grill turkey parts the same way as chicken parts but cook at medium heat. Since turkey is less delicate in taste than chicken, marinating times can be longer.

Turkey breasts grilled with fresh herbs (for example, thyme, sage, lemon grass or rosemary) tucked under the skin make an exotic meal requiring little attention. Simply loosen the skin, place the fresh herbs underneath, skewer the skin back in place, brush lightly with olive oil and start the cooking. The aroma is enticing, the taste is tantalizing, and you are left with very little cleanup.

Marinating poultry cuts before grilling is a good idea, and not just for the taste. Meats cooked at high temperatures produce substances called heterocyclic amines that promote cancer. A study underwritten by the National Cancer Institute of the United States shows that a whole chicken breast, marinated in olive oil, cider vinegar, brown sugar, lemon juice, garlic, mustard and salt and grilled on a propane gas grill for 30 minutes, produced fewer heterocyclic amines than unmarinated chicken grilled the same way. Marinating reduced some of these carcinogenic substances by 90 percent. (*University of California at Berkeley Wellness Letter*, July, 1997). Be sure to boil remaining marinade in order to destroy any harmful bacteria left over from the raw poultry before using the marinade as a sauce or brushing it on poultry during grilling.

Larger whole chickens and turkeys should be cooked by indirect grilling (page 7) on medium heat. Cover the bird with foil after removing it from the grill and allow 15 or 20 minutes standing time before carving. Feeling adventurous? Try adding aromatic wood chips such as mesquite to the grill for real wood-smoke flavor. Follow the suppliers instructions. Alternatively, fill the cavity of the bird with fresh rosemary or thyme and slices of lemon for exciting herb and citrus flavors.

As with any other raw meat, proper storage and handling of poultry is important. Keep poultry clean and keep it cold until you cook it. Before marinating or cooking poultry, rinse and pat dry. Wash and dry your hands before and after handling raw meat. Most poultry can be stored in the refrigerator for up to 48 hours, or in the freezer for up to 6 months. Refrigerate leftovers promptly.

INDIRECT GRILLING

Your turkey is done if the legs move easily when twisted and the juices run clear. Let turkey stand covered with foil for 15 to 20 minutes before carving.

Cut	Total Cooking Time	Grill Temperature	Doneness
Whole Turkey – unstuffed			
8–10 lb (3.5–4.5 kg)	1 1/2 hours	medium	thermometer is 170°F (70°C)
10–12 lb (5–5.5 kg)	1 3/4 hours	medium	thermometer is 170° (70°C)
12-16 lb (5.5–7.0 kg)	2 hours	medium	thermometer is 170°F (70°C)
Whole Turkey Breast, 2 lb (1 kg)	1 3/4 hours	medium-low	thermometer is 170°F (70°C)

Mediterranean Stuffed Chicken Breasts

Mediterranean flavors of olive, oregano, Parmesan and garlic permeate these succulent chicken breasts. Sliced, the breasts display the attractive marbling of the stuffing. Plan for leftovers. These chicken breasts are as good, if not better, served cold, a day later.

Stuffing

1 cup	soft bread crumbs	250 mL
¼ cup	milk	50 mL
¼ cup	finely chopped black olives	50 mL
1	egg	1
¼ cup	grated Parmesan cheese	50 mL
2 tbsp	chopped fresh parsley	25 mL
1½ tsp	dried oregano or 2 tbsp (25 mL) fresh	7 mL
1	clove garlic, minced	1
	Salt and freshly ground pepper	

Chicken

4	boneless, skinless chicken breast halves	4
½ cup	dried bread crumbs	125 mL

Wine Sauce

1 cup	dry white wine	250 mL
2 tbsp	capers, rinsed and drained	25 mL
1 tbsp	melted butter or margarine	15 mL
½ cup	chicken broth	125 mL
1 tbsp	each: cornstarch and chopped fresh parsley	15 mL

1 *For stuffing:* In small bowl, soak bread in milk for 5 minutes. Stir in olives, egg, cheese, parsley, oregano, garlic, and salt and pepper to taste.

2 *For chicken:* Cut a pocket in the thickest part of each chicken breast, fill with some of the stuffing and close with toothpicks. Coat chicken evenly with dried bread crumbs.

3 Preheat grill on medium-high. Place chicken breasts on oiled grill rack. Close lid and cook (use Direct Grilling, page 7) for about 3 minutes per side or until brown. Lower heat to medium, continue cooking until meat is tender and no longer pink inside.

4 *For sauce:* Meanwhile, in small saucepan, combine wine, capers and butter. Heat for 5 minutes or until hot. Combine chicken broth, cornstarch and parsley; stir into wine mixture; cook for 5 minutes or until slightly thickened, stirring often.

5 Remove chicken breasts from grill to cutting board. Cover with foil for 5 minutes. Carve each breast crosswise into slices and place on heated serving platter. Pour some warm sauce over chicken and pass extra sauce.

Makes 4 servings.

Suggested Menu: Serve with Caramelized Leeks and Onions (page 163) or buttered cooked noodles, Grilled Eggplant (page 168), and a sliced French baguette.

Maple Cranberry Chicken
Quarters, page 75

Maple Cranberry Chicken Quarters

Maple and cranberry flavors give chicken quarters a special lift. The cranberry theme carries through to the accompanying salsa. Chicken legs or breasts can be substituted for the quarters.

Maple Cranberry Glaze

| ½ cup | maple syrup | 125 mL |
| ¼ cup | dried cranberries | 50 mL |

Chicken

2 lb	chicken leg quarters (both thigh and drumstick)	1 kg
1 tbsp	each: canola oil and vinegar	15 mL
	Salt and freshly ground pepper	
1 cup	Mexican Cranberry Salsa (page 18)	250 mL
	Fresh cilantro sprigs	

1 *For glaze:* In small saucepan, cook maple syrup and cranberries for 5 minutes or until fruit is softened. Place mixture in food processor or blender; purée until smooth and set aside.

2 Preheat grill on medium-high. Combine oil and vinegar; use to brush chicken. Place chicken on oiled grill rack. Close lid and cook (use Indirect Grilling, page 7) on medium for 50 to 60 minutes or until chicken is tender and no longer pink inside. Brush often with glaze during last 15 minutes of cooking.

3 Garnish chicken with Mexican Cranberry Salsa and fresh cilantro sprigs.
Makes 4 servings.

Suggested Menu: Our family enjoys Grilled Sweet Potatoes (page 169) and a green vegetable such as green beans or snow peas. For an easy and fun dessert, try Grilled Fruit and Maple Pizza (page 215).

Tip: Do not refreeze completely thawed, uncooked chicken. Once chicken is thawed, keep it refrigerated and cook it within 48 hours.

Chicken Mushroom Burgers

These burgers are a real hit with all ages. A 12 year old granddaughter, who is always suspicious about anything different in foods, asks for these whenever she visits.

1 lb	lean ground chicken	500 g
1½ cups	finely chopped mushrooms	375 mL
2	green onions, chopped	2
1 to 2	cloves garlic, minced	1 to 2
¼ cup	oat bran	50 mL
1¼ tsp	dried tarragon	6 mL
	or 1 tbsp (15 mL) fresh	
½ tsp	salt	2 mL
⅛ tsp	freshly ground pepper	0.5 mL
6	whole wheat buns, halved	6

Garnishes

tomato slices, alfalfa sprouts or leaf lettuce, cranberry sauce, mustard, light mayonnaise

1 In bowl, combine chicken, mushrooms, onions, garlic, oat bran and seasonings. Lightly shape into 6 patties, about ½-inch (1 cm) thick.

2 Preheat grill on medium-high. Place patties on oiled grill rack. Close lid and cook (use Direct Grilling, page 7) for about 6 minutes per side or until brown and chicken is no longer pink inside.

3 During last part of cooking, place buns at back of grill to warm. Fill each bun with a cooked pattie, top with choice of garnishes.
Makes 6 servings.

Suggested Menu: Serve with Grilled Asparagus (page 168) or Asparagus Salad with Creamy Dressing (page 174), crinkle cut potatoes with a garnish of chopped fresh mint, and iced mineral water with lemon.

Tip: A little care for your chicken is in order. After handling raw chicken, wash your hands and all utensils with hot soapy water and rinse well.

After grilling always put burgers on a clean plate; never use a plate that held the raw burgers.

Chicken Mushroom Burgers,
page 76

Middle Eastern Chicken Burgers with Yogurt Sauce

The flavors of India – curry, cumin and coriander – permeate these burgers and their matching yogurt sauce.

Yogurt Sauce

2 cups	plain yogurt	500 mL
2	small onions, coarsely chopped	2
2 tbsp	olive oil	25 mL
4	cloves garlic	4
1 cup	loosely packed cilantro leaves	250 mL
1 tsp	each: coriander seeds and ground cumin	5 mL
½ tsp	crushed red pepper flakes	2 mL
	Salt and freshly ground pepper	

Chicken Burgers

1	egg, beaten	1
¼ cup	dried bread crumbs	50 mL
2	green onions, thinly sliced	2
1	clove garlic, minced	1
½ tsp	each: cumin and salt	2 mL
¼ tsp	freshly ground pepper	1 mL
1 lb	lean ground chicken or turkey	500 g
6	whole wheat sesame burger buns, split	6

Garnishes

lettuce leaves, sliced red onion rings, pickled banana peppers

1 *For sauce:* In food processor, process yogurt, onions, oil, garlic, cilantro and seasonings until almost smooth; add salt and pepper to taste. Cover and refrigerate.

2 *For burgers:* In bowl, combine egg, bread crumbs, onions, garlic and seasonings. Mix in chicken; lightly shape into 6 patties, about ½-inch (1 cm) thick.

3 Preheat grill on medium. Place patties on oiled grill rack. Close lid and cook (use Direct Grilling, page 7) for 6 to 7 minutes per side (about 8 for turkey) or until brown and burger is no longer pink inside; turn once.

4 During last part of cooking, place buns at back of grill to warm. Fill each bun with a cooked pattie, top with lettuce, onion, banana peppers and Yogurt Sauce.

Makes 6 servings.

> **Tip:** Do not thaw frozen poultry at room temperature – bacteria will thrive. The microwave oven provides an ideal way to defrost poultry. Allow 3 to 5 minutes per pound (500 g). Cover with waxed paper and thaw on defrost cycle; rotate occasionally.

Rock Cornish Hens and Vegetables en Papillote

The flavors in this recipe are reminiscent of Provençal cooking. The *en papillote* cooking method (here, in a foil pouch) provides an interesting transfer of flavors between the hens and the vegetables. Each serving is cooked in a neat package. Once everything is assembled, sit back and relax-dinner will be ready in about an hour and a half.

Hens

3	Rock Cornish hens, thawed	3
2	cloves garlic, halved	2

Stuffing

2 tbsp	butter or margarine	25 mL
1 cup	chopped onion	250 mL
2 cups	sliced mushrooms	500 mL
1	large tomato, diced	1
1 tbsp	each: dried tarragon and parsley or 3 tbsp (45 mL) chopped fresh	15 mL
½ tsp	each: dried thyme and salt	2 mL
¼ tsp	freshly ground pepper	1 mL
¼ cup	dried bread crumbs	50 mL

Vegetables

1½	medium zucchini, halved lengthwise and crosswise	1½
12	baby carrots, trimmed	12
1	medium red onion, cut into wedges	1
½	sweet red pepper, cut into wide strips	½
3	medium potatoes, halved	3
1	large stalk celery, cut into 6 pieces	1
	Fresh tarragon	

1 *For hens:* Wash and dry. Rub cut side of garlic over cavity and outer skin of each hen; crush garlic.

2 *For stuffing:* In skillet, melt butter over medium-high. Add crushed garlic and onion; cook for about 5 minutes. Add mushrooms; cook until mushrooms are softened and liquid has evaporated. Combine mushroom mixture, tomato and seasonings; stir in bread crumbs. Spoon stuffing into cavity of each hen; truss with skewers and kitchen cord. Arrange each hen in center of large piece of foil or in aluminum foil pans.

3 *For vegetables:* Scatter zucchini, carrots, red pepper, onions, potatoes and celery around each hen; add extra tarragon. Sprinkle lightly with salt and pepper. Close foil securely around hen and vegetables.

5 Preheat grill on medium-high. Place foil packages on grill rack. Close lid and cook (use Indirect Grilling, page 7) for about 1½ hours or until hen juices run clear and vegetables are tender.

6 Remove packages from grill. Open foil, split hens down backbone and serve each half with an assortment of vegetables.

Makes 6 servings.

Tip: Of course, no drip pan is required when cooking *en papillote*.

Rock Cornish Hens with Sherry-Peach Glaze

Celebrate the summer peach season with this glaze and salsa. They are quite sensational with the grilled Cornish game hens. The salsa also goes well with chicken breasts and chicken burgers.

2	Rock Cornish hens (1½ lb/750 g each)	2
	Canola oil and fresh rosemary sprigs	

Sherry-Peach Glaze

⅓ cup	peach preserves or jam	75 mL
1 tbsp	sherry or lemon juice	15 mL
1 tsp	dried rosemary or 1 tbsp (15 mL) fresh	5 mL

Peach 'n' Pepper Salsa

2 cups	chopped peeled peaches (2 medium)	500 mL
½ cup	each: chopped sweet red and green pepper	125 mL
¼ cup	each: finely chopped red onion and chopped fresh cilantro	50 mL
½	jalapeño pepper, chopped	½
1	clove garlic, crushed	1
1 tbsp	each: lime juice and rice vinegar	15 mL
1 tsp	liquid honey	5 mL
	Fresh rosemary sprigs	

1 Rinse and prepare hens for grilling; brush lightly with oil, sprinkle rosemary in cavity.

2 Preheat grill on medium-high. Place hens in center of oiled grill rack, bone side down. Close lid and cook (use Indirect Grilling, page 7) for about 1½ hours or until meat is tender and no longer pink inside.

3 *For glaze:* In small saucepan, melt preserves; stir in sherry and rosemary. Brush hens with glaze during last 15 minutes of cooking.

4 *For salsa:* Meanwhile, in medium bowl, combine peaches, sweet peppers, onion, cilantro, jalapeño pepper and garlic. Stir in lime juice, vinegar and honey. Cover and refrigerate.

5 Remove hens from grill, cover with foil for 5 minutes before cutting through backbone. Lay each half on large warm platter, garnish with rosemary. Serve with salsa.

Makes 4 servings and 3 cups (750 mL) salsa.

Suggested Menu: Accompany Rock Cornish Hens with Creamed Spinach (page 155) on a bed of cooked lentils. An alternative menu with Lemon Mashed Potatoes (page 164) and steamed spinach makes a colourful meal. Grilled fresh peach halves brushed occasionally with balsamic vinegar provide an exciting garnish along with the salsa.

Tip: Since jalapeño peppers vary greatly in heat levels, add them to taste.

Rock Cornish Hens with Sherry-Peach Glaze, page 80

Quails with Lemon Marinade

A lemon marinade is ideal for this delicately flavored fowl. Hearty appetites should be able to deal with two of these small birds-hence my suggestion that this recipe makes two to four servings, depending on appetite. It's an easy recipe to double.

| 4 | quails (6 oz/180 g) each | 4 |

Lemon Marinade

⅓ cup	lemon juice	75 mL
1 tsp	grated lemon peel	5 mL
4 tsp	brown sugar	20 mL
1 tbsp	chopped fresh parsley	15 mL
1 tbsp	olive oil	15 mL
2	cloves garlic, crushed	2
1 tsp	dried oregano or 1 tbsp (15 mL) chopped fresh	5 mL
½ tsp	salt	2 mL
¼ tsp	freshly ground pepper	1 mL

1 Remove backbone and breastbone from quails (or better still, ask the butcher to do this). Rinse and pat dry. Thread soaked wooden skewers through meat to help quail remain flat during grilling.

2 *For marinade:* In bowl, whisk together lemon juice and peel, sugar, parsley, oil, garlic, oregano, salt and pepper. Place quails in a large resealable plastic bag. Pour lemon mixture into bag, turn to coat and reseal. Refrigerate for about 30 minutes; turn bag occasionally.

3 Remove quails from marinade; reserve marinade. Place marinade in small saucepan, bring to a boil, reduce heat and cook for 5 minutes; keep warm.

4 Preheat grill on medium-high. Place quail on oiled grill rack, skin side down. Close lid and cook (use Indirect Grilling, page 7) for 30 minutes or until meat is tender and no longer pink. Baste often with warm marinade. Remove quails from grill, cover with foil for 5 minutes.
Makes 2 to 4 servings.

Suggested Menu: Serve on a bed of Warm Spinach and Radicchio Salad (page 190).

Tip: It is wise not to marinate poultry in an acid mixture any longer than 30 minutes since the meat requires flavor enhancement rather than tenderizing. Longer marinating in acids such as citrus juices and vinegar starts to "cook" the meat and changes the texture. This is also true for marinating fish.

Lemon Chicken Drumsticks

Lemon flavor highlights come from both the marinade and the sauce. Trimming fat and skin from the drumsticks reduces calories and allows the marinade to be absorbed by the chicken so that it remains moist.

Marinade

¼ cup	lemon juice, divided	50 mL
3 tbsp	Dijon mustard	45 mL
1	clove garlic, crushed	1
4	chicken drumsticks (about 1 lb/500 g)	4

Lemon Sauce

2 tbsp	each: low-fat mayonnaise and barbecue sauce	25 mL
1 tsp	chili powder	5 mL
1 tsp	grated lemon peel	5 mL
¾ cup	coarse bread crumbs	175 mL
1 tsp	each: dried oregano and basil	5 mL
	Lemon slices	

1 *For marinade:* In medium bowl, combine 3 tbsp (45 mL) lemon juice, mustard and garlic. Trim and discard skin and excess fat from chicken. Add chicken to marinade and turn to coat evenly. Cover and refrigerate for at least 30 minutes.

2 *For sauce:* In bowl, combine remaining lemon juice, mayonnaise, barbecue sauce, chili powder and lemon peel; cover and refrigerate.

3 In shallow pan, combine bread crumbs, oregano and basil. Remove chicken from marinade; discard marinade. Dip chicken in bread crumb mixture.

4 Preheat grill on medium. Place chicken on oiled grill rack. Close lid and cook (use Indirect Grilling, page 7) for 30 to 40 minutes or until chicken is tender and no longer pink inside; turn several times.

5 Serve chicken with chilled sauce and sliced lemon.

Makes 4 servings.

Tip: To remove all skin and fat from poultry, use a sharp knife or poultry shears.

Duck Breasts with Mango Orange Sauce,
page 85, on Wild Rice Crêpes, page 188

Duck Breasts with Mango Orange Sauce

Mangos and oranges make a marvelous sauce to grace grilled duck breasts. Duck can be a challenge to cook. The breast may be perfectly done to medium-rare while the legs are still undercooked. The classic solution, taken here, is to cook and serve only the breasts and keep the legs for another occasion.

| 2 | whole boneless duck breasts (12 oz/375 g each) | 2 |

Marinade

½ cup	dry white wine	125 mL
⅓ cup	orange marmalade	75 mL
1 tbsp	canola oil	15 mL
1	clove garlic, minced	1
1 tsp	ground summer savory	5 mL
¼ tsp	freshly ground pepper	1 mL

Mango Orange Sauce

1	ripe mango, peeled and sliced	1
½ cup	orange juice	125 mL
¼ cup	liquid honey	50 mL
1 tsp	each: chopped fresh gingerroot and orange peel	5 mL
¼ tsp	salt	1 mL
⅛ tsp	white pepper	0.5 mL
	Mango slices	

1 Place duck in shallow nonreactive dish or resealable plastic bag.

2 *For marinade:* In small bowl, combine wine, marmalade, oil, garlic, savory and pepper. Pour over duck, turn to coat, cover and refrigerate for 4 hours or overnight; turn occasionally.

3 *For sauce:* In small saucepan, combine mango, orange juice, honey, gingerroot, peel, salt and pepper. Bring to boil, reduce heat and cook for about 5 minutes or until fruit is soft. Remove from heat, cool slightly. Place in food processor or blender and purée until smooth. Return to saucepan and keep warm.

4 Remove duck from marinade; reserve marinade. Place marinade in small saucepan; bring to a boil, reduce heat and cook for 5 minutes; keep warm. Score duck skin in crisscross pattern with sharp knife.

5 Preheat grill on medium-high. Place duck on oiled grill rack. Close lid and cook (use Direct Grilling, page 7) for about 5 minutes per side or until tender and no longer pink inside; brush often with warm marinade.

6 Remove duck from grill, remove skin and discard; slice meat thinly. Fan duck slices on warm plates and garnish with a spoonful of Mango Orange Sauce and sliced mango.

Makes 4 servings.

Suggested Menu: Serve duck with Wild Rice Crêpes (page 188). This menu is absolutely ideal as a dinner for guests, and family will enjoy it also. The warm sliced duck can also be used for a warm duck salad.

Tip: Since duck is high in fat, place a grilling pan with cold water below the grill rack to prevent flare-ups during cooking

Chicken with Oriental Marinade

Plum sauce gives an Oriental accent to chicken breasts, a longtime grill favorite. Experiment with different mustards to put a new spin to this simple glaze.

Marinade

½ cup	plum sauce	125 mL
3 tbsp	soy sauce	45 mL
1	piece gingerroot (1 inch/2.5 cm), minced	1
2 tsp	sesame oil	10 mL
2	cloves garlic, crushed	2
2 tsp	grainy mustard	10 mL

Chicken

4	boneless, skinless chicken breast halves	4
4	green onion fans	4

1 *For marinade:* In bowl, combine plum and soy sauce, gingerroot, oil, garlic and mustard; stir well.
2 Place chicken breasts in resealable plastic bag; pour plum mixture over chicken and refrigerate for 1 hour or longer depending on depth of flavor desired. Remove chicken from marinade; reserve marinade. Place marinade in small saucepan, bring to a boil, reduce heat and cook for 5 minutes; keep warm.
3 Preheat grill on medium-high. Place chicken on oiled grill rack. Close lid and cook (use Direct Grilling, page 7) for about 15 minutes or until

meat is tender and no longer pink inside. Brush occasionally with warm marinade; turn once. Serve with onion garnish.
Makes 4 servings.

Suggested Menu: Accompany these chicken breasts with an Oriental-flavored rice, a noodle salad with water chestnuts and snow peas sautéed in sesame and olive oil, or Szechwan Vegetable Salad (page 177).

Tip: If plum sauce is very thick, thin it with 2 tbsp (25 mL) pineapple or orange juice.

Chicken Breast with Creamy Peppercorn Sauce

The fresh, pungent pepper flavor of the green and black peppercorn sauce gives an exciting lift to grilled chicken breasts.

Creamy Peppercorn Sauce

¼ cup	white wine vinegar	50 mL
¼ cup	sweet white wine (such as Sauterne)	50 mL
1 tbsp	each: black and dried green peppercorns	15 mL
1¼ cups	heavy cream	300 mL
6	boneless, skinless chicken breast halves	6
	Fresh chives	

1 *For sauce:* In heavy saucepan, cook vinegar, wine and peppercorns on medium-high for 10 minutes or until reduced to a glaze. Stir in cream, reduce heat and simmer for 5 minutes or until reduced to about 1¼ cups (300 mL); keep warm.

2 Preheat grill on medium-high. Place chicken on oiled grill rack. Close lid and cook (use Direct Grilling, page 7) for 12 to 15 minutes or until tender and no longer pink inside; turn once. Remove chicken from grill and serve with warm Creamy Peppercorn Sauce and a garnish of chives.
Makes 6 servings.

Suggested Menu: Serve warm over assorted greens, or accompany the chicken with Endive Salad with Grilled Red Onions (page 174), steamed broccoli and whole wheat rolls. A bowl of Cucumber Vichyssoise with Dill (page 25) as a starter is a nice addition.

DIRECT GRILLING

Rosemary Grilled Chicken with Citrus Salsa

The real beauty of boneless skinless chicken breasts is their simplicity of preparation. They come ready to go. Try marinating them in this simple rosemary-wine mixture and serve with a tangy salsa.

Marinade

½ cup	fresh rosemary sprigs	125 mL
⅔ cup	dry white wine	150 mL
2 tbsp	canola oil	25 mL
½ tsp	each: freshly ground pepper and paprika	2 mL
2	cloves garlic, minced	2

Chicken

6	boneless, skinless chicken breast halves	6
1 cup	Citrus Salsa (page 39, omit jalapeño pepper) Orange twists	250 mL

1 *For marinade:* In small bowl, combine rosemary, wine, oil, pepper, paprika and garlic. Place chicken in shallow nonreactive dish in single layer. Pour marinade over chicken; turn to coat. Cover and refrigerate for up to 4 hours.

2 Preheat grill on medium-high. Remove chicken and rosemary from marinade; reserve rosemary sprigs and discard the rest of the marinade. Place chicken on oiled grill rack. Close lid and cook (use Direct Grilling, page 7) for 6 to 8 minutes per side or until chicken is no longer pink inside. After chicken has been turned, sprinkle reserved rosemary on cooked side of chicken.

3 Serve chicken with a spoonful of Citrus Salsa and an orange twist.
Makes 6 servings.

Suggested Menu: Accompany the chicken with frenched green beans, Grilled New Potatoes (page 169) and if time permits, Artichoke Salad (page 176).

Yucatan Chicken with Guacamole

Hot peppers and oregano give these chicken breasts a Mexican flavor. A tomato slice and an oregano sprig are sandwiched within each breast.

3	boneless, skinless whole chicken breasts (about 2 lb/1 kg)	3

Chili Paste

3 tbsp	each: tomato paste and water	45 mL
2 tbsp	chili powder	25 mL
1 tbsp	rice vinegar	15 mL
1 tbsp	minced jalapeño pepper	15 mL
2	cloves garlic, minced and mashed	2
½ tsp	each: dried oregano and salt	2 mL
2	firm medium tomatoes	2
6	fresh oregano sprigs	6
	Jalapeño pepper	
	Red chili pepper	

1 Rinse chicken, pat dry and remove excess fat and discard; halve breasts and set aside.

2 *For paste:* In small bowl, stir together tomato paste, water, chili powder, vinegar, jalapeño pepper, garlic, oregano and salt to make a thick paste. Place chicken in shallow nonreactive dish large enough to hold chicken in one layer; coat chicken with chili paste. Cover and refrigerate for at least 3 hours or overnight.

3 With a knife, remove stem end of tomatoes; cut each tomato into three 1-inch (2.5 cm) slices. Arrange 1 tomato slice and 1 oregano sprig on wide end of each chicken breast; fold narrow end over to sandwich tomato and oregano. Thread a skewer through ends of chicken breast and then through folded side, letting pointed end of skewer extend about 2 inches (5 cm) beyond chicken breast. Repeat with remaining tomatoes, oregano and chicken.

4 Preheat grill on medium-high. Place chicken, thick end down, on oiled grill rack. Close lid and cook (use Direct Grilling, page 7) for about 10 minutes; turn and cook on second side until chicken is tender and no longer pink inside. Remove chicken and garnish with jalapeño chili peppers and red chili peppers.
Makes 6 servings.

Suggested Menu: For an authentic "south of the border " taste, serve with crisp corn tortillas, Guacamole (page 46), and Mexican Corn Salad (page 190).
Tip: The longer the marinating time, the more distinctive the depth of spice flavor.

Yucatan Chicken with Guacamole, page 88

Polynesian Honey Turkey Drumsticks

Pineapple juice and gingerroot give an exotic Polynesian twist to ordinary turkey drumsticks.

Marinade

½ cup	pineapple juice	125 mL
¼ cup	liquid honey	50 mL
3	cloves garlic, crushed	3
3 tbsp	Worcestershire sauce	45 mL
1	piece gingerroot (1 inch/2.5 cm long), finely chopped	1
½ tsp	each: salt and paprika	2 mL
¼ tsp	freshly ground pepper	1 mL

Turkey

3	turkey drumsticks (about ¾ lb/375 g each)	3
	Snipped fresh chives	

1 *For marinade:* In small bowl, combine pineapple juice, honey, garlic, Worcestershire sauce, gingerroot, salt, paprika and pepper.

2 Place drumsticks in large resealable plastic bag; pour marinade over drumsticks; turn to coat. Refrigerate for at least 6 hours or overnight. Remove drumsticks from marinade; reserve marinade. Place marinade in small saucepan, bring to a boil, reduce heat and cook for 5 minutes; keep warm.

3 Preheat grill on medium. Place drumsticks on oiled grill rack. Close lid and cook (use Indirect Grilling, page 7) for about 1½ hours or until drumsticks are tender and no longer pink inside. Brush occasionally during final 20 minutes with warm marinade.

4 Remove drumsticks from grill; cover with foil and let stand for 10 minutes. Slice meat, arrange on plate and sprinkle with chives.
Makes 4 to 6 servings.

> **Tip:** Never pierce turkey with a fork. Instead, turn it with a spatula or tongs to retain the juice. Brush on marinade during final 15 to 20 minutes of grilling to prevent burning.

Peppered Orange Turkey Breast

Marinated in Peppered Orange Marinade and slowly grilled on the barbecue, turkey breast is moist and flavorful. Basting with extra marinade during grilling adds more flavor.

Peppered Orange Marinade

1	dried chili pepper, seeded and coarsely chopped	1
1 cup	chicken broth	250 mL
1 tbsp	achiote powder* (optional)	15 mL
1½ tsp	dried oregano	7 mL
2 cups	orange juice	500 mL
2 tbsp	lime juice	25 mL
1 to 2 tsp	hot pepper sauce	5 to 10 mL
	Salt and freshly ground pepper	

Turkey

1	whole turkey breast (about 4 lb/2 kg)	1
1 cup	loosely packed fresh cilantro	250 mL
1	medium onion, quartered	1
1	lemon, quartered	1
1½ cups	mesquite or hickory chips	375 mL

1 *For marinade:* In small saucepan, combine chili pepper, broth, achiote (if using) and oregano. Simmer for about 30 minutes or until chili pepper starts to soften. Remove from heat and purée. Stir in orange and lime juice and hot pepper sauce; refrigerate one-half of the marinade.

2 Place turkey breast in a resealable plastic bag or shallow nonreactive dish. Pour remaining marinade over turkey and turn to coat. Refrigerate for 12 hours or overnight; turn occasionally.

3 Remove turkey from marinade; reserve marinade. In small saucepan, bring marinade to a boil, reduce heat and cook for 5 minutes; keep warm. Place cilantro, onion and lemon in breast cavity.

4 Preheat grill on medium. Place breast on oiled grill rack, skin side down; reduce heat to medium-low. Close lid and cook (use Indirect Grilling, page 7) for about 1¾ hours or until thermometer registers 170°F (77°C) and turkey is well browned and meat no longer pink; turn several times. Brush turkey occasionally with warm marinade.

5 Remove turkey from grill to carving board; cover with foil for 10 to 15 minutes before slicing. Carve meat on diagonal. Heat refrigerated marinade and serve with turkey.
Makes 6 to 8 servings.

*Achiote is a powder made from the seeds of the annotto tree and is available in East Indian, Caribbean and Spanish supply stores. Its rusty-red color enhances foods.

Suggested Menu: Serve the turkey breast with toasted corn bread, a salad of diced fresh pineapple and other tropical fruits flavored with fresh mint, and perhaps cooked black beans and rice.

Tips:

1 This same procedure can be followed for a small whole turkey or large chicken equally well.

2 When is a turkey breast fully cooked? When the thickest part turns from pink to white.

3 Labels on fresh poultry must give the year, month and day of packaging. Select a fresh turkey breast packaged the day you are in the store. At home, place turkey in refrigerator or freezer immediately.

4 Store cooked turkey in a covered container, plastic bag or aluminum foil for up to 4 days in the refrigerator or up to 3 months in the freezer.

Dijon Halibut with Provençal Sauce, top, page 98, and Ginger Sesame Salmon Steaks, page 95

CHAPTER 4

Fish and Seafood on the Grill

FISH IS ONE OF the most satisfying foods to cook on the grill. Cooking times are short and the results can be spectacular. The recipes in this chapter do wonderful things to fish and seafood. Grilled Mango and Citrus Fish Fillets (page115) is an amazing combination of fruit and fish. Tandoori Scallops with Vegetables (page 110) is an interesting simulation of an Indian classic. The Wine and Olive Sauce for the Fish Steaks (page 104) is divine.

The most important thing to know in grilling seafood is what variety to use. Choose a fish that has a firm, meaty texture so it won't fall apart while grilling. From the ocean, grouper, tuna, salmon, arctic char, swordfish, halibut, scallops, and shrimp are the most suitable. Add to this fresh water whitefish, splake and pickerel. However, any of the more delicate textured fish are also fine for grilling *en papillote*.

Fish has been called the griller's greatest challenge. The problem lies in getting it off the grill. To ensure easy removal of the cooked fish, spray or oil the rack lightly before placing it over the fire. Make sure the grill grate is very hot when you put the fish on it. Leave the fish for a few minutes before moving it. This allows a sear to develop

DIRECT GRILLING

Cook all fish for 10 minutes per inch (2.5 cm) of thickness or until it flakes easily with a fork and is opaque.
Cook all seafood until it is opaque.

Fish or Seafood	Weight/Thickness	Grill Temperature	Time
Fillets and steaks	1/2–1 inch (1–2.5 cm)	medium-high	10 min/inch (2.5 cm)
Lobster tails	6 oz (180 g)	medium-high	6–8 minutes
	8 oz (250 g)	medium-high	12–15 minutes
Scallops for kebabs	12–15 per lb (500 g)	medium-high	about 6 minutes
Shrimp	medium	medium-high	6–8 minutes
	jumbo	medium-high	12–15 minutes

between the fish and the grill rack, which further helps prevent sticking. Be sure the rack is clean; residue from a previous meal could interfere with the delicate flavor of seafood.

Cook difficult-to-handle seafood in a fish basket or on a perforated tray placed on the grill rack. In most instances, fish should be cooked by direct grilling (page 7). However, indirect grilling (also page 7), should be used for whole fish and fish *en papillote*. In the case of whole fish, the skin and bones help keep the fish moist and flavorful.

Fish contains a lot of moisture. To ensure it does not dry out and become tough, grill fish quickly on medium-high heat. Be careful to not overcook. Start checking a few minutes before you think it may be done. Fish is done when it is firm to the touch, flakes easily and is opaque; under-cooked fish appears shiny and semitranslucent. The rule for cooking fish developed by The Canadian Department of Fisheries and Oceans is to measure the fish at its thickest part; cook for 10 minutes per inch (2.5 cm) of thickness at medium-high on the grill. Turn steaks and skinless fillets halfway through the cooking time. Don't turn fillets with skin; instead, leave them skin side down. The skin will protect the flesh from the direct heat and is easily removed before serving.

Planked fish is a moist and flavorful way to grill fish fillets. Place the fillet on an untreated, water-soaked cedar plank about 8 x 18 x 2 inches (20 x 45 x 5 cm). Place the plank directly on the grill rack and cook by the direct grill method (page 7). Spray the wood occasionally if it starts to smoke or flame. You will never have to turn the fish or wonder if it is burning. The cedar plank can be reused several times.

INDIRECT GRILLING

Fish or Seafood	Weight/Thickness	Grill Temperature	Time
Whole fish	about 1 1/2 lb (750 g)	medium-high	10 min/inch (2.5 cm) thickness
Fillets and steaks in foil with vegetables	1/2–1 inch (1–2.5 cm)	medium-high	10 min/inch (2.5 cm) thickness

Ginger Sesame Salmon Steaks

Ginger has a special affinity with grilled salmon. The combination of pungent ginger with the sweet nutty flavor of sesame adds an exciting dimension to this magnificent fish. You can substitute any firm-fleshed fish such as grouper, tuna or halibut.

Ginger Seasame Baste

1 tbsp	sesame seeds, toasted (see below)	15 mL
1 tbsp	minced gingerroot	15 mL
2	cloves garlic, crushed	2
4 tsp	sesame oil	20 mL
1 tbsp	soy sauce	15 mL

Fish

4	salmon steaks (1 inch/2.5 cm thick) about 2 lb/1kg	4
	Salt and lemon pepper	
	Lemon wedges	

1 *Baste:* In small bowl, combine sesame seeds, gingerroot, garlic, oil and soy sauce; set aside.

2 Season salmon lightly with salt and lemon pepper. Preheat grill on medium-high. Place salmon on oiled grill rack and brush with reserved sesame mixture. Close lid and cook (use Direct Grilling, page 7) for about 10 minutes (10 minutes per inch/2.5 cm of thickness) or until fish is opaque and flakes easily with a fork; turn once. Remove fish from grill and serve with lemon wedges. *Makes 4 servings.*

Suggested Menu: Whole baby beets with fresh dill and braised cucumbers complete this flavorful salmon dinner.

Tip: Toast sesame seeds in a small heavy skillet over low heat. Watch carefully as they will burn if left too long; shake pan occasionally.

Whole Fish with Orange Dill Sauce

Whether your whole fish is an ocean swimmer or a fresh water one, the same cooking techniques apply. Cooking times are based on the thickness of the fish. Measure the fish at the thickest part and then cook, covered, for 10 minutes per inch (2.5 cm) of thickness at high heat – 450°F (230°C) whether over hot coals or at high on a gas barbecue.

Orange Marinade

¾ cup	orange juice	175 mL
2 tbsp	olive oil	25 mL
1 tbsp	minced fresh dill or	15 mL
	1 tsp (5 mL) dried	
⅛ tsp	freshly ground pepper	0.5 mL

Fish

4–6 lb	whole fish (salmon, whitefish,	2–3 kg
	snapper, cod) cleaned and head removed	
	Fresh dill sprigs	

Orange Dill Sauce

¼ cup	softened butter or margarine	50 mL
1 tsp	grated orange peel	5 mL
1 tsp	minced fresh dill	5 mL
	or ¼ tsp (1 mL) dried	
¼ tsp	salt	1 mL
⅛ tsp	freshly ground pepper	0.5 mL

1 *For marinade:* In small bowl, combine juice, oil, dill and pepper. Wipe fish with paper toweling; pat dry. Place fish in shallow nonreactive dish. Arrange fresh dill sprigs inside cavity of fish. Pour marinade over fish, turn to completely coat. Cover and refrigerate for several hours depending on size of fish.

2 Preheat grill on medium-high. Remove fish from marinade; discard marinade. Place fish in grill basket or on oiled grill rack. Close lid and cook (use Indirect Grilling, page 7) for about 20 minutes (10 minutes per inch/2.5 cm of thickness) or until fish is opaque and flakes easily with a fork; turn once. Remove skin and backbone and discard. Cut fish into serving pieces.

3 *For sauce:* Meanwhile, combine butter, orange peel, dill, salt and pepper. Spoon Orange Dill Sauce over each serving of fish.

Makes 6 to 8 servings.

Alternate cooking technique: Place fish on heavy-duty foil. Add lemon or orange slices for extra flavor and moisture. Close foil securely and proceed as above.

Suggested Menu: New red-skinned boiled potatoes, steamed snow peas and carrots, multigrain bread, a chilled dry Italian white wine such as an Orvieto, and a lemon pudding complete this wonderful meal.

Whole Fish with Orange Dill Sauce, page 96

Dijon Halibut with Provençal Sauce

The French certainly have a flair for food and this recipe is an excellent example.

Provençal Sauce

1 tbsp	olive oil	15 mL
1	medium onion, chopped	1
3 cups	cubed unpeeled eggplant	750 mL
1	medium zucchini, cubed	1
2	medium tomatoes, cut in large dice	2
1	sweet green pepper, seeded and diced	1
3	cloves garlic, minced	3
½ cup	chopped fresh basil or 2 tbsp (25 mL) dried	125 mL
	Salt and freshly ground pepper	

Fish

⅓ cup	plain yogurt	75 mL
3 tbsp	Dijon mustard	45 mL
2 lb	halibut (1 inch/2.5 cm thick)	1 kg
	Lemon wedges	

1 *For sauce:* In large nonstick skillet, heat oil over medium-high heat. Cook onion for 5 minutes. Add eggplant, zucchini, tomatoes, green pepper and garlic. Cook, uncovered, for about 30 minutes or until mixture is thickened. Stir in basil and salt and pepper to taste; keep warm.

2 Combine yogurt and mustard; spread evenly over both sides of halibut.

3 Preheat grill on medium-high. Place fish on oiled grill rack; close lid and cook (use Direct Grilling, page 7) for 10 minutes (10 minutes per inch/2.5 cm of thickness) or until fish is opaque and flakes easily with a fork; turn once. Transfer fish to warmed plates and serve with Provençale Sauce and a lemon wedge.

Makes 4 servings.

Suggested Menu: A cooked fresh pasta along with crusty baguette slices complete this exciting meal.

Oriental Grilled Salmon

Salmon, highlighted with the flavors of this unique Oriental marinade, becomes a springtime feast with asparagus wrapped in a creamy sauce and new boiled potatoes.

Oriental Seafood Marinade

⅓ cup	canola oil	75 mL
2 tbsp	light soy sauce	25 mL
1 tsp	garlic powder	5 mL
¼ tsp	freshly ground pepper	1 mL
¼ cup	rye whisky	50 mL
2 tsp	brown sugar	10 mL

Salmon

4	salmon fillets (about 1½ lb/ 750 g)	4

1 *For marinade:* In small bowl, combine oil, soy sauce, garlic powder, pepper, rye and sugar; mix well.

2 Place salmon in resealable plastic bag or nonreactive shallow dish; pour marinade over fish, turn to coat; cover and refrigerate for 2 to 4 hours. Turn salmon occasionally.

3 Remove salmon from marinade; reserve marinade. Place marinade in small saucepan, bring to a boil, reduce heat and cook for 5 minutes; keep warm.

4 Preheat grill on medium-high. Place fish on oiled grill rack. Close lid and cook (use Direct Grilling, page 7) for about 10 minutes (10 minutes per inch/2.5 cm of thickness) or until fish is opaque and flakes easily with a fork. Baste occasionally with reserved warm marinade.

Makes 4 servings.

Tip: Thread 2 water-soaked bamboo skewers through each fish fillet to make it easier to remove fish from grill.

DIRECT GRILLING

Salmon Steaks with Mustard Sauce and Almonds

This exciting combination of a mild and creamy mustard sauce with salmon and a crunch of toasted slivered almonds is perfect. You can also use grouper, whitefish, tuna, sea bass, halibut or snapper.

Creamy Mustard Sauce

½ cup	low-fat sour cream	125 mL
⅓ cup	light mayonnaise	75 mL
2 tsp	each: Dijon mustard and lemon juice	10 mL
¼ tsp	each: dried thyme and freshly ground pepper	1 mL
2 tbsp	fresh snipped chives	25 mL

Fish

6	salmon steaks, (¾ inch/2 cm thick)	6
⅓ cup	sliced toasted almonds	75 mL
	Fresh snipped chives	

1 *For sauce:* In small saucepan, combine sour cream, mayonnaise, mustard, lemon juice, thyme and pepper. Cook on low heat until hot; stir frequently. Stir in chives and keep warm. (Alternatively, microwave sauce in microwaveable container on medium-low [40%] for 2 to 3 minutes; stir occasionally.)

2 Preheat grill on medium-high. Place salmon on oiled grill rack. Close lid and cook (use Direct Grilling, page 7) for about 5 minutes per side or until fish is opaque and flakes easily with a fork (10 minutes per inch/2.5 cm of thickness).

3 To serve, spoon Creamy Mustard Sauce over each salmon steak. Sprinkle with toasted almonds and garnish with extra snipped chives.

Makes 6 servings.

Suggested Menu: Serve this dish on a bed of bright vegetables with one of the many interesting packaged rice mixtures and either Spring Greens with Strawberries (page 178) or a tossed green salad.

Swordfish Steak with Lemon Caper Sauce

This simple, traditional approach is particularly appropriate for the mild flavored yet dense meat-like nature of swordfish, but it could become your favorite for any firm-fleshed fish.

Lemon Caper Sauce

1 tsp	salt	5 mL
2 tbsp	lemon juice	25 mL
1 tbsp	chopped fresh oregano or 1 tsp (5 mL) dried	15 mL
3 tbsp	olive oil	45 mL
1 tbsp	capers, drained and washed	15 mL
¼ tsp	freshly ground pepper	1 mL

Fish

4	swordfish steaks (½ inch/1 cm thick) about 2 lb/1 kg	4

1 *For sauce:* Place salt in small bowl; stir in lemon juice until salt has dissolved. Add oregano, then slowly whisk in oil until creamy. Add capers and pepper; set aside.

2 Preheat grill on medium-high. Place fish on oiled grill rack. Close lid and cook (use Direct Grilling, page 7) for about 6 minutes (10 minutes per inch/2.5 cm of thickness) or until fish is opaque and flakes easily with a fork; turn once. Transfer fish to warmed plates. Prick fish with a fork in several places and drizzle with reserved Lemon Caper Sauce.
Makes 4 servings.

Suggested Menu: This tangy fish recipe calls for a brisk, fragrant, refreshing white wine. Start with Chunky Gazpacho (page 24) and serve Double Cheese-topped Potatoes (page 166) and a green salad with the fish.

Grouper with Gazpacho Sauce

The Gazpacho Sauce makes this recipe. Although it is a bit of extra work, it is well worth the effort. Any firm-fleshed fish can be substituted for grouper.

Gazpacho Sauce

¼ cup	finely chopped onion	50 mL
1	clove garlic, minced	1
1 tbsp	olive oil	15 mL
1½ cups	chopped ripe tomatoes (about 3)	375 mL
¼ cup	finely chopped sweet yellow pepper	50 mL
2 cups	tomato juice	500 mL
½ cup	fish stock or vegetable bouillon	125 mL
2 tbsp	balsamic vinegar	25 mL
½ tsp	Worcestershire sauce	2 mL
	Salt and freshly ground pepper	

Fish

6	grouper, sea bass, red snapper or whitefish fillets (about 1½ lb/750 g)	6
	Fresh rosemary sprigs	

1 *For sauce:* In large heavy saucepan, cook onion and garlic in oil over medium-low heat until softened; stir occasionally. Add tomatoes, yellow pepper, tomato juice, stock, vinegar and Worcestershire sauce. Bring to a boil, reduce heat and simmer, uncovered, for 30 to 40 minutes, or until sauce is thickened. Season to taste with salt and pepper. Remove from heat and cool slightly. Taste and stir in additional vinegar and Worcestershire sauce, if needed. (Sauce may be made 1 day ahead, covered and chilled.)

2 Preheat grill on medium-high. Place fish in basket or directly on oiled grill rack. Close lid and cook (use Direct Grilling, page 7) for about 5 minutes per side (10 minutes per inch /2.5 cm of thickness) or until fish is opaque and flakes easily with a fork.

3 Spoon ¼ cup (50 mL) Gazpacho Sauce around edge of each plate, place fish in center and top with rosemary sprigs.

Makes 6 servings

Suggested Menu: Serve with Orzo Spinach Pilaf (page 186) and Grilled Zucchini and Yellow Squash (page 169).

Tip: Fish stock is available frozen at seafood stores or specialty foods shops.

Lemon-Herb Grilled Whitefish

Lemon and herbs, an ageless combination with fish, is given a modern twist in this recipe with a touch of vermouth and Dijon mustard. Other firm-fleshed fish such as sea bass, halibut, swordfish, orange roughy and grouper can also be used.

Lemon-Herb Marinade

2 tbsp	olive or canola oil	25 mL
2 tbsp	dry vermouth or white wine	25 mL
1 tbsp	lemon juice	15 mL
1 tbsp	each: chopped fresh chives and dill or 1 tsp (5 mL) dried	15 mL
2 tsp	grated lemon peel	10 mL
1 tsp	Dijon mustard	5 mL
	Salt and white pepper	

Fish

4	whitefish fillets (about 4 oz/125 g each)	4
8	slices red onion	8
	Fresh dill sprigs and lemon wedges	

1 *For marinade:* In small bowl, combine oil, vermouth, lemon juice, chives, dill, lemon peel, mustard, salt and pepper. Place fish and onion in a shallow nonreactive dish or resealable plastic bag. Pour marinade over fish; turn fish and onion to coat well. Marinate in refrigerator for 30 minutes; turn fish occasionally.

2 Remove onion and fish from marinade; reserve marinade. In small saucepan, bring marinade to a boil; reduce heat and cook for 5 minutes; keep warm.

3 Preheat grill on medium-high. Place onion and fish on oiled grill rack. Close lid and cook (use Direct Grilling, page 7) for about 10 minutes (10 minutes per inch/2.5 cm of thickness) or until fish is opaque and flakes easily with a fork and onion is tender; turn once. Brush occasionally with warm marinade.

4 Serve fish and onion garnished with fresh dill and lemon wedges.
Makes 4 servings.

Suggested Menu: Serve with Grilled Fennel (page 168) and Grilled Zucchini (page 169) and fluffy rice.

Lemon-Herb Grilled Whitefish, page 102

Fish Steaks with Wine and Olive Sauce

Tomatoes, basil, oranges and olives – all flavors of the Mediterranean – come through in this superb sauce. Use a firm-fleshed fish such as sea bass, perch, tuna, salmon or snapper.

Wine and Olive Sauce

1 tsp	fennel seeds	5 mL
2	cloves garlic, minced	2
⅓ cup	dry white wine	75 mL
¼ cup	each: sliced green and black kalamata olives	50 mL
1 tbsp	orange juice	15 mL
1 tsp	grated orange peel	5 mL
⅛ tsp	crushed red pepper flakes	0.5 mL
1	medium tomato, diced	1

Fish

4	fish steaks (about 1 lb/500 g, ¾ inch/2 cm thick)	4
	Salt and freshly ground pepper	
	Fresh basil leaves	

1 *For sauce:* In nonstick skillet, over high heat, sauté fennel and garlic for 3 minutes or until seeds are toasted. Reduce heat to medium; stir in wine, green and black olives, orange juice and peel and pepper flakes. Cook until liquid is reduced. Allow to cool slightly before stirring in tomato; set aside.

2 Preheat grill on medium-high. Sprinkle fish lightly with salt and pepper. Place fish on oiled grill rack or in fish basket. Close lid and cook (use Direct Grilling, page 7) for about 5 minutes per side or until fish is opaque and flakes easily with a fork (10 minutes per inch/2.5 cm of thickness).

3 Serve fish with Wine and Olive Sauce; garnish with fresh basil.

Makes 4 servings and 1¼ cups (300 mL) sauce.

Suggested Menu: A robust dish like this calls for a brisk, fragrant Italian white wine such as a Soave. These fabulous flavors of Italy belong with Orzo Spinach Pilaf (page 186), a green salad and crusty country bread.

Fish Steaks with Wine and Olive Sauce

Fish and Mushrooms en Papillote

Use sea bass, red snapper, whitefish, salmon, perch or other firm-fleshed fish for this easy recipe. Grilling *en papillote* (in a package) assures a moist and juicy as well as tidy result. In this recipe we replace the traditional greased parchment paper with more readily available aluminum foil.

4	fish fillets (about 1 lb/500 g)	4
2	chopped green onions	2
2	large shiitake mushrooms, sliced	2
¼ cup	chopped fresh parsley	50 mL
¼ cup	dry white wine	50 mL
2 tsp	olive oil	10 mL
1	clove garlic, minced	1
¼ tsp	each: dried thyme and salt	1 mL
⅛ tsp	freshly ground pepper	0.5 mL

1 Cut 4 pieces of aluminum foil 2 inches (5 cm) longer than fish fillets and twice as wide. Center one fillet on each piece; divide onions, mushrooms and parsley over fish.

2 In small bowl, combine wine, oil, garlic, thyme, salt and pepper; drizzle over each fillet. Fold foil over fish and seal with double fold; tuck ends under to seal securely.

3 Preheat grill on medium-high. Place each package on grill rack. Close lid and cook (use Indirect Grilling, page 7) for about 15 minutes (10 minutes per inch /2.5 cm of package thickness) or until fish is opaque and flakes easily with a fork and vegetables are tender; turn once.
Makes 4 servings.

Suggested Menu: Open the fish parcels and serve over fluffy rice. Accompanied with Watercress and Bean Sprout Salad (page 182) and steamed snow peas and red pepper strips, this meal becomes a veritable feast.

Fish and Mushrooms en Papillote

Tuna Steaks with Tomato-Basil Coulis

Grilled tuna steaks are always superb, but a flavorful tomato sauce makes them even more appealing.

Tomato Basil Coulis

1 tbsp	olive oil	15 mL
2	medium shallots, finely chopped	2
4	medium tomatoes, peeled and coarsely chopped	4
½ cup	light sour cream	125 mL
1 tbsp	all-purpose flour	15 mL
½ tsp	salt	2 mL
¼ tsp	freshly ground pepper	1 mL
½ cup	loosely packed fresh basil leaves, chopped	125 mL

Fish

4	tuna steaks (about 1½ lb/750 g)	4
	Fresh basil leaves	

1 *For coulis:* In large nonstick skillet, heat oil over medium-high heat. Cook shallots for 2 minutes or until softened. Add tomatoes; reduce heat to low and cook gently, uncovered, for 25 minutes or until tomatoes have thickened into a sauce-like consistency. Combine sour cream and flour and stir gradually into hot mixture. Cook, stirring frequently, until sauce has thickened. Add salt and pepper; cover and keep sauce warm. Just before serving, stir in chopped basil.

2 Meanwhile, preheat grill on medium-high. Place tuna on oiled grill rack. Close lid and cook (use Direct Grilling, page 7) for about 10 minutes (10 minutes per inch/2.5 cm of thickness) or until fish is opaque and flakes easily with a fork; turn once.

3 Spoon a generous amount of sauce on 4 warm plates. Place tuna steaks on sauce, garnish with several leaves of fresh basil and serve.
Makes 4 servings.

Suggested Menu: Serve with spinach fettuccini, a Caesar salad and crusty rolls. Fresh fruit with warm Sabayon Sauce (page 218) provides a light finish to a wonderful meal.

Lemon Tuna Steaks with Gremolata

Gremolata, made with minced parsley, lemon peel and garlic, is more of a garnish than a sauce. Traditionally it is used to sprinkle over veal dishes such as *osso buco*. In this recipe, *gremolata* adds a wonderful fresh flavor to grilled tuna.

Gremolata

½ cup	finely chopped fresh parsley	125 mL
2 tsp	grated lemon zest	10 mL
2	cloves garlic, finely chopped	2

Fish

| 4 | tuna steaks (¾ inch/2 cm thick) | 4 |

Salt and freshly ground pepper

Lemon wedges

1 *For* gremolata: In small bowl, combine parsley, lemon zest and garlic; mix well and reserve.

2 Preheat grill on medium-high. Sprinkle fish lightly with salt and pepper. Place on oiled grill rack. Close lid and cook (use Direct Grilling, page 7) for about 5 minutes per side (10 minutes per inch/2.5 cm of thickness) or until fish is opaque and flakes easily with a fork.

3 Garnish each steak with *gremolata* and a lemon wedge.

Makes 4 servings.

> **Suggested Menu:** We often serve this recipe with Grilled Asparagus (page 168), new red potatoes, a spinach and orange side salad, and Herbed Italian Loaf (page 27).

DIRECT GRILLING

Halibut Fillets with Roasted Red Pepper Mayonnaise

The flavor of roasted red peppers complements grilled fish beautifully. Any left? This mayonnaise makes a marvelous dip for vegetable crudités.

Red Pepper Mayonnaise

1 cup	bottled roasted red peppers, drained	250 mL
⅓ cup	light mayonnaise	75 mL
2 tbsp	Dijon mustard	25 mL
2	cloves garlic, minced	2
1 tsp	lemon juice	5 mL
	Salt and freshly ground pepper	
1 cup	packed fresh basil leaves, chopped	250 mL

Fish

| 4 | halibut steaks (¼ lb/125 g each) | 4 |

1 *For mayonnaise:* In blender or food processor, purée red peppers, mayonnaise, mustard, garlic and lemon juice until smooth. Add salt and pepper to taste. Reserve 2 tbsp (25 mL) mayonnaise mixture. Combine remaining mayonnaise mixture with basil.

2 Preheat grill on medium-high. Pat halibut dry. Spread reserved 2 tbsp (25 mL) mayonnaise mixture on one side of the halibut steaks and place, mayonnaise side down, on oiled grill rack. Close lid and cook (use Direct Grilling, page 7) for 5 to 6 minutes. Turn fish and cook for 3 to 4 minutes or until fish is opaque and flakes easily with a fork. (Total cooking time will be 10 minutes per inch/2.5 cm of thickness.)

3 Serve halibut with Red Pepper Mayonnaise.

Makes 4 servings

> **Suggested Menu:** Choose a rice or pasta accompaniment from the selections in Chapter 8. A fresh young Italian white wine such as an Orvieto is excellent with these pungent flavors.
>
> **Tip:** If preferred, grill your own sweet red peppers; (see page 169).

Shrimp-stuffed Fish Fillets with Coconut Sauce,
page 109

Shrimp-stuffed Fish Fillets with Coconut Sauce

Go Polynesian with these attractive and tasty fish rollups.

Shrimp Rice Filling

10	fresh or frozen cooked shrimp, shelled, cleaned and chopped	10
1 cup	cooked long grain rice	250 mL
½ cup	shredded unsweetened coconut	125 mL
	Salt and lemon pepper	
4	sole, turbot, halibut or whitefish fillets (about ¼ lb/125 g each)	4

Coconut Sauce

½ cup	coconut milk	125 mL
½	small onion, finely chopped	½
1	clove garlic, minced	1
2 tsp	each: cornstarch and lime juice	10 mL
½ tsp	chili powder	2 mL
	Salt and lemon pepper	
	Flaked coconut	

1 *For filling:* In small bowl, combine shrimp, rice, coconut, salt and lemon pepper to taste; set aside.

2 Wipe fish fillets with paper toweling. Place fillets between two sheets of waxed paper; flatten each with a rolling pin. Place some filling along center of each fillet. Roll from narrow end; secure with toothpicks.

3 Preheat grill on medium-high. Place fish rolls on oiled grill rack. Close lid and cook (use Indirect Grilling, page 7) for about 20 minutes (10 minutes per inch/2.5 cm of thickness of rolls), or until fish is opaque and flakes easily with a fork.

4 *For sauce:* Meanwhile, in small saucepan, combine coconut milk, onion and garlic; cook on low heat until onion is tender. Stir in cornstarch, lime juice, chili powder, salt and lemon pepper to taste. Cook until slightly thickened; keep warm.

5 Place fish rolls on warm plates, drizzle with sauce and garnish with extra coconut.

Makes 4 servings.

Suggested Menu: Serve with sautéed snow peas, sweet red pepper strips and *enoki* mushrooms.

Tandoori Scallops with Vegetables

The term *tandoori* refers to an Indian style of cooking using a traditional clay and brick *tandoor* oven with a rounded top. Before cooking, meat, fish or seafood is marinated in a mixture of such spices as ground ginger, cumin, coriander, turmeric and paprika stirred into plain yogurt. In the following recipe, the *tandoor* oven is replaced by a covered grill.

Tandoori Marinade

½ cup	plain yogurt	125 mL
2 tbsp	lemon juice	25 mL
1 tsp	each: ground cumin, coriander,	5 mL
	paprika, turmeric, cayenne and salt	
1	clove garlic, crushed	1

Seafood

1 lb	sea scallops	500 g
2 tsp	cornstarch	10 mL
½ lb	snow peas, trimmed	250 g
4	carrots, sliced diagonally	4
½ lb	mushrooms	250 g
2 tsp	olive oil	10 mL
	Coconut Rice (recipe follows)	
	Fresh cilantro	

1 *For marinade:* In small bowl, combine yogurt, lemon juice, spices and garlic; mix well and reserve.

2 Wash scallops and pat dry. Coat scallops thoroughly with reserved marinade. Cover and refrigerate for 2 hours.

3 Remove scallops from marinade; reserve marinade. In small saucepan, stir cornstarch into reserved marinade. Cook over low heat until thickened and smooth; keep warm.

4 Steam snow peas and carrots; lightly sauté mushrooms in oil.

5 Meanwhile, preheat grill on medium-high. Thread scallops onto 4 metal or soaked wooden skewers. Place kebabs on oiled grill rack. Close lid and cook (use Direct Grilling, page 7) for 5 to 6 minutes or until scallops are opaque and done; turn once.

6 Remove scallops from skewers. Serve scallops on a bed of cooked Coconut Rice surrounded with vegetables. Drizzle lightly with warm sauce and add a garnish of fresh cilantro.
Makes 4 servings.

Coconut Rice is a great accompaniment to these scallops. Combine 3 cups (750 mL) cooked Oriental rice with 2 tbsp (25 mL) grated coconut, 2 tbsp (25 mL) coconut milk, and 1 tbsp (15 mL) minced gingerroot.

Tandoori Scallops with Vegetables

Parmesan-crusted Shrimp and Scallops

This exciting way to coat seafood combines the rich sharpness of Parmesan cheese with the delicate flavors of shrimp and scallops. The coating also seals in the juices of the shrimp and scallops while they grill. Top it all off with a Lemon Basil Sauce.

Lemon Basil Sauce

3 tbsp	butter or margarine	45 mL
1 tbsp	lemon juice	15 mL
1 tsp	grated lemon peel	5 mL
1 tbsp	each: snipped fresh chives and basil	15 mL

Coating

½ cup	finely crushed melba toast crumbs	125 mL
4 tsp	grated Parmesan cheese	20 mL
1 tbsp	finely chopped fresh parsley	15 mL
¼ tsp	each: paprika, freshly ground pepper and salt	1 mL

Seafood

1 lb	sea scallops	500 g
12	jumbo shrimp, shells removed	12
2 tbsp	melted butter or margarine	25 mL

1 *For sauce:* In small saucepan, combine butter, lemon juice and peel; heat until butter is melted. Remove from heat and stir in chives and basil; keep warm.

2 *For coating:* In resealable plastic bag, combine melba crumbs, cheese, parsley, paprika, pepper and salt. Brush scallops and shrimp with melted butter. Place in plastic bag; shake to coat.

3 Preheat grill on medium-high. Place seafood on oiled grill rack or in fish basket. Close lid and cook (use Direct Grilling, page 7) for about 6 minutes per side or until shrimp and scallops are opaque and cooked; turn once. Serve with warm Lemon Basil Sauce.

Makes 4 to 6 servings.

Suggested Menu: Definitely serve with a seasoned cooked rice, a green salad and possibly an olive or herbed focaccia bread.

Tip: Normally shrimp is grilled with the shell on to obtain the juiciest shrimp. However, in this recipe the crumb coating seals in the juices. Leave tail intact when grilling to provide a handle when eating. If buying frozen shrimp, look for bags marked "zipper-backed" for easy peeling.

Lobster Tails with Chive Lemon Sauce

Entertaining with style! This is one of the most elegant, yet easiest dinners.

Lobster

4	medium frozen or fresh lobster tails	4
	(about 6 oz/180 g each)	
	Juice and peel of 1 lemon	
2 tbsp	olive oil	25 mL
1 tsp	paprika	5 mL

Chive Lemon Sauce

½ cup	butter	125 mL
1 tbsp	lemon juice	15 mL
1 tsp	grated lemon peel	5 mL
1 tbsp	snipped fresh chives	15 mL
	Lemon wedges	

1 Thaw lobster if frozen; wash and pat dry with paper toweling. To butterfly the lobster tail (so it will lie flat during grilling), using kitchen scissors, cut lengthwise through centers of hard top shells and meat; do not cut through the undershell. Press tails open.

2 In small bowl, combine lemon juice and peel, oil and paprika; brush on exposed lobster meat.

3 Preheat grill on medium-high. Place tails, meat side down, on oiled grill rack. Close lid and cook (use Direct Grilling, page 7) for 6 to 8 minutes or until lobster is opaque; turn once.

4 *For sauce:* In small saucepan, melt butter, lemon juice and peel. Remove from heat, add chives and keep warm.

5 Serve lobster tails on individual warmed plates with a lemon wedge and a small dish of sauce for dipping.

Makes 4 servings.

Suggested Menu: To complete your lobster dinner, start with Cucumber Vichyssoise with Dill (page 25), then accompany these succulent tails with a lightly dressed coleslaw, crusty rolls and Grilled Basil Tomatoes (page 167).

Stuffed Rainbow Trout with Dilled Sauce

The delicate flavors of the crabmeat stuffing and the trout complement each other beautifully, and the lemon gives a gentle zip to both. The foil wrapping keeps the fish moist throughout the grilling and helps to secure the stuffing.

Crab Stuffing

1	small onion, finely chopped	1
1	stalk celery, finely chopped	1
1 tbsp	butter or margarine	15 mL
1	can (4.5 oz/128 g) crabmeat, drained and coarsely chopped	1
1½ cups	cooked rice	375 mL
1 tbsp	each: lemon juice and finely chopped fresh parsley	15 mL
1 tsp	grated lemon peel	5 mL
	Salt and freshly ground pepper	

Fish

6	rainbow trout fillets (1½ lb/750 g)	6

Dilled Mayonnaise

½ cup	each: light mayonnaise and plain yogurt	125 mL
2 tsp	lemon juice	10 mL
2 tsp	chopped fresh dill or ½ tsp (2 mL) dried	10 mL
⅛ tsp	each: salt and freshly ground pepper	0.5 mL
	Fresh dill sprigs	

1 *For stuffing:* In medium skillet, cook onion and celery in butter over medium-high heat for 5 minutes or until softened. Remove from heat and stir in crabmeat, rice, lemon juice, parsley, peel, and salt and pepper. Divide stuffing over three fish fillets; top with other three. Secure with toothpicks or string. Wrap each stuffed fillet loosely in several layers of aluminum foil and close to form secure packages.

2 *For mayonnaise:* In small bowl, combine mayonnaise, yogurt, lemon juice, dill, salt and pepper; set aside.

3 Preheat grill on medium-high. Place foil packages on grill rack. Close lid and cook (use Indirect Grilling, page 7) for about 45 minutes or until fish is opaque and flakes easily with a fork (10 minutes per inch/2.5 cm of package thickness); turn once.

4 Cut each filled fillet in half. Serve with a spoonful of Dilled Mayonnaise and fresh dill sprigs.
Makes 6 servings.

Tip: For a change, replace crabmeat with either chopped baby shrimp or smoked salmon.

Tuscan-style Grilled Fish Fillets

The flavors of Tuscany make a Mediterranean delicacy out of any firm-fleshed fish fillet.

2 tbsp	lemon juice	25 mL
1 tsp	salt	5 mL
2 tbsp	extra virgin olive oil, divided	25 mL
2 tbsp	chopped fresh basil	25 mL
1/8 tsp	freshly ground pepper	0.5 mL

Tuscan Sauce

1/4 cup	finely chopped onion	50 mL
2	cloves garlic, crushed	2
1	large tomato, cubed	1
2 tsp	capers, drained and rinsed	10 mL
	Freshly ground pepper	

Fish

4	red snapper, sea bass, salmon or perch fillets (1 1/2 lb/750 g)	4

1 In small bowl, stir together lemon juice and salt until salt is dissolved. Add 1 tbsp (15 mL) oil, basil and pepper; set aside.

2 *For sauce:* In nonstick skillet, sauté onion and garlic in remaining oil for about 5 minutes. Stir in tomato, capers and pepper to taste. Cook over low heat until tomatoes have thickened into a sauce-like consistency; keep warm.

3 Preheat grill on medium-high. Drizzle fish with lemon-basil mixture. Place fish on oiled grill rack. Close lid and cook (use Direct Grilling, page 7) for 10 minutes per inch (2.5 cm) of thickness or until fish is opaque and flakes easily with a fork. Serve with Tuscan Sauce.
Makes 4 servings.

Suggested Menu: A creamy spinach risotto dish would be perfect with this fish recipe. Prepare your favorite risotto recipe and stir in some chopped spinach part way through the cooking. Finish with a generous sprinkling of grated Parmesan cheese. A romaine lettuce salad and a light Italian red wine complete the scene.

Grilled Mango and Citrus Fish Fillets

Citrus flavors and fish are natural partners. Grilled mango slices add taste and eye appeal.

Mango and Citrus Marinade

⅓ cup	each: orange, lemon and lime juice	75 mL
¼ cup	marmalade	50 mL
½ tsp	granulated sugar	2 mL
½	medium onion, finely chopped	½
1	piece gingerroot (1 inch/2.5 cm), grated	1

Fish

6	salmon, orange roughy, sea bass or halibut fillets (¼ lb/125 g each)	6
½ cup	fresh cilantro, chopped	125 mL
2	mangoes, peeled and sliced	2
	Vegetable oil	

1 *For marinade:* In blender or food processor, process juices and marmalade until well blended. Pour ½ cup (125 mL) juice mixture into a bowl; stir in sugar until dissolved and reserve.

2 Add onion and gingerroot to remaining mixture in blender; process until smooth. Transfer onion mixture to shallow nonreactive dish. Arrange fillets in single layer over mixture; turn to coat and sprinkle with cilantro. Cover and refrigerate for 1 hour.

3 Preheat grill on medium-high. Remove fish from marinade; discard marinade. Place fish on oiled grill rack, skin side down. Close lid and cook (use Direct Grilling, page 7) until fish is opaque and flakes easily with a fork (10 minutes per inch/2.5 cm thickness). At same time, place sliced mango on grill rack, brush lightly with oil and cook until grill marks appear and mango is heated.

4 Remove fish to a heated serving platter. Drizzle with reserved juice mixture and serve with mango slices.

Makes 6 servings.

Suggested Menu: A fluffy aromatic rice such as Thai or basmati and asparagus are perfect companions to this fish.

Tip: It is wise not to marinate fish in an acid mixture any longer than 30 minutes. Longer marinating in mixtures containing citrus juices or vinegar tends to "cook" the fish and change the texture. This is also true for marinating poultry.

Scallop and Shrimp Kebabs with Vegetables, page 128

CHAPTER 5

Kebab Grilling

KEBABS, A METHOD OF open-air cooking, can be traced back to the mountain people of the Caucasus who impaled meat on their swords and roasted it over an open fire. Today, skewers have replaced swords and grills have been substituted for the open fire. Kebabs have become a chic style of cooking in North America.

The popularity of kebabs is well deserved. Their festive appearance and interesting mingling of different flavors turns dinner into a party any night of the week. In spite of their exotic nature, they are an inexpensive way to serve a crowd. Since meats are cut into small pieces and stretched with vegetables, they go further than the same quantity served as a steak, chop or chicken breast. Furthermore small pieces of meat are ideal for marinating, so that economical cuts can be readily used. Now that smaller meat servings are part of current healthy recommendations, kebabs fit right in.

In this chapter, you'll find an exciting, eclectic

DIRECT GRILLING

All cooking times assume using closed lid grilling. If using open lid grilling, allow extra time.

Cut and Thickness	Total Time	Grill Temperature
Beef 1 to 1 1/2-inch (2.5 to 3 cm) cubes	about 10 minutes	medium
Pork 1-inch (2.5 cm) cubes	about 20 minutes or until juices run clear	medium-low to medium
Lamb 1-inch (2.5 cm) cubes	10 minutes brown with some pink inside	medium
Turkey 1-inch (2.5 cm) cubes	about 20 minutes or no longer pink	medium-high
Chicken 1-inch (2.5 cm) cubes	10 to 12 minutes or no longer pink	medium-high
Venison	6 to 8 minutes for medium-rare	medium-high
Fish 1-inch (2.5 cm) cubes	about 10 minutes	medium-high
Shrimp and scallops	about 10 minutes	medium-high

selection of meat, seafood, poultry and vegetarian kebabs. Meat selections include venison, beef, and a pork recipe with apples and a wonderful Calvados marinade (page 122). Seafood skewers include swordfish, tuna, shrimp and scallops, and you can always substitute turkey in the chicken kebab recipes. Tofu is the basis for the two vegetarian recipes. Fruits as well as vegetables are skewered with meats, as in our Marinated Tofu, Melon and Green Onion Kebabs (page 134) and Polynesian Chicken Mango Kebabs (page 133).

Skewers of some kind are essential for kebab grilling. They come in many sizes in wood or metal. The inexpensive wooden ones are great for a crowd, so that everyone can have their own skewer. Wooden skewers must be soaked in warm water for about 15 minutes to prevent charring and burning during grilling. To further reduce charring, arrange food so it covers most of the wood. However, even with all precautions taken, there is almost always some charring, so wooden skewers cannot be reused. Food cooks faster on metal skewers than on wooden ones because the metal conducts the heat into the middle of the food. Also, while metal skewers are more expensive than wooden ones, they are reusable.

When threading meat on skewers, leave some space between the pieces to allow the meat to cook more evenly. Since the meat is cut into small pieces, less tender cuts require only a short marinade to be full of flavor and a short grilling time to be succulent and tender. No marinating is required for tender cuts unless desired for flavor. Kebabs are always cooked by direct grilling (page 7). See the chart below for cooking times and temperatures. During cooking, turn kebabs several times. Partially precook less tender vegetables such as onions, carrots, potatoes and broccoli before placing them on skewers with meat to ensure they will be properly cooked when the meat is done (for example, see pork kebabs on page 122). Other vegetables, such as cherry tomatoes, zucchini, sweet peppers and mushrooms do not require precooking.

Beef Kebabs with Red Pepper Sauce

Dip cooked beef kebabs into this smoky, roasted pepper sauce at serving time. Before grilling, rub beef with herbs for a wonderful and full-flavored meat.

Red Pepper Sauce

3	large sweet red peppers	3
1 tbsp	balsamic vinegar	15 mL
1	clove garlic	1
½ tsp	salt	2 mL
¼ tsp	freshly ground pepper	1 mL
2 tbsp	chopped Italian parsley	25 mL

Beef and Rub

1½ lb	rib, sirloin, strip loin	750 g
	or tenderloin steak (¾ inch/2 cm thick)	
3	cloves garlic, minced	3
1 to 2 tsp	dried herbs	5 to 10 mL
	(thyme, basil, oregano or rosemary)	
	or 1 to 2 tbsp (15 to 25 mL) fresh	
	Salt and freshly ground pepper	

1 *For sauce:* Either cut peppers in half and remove seeds or leave them whole. Preheat grill on medium-high. Place peppers on oiled grill rack. Close lid and cook (use Direct Grilling, page 7) for about 20 minutes or until skins are blistered on all sides; turn often. Place hot peppers in a paper bag to cool for about 15 minutes. Peel away the blackened skin.

2 In food processor, purée peppers, vinegar, garlic, salt and pepper until almost smooth. Stir in parsley. Cover and refrigerate until ready to use.

3 *For beef and rub:* Remove excess fat from beef and discard. Cut beef into ¾-inch (2 cm) cubes and place in shallow nonreactive dish. In small bowl, combine garlic, herbs, salt and pepper; press mixture evenly over all sides of beef. (Rub it in with your fingers, if necessary.)

4 Thread beef cubes onto 6 metal or soaked wooden skewers. Preheat grill on medium. Place kebabs on oiled grill rack. Close lid and cook (use Direct Grilling, page 7) for about 10 minutes or until meat is cooked to desired stage of doneness; turn kebabs three times.

5 Remove beef from skewers and serve with Red Pepper Sauce for dipping.

Makes 6 servings and about 1 cup (250 mL) sauce.

Suggested Menu: Potatoes and Onions in a Pouch (page 155) can be grilled at the same time as the kebabs. Toss a green salad with Creamy Buttermilk Dressing (page 180).

Tip: Store Red Pepper Sauce for up to 3 days in the refrigerator or freeze for longer storage. It is most flavorful when brought to room temperature before serving.

Gingered Beef Kebabs with Mushrooms and Red Pepper

This recipe was inspired by the Beef Information Bureau Winning Tastes of Beef special issue of *Canadian Living* magazine. I have taken a few liberties with the recipe. I hope you will enjoy it.

1½ lb	round or sirloin steak	750 g
	(¾ inch/2 cm thick)	
½ cup	soy sauce	125 mL
1	piece gingerroot	1
	(1 inch/2.5 cm), minced	
2	cloves garlic, crushed	2
1	medium sweet red pepper,	1
	cut into squares	
24	medium mushrooms, trimmed	24
2 tbsp	liquid honey	25 mL
3 cups	cooked rice	750 mL
	(1 cup/250 mL raw)	
¼ cup	chopped fresh parsley	50 mL
	Salt and freshly ground pepper	

1 Remove excess fat from beef and discard. Cut beef into ¾-inch (2 cm) cubes and place in resealable plastic bag.

2 In bowl, combine soy sauce, gingerroot and garlic. Pour over beef; turn to coat and refrigerate for up to 6 hours; turn beef occasionally.

3 Remove beef from marinade; reserve marinade. Thread beef, red pepper and mushrooms alternately onto 6 metal or soaked wooden skewers. In small saucepan, combine marinade and honey; bring to a boil, reduce heat and simmer for 5 minutes; keep warm.

4 Preheat grill on medium. Place kebabs on oiled grill rack. Close lid and cook (use Direct Grilling, page 7) for about 10 minutes or until vegetables are golden brown and meat is medium-rare; turn three times, brushing with warm marinade.

5 Combine cooked rice and parsley, season to taste with salt and pepper. Remove meat and vegetables from skewers and serve over parsley rice. *Makes 6 servings.*

Suggested Menu: Here is another menu idea. Make a couscous salad using the recipe for Pine Nut Couscous (page 186) served cold with halved grapes and a sprinkle of fresh thyme to set off the beef and red pepper kebabs. Add Pickled Onions (page 203) as a condiment.

Gingered Beef Kebabs with Mushrooms
and Red Pepper, page 120

Calvados Pork Kebabs with Apples and Vegetables

Apples, apple juice and Calvados, an eau-de-vie distilled from apples, complement pork in this exciting kebab.

1½ lb	boneless pork (shoulder or tenderloin)	750 g
½ cup	apple juice	125 mL
¼ cup	Calvados or brandy	50 mL
2	cloves garlic, crushed	2
1 tsp	ground cinnamon	5 mL
½ tsp	each: ground nutmeg and ginger	2 mL
1	large onion, cut into wedges	1
1 cup	broccoli florets	250 mL
2	medium carrots, cut into 1-inch (2.5 cm) chunks	2
1 tbsp	liquid honey	15 mL
2	firm apples, cored and thickly sliced	2

1 Cut pork into 1-inch (2.5 cm) cubes. Remove excess fat and discard. Place in resealable plastic bag.

2 In bowl, combine apple juice, Calvados, garlic, cinnamon, nutmeg and ginger. Pour over pork, turn to coat; refrigerate for 4 hours or overnight.

3 Partially cook onion, broccoli and carrot pieces individually until barely tender; drain and reserve.

4 Remove pork from marinade; reserve marinade. Place marinade in small saucepan; stir in honey and bring to a boil. Reduce heat and simmer for 5 minutes; keep warm.

5 Preheat grill on medium. Thread pork, apple, onion, broccoli and carrot alternately onto 6 metal or soaked wooden skewers. Place kebabs on oiled grill rack. Close lid and cook (use Direct Grilling, page 7) for about 20 minutes or until vegetables and apples are tender, pork is browned and juices run clear. Turn several times, brushing with warm marinade.

Makes 6 servings.

Suggested Menu: Since there is such a variety of vegetables on the skewers, boiled new potatoes and a small salad are all that is necessary to complete this menu.

Tip: For variety, replace the apple slices with pineapple and any of the vegetables with sweet red pepper squares and green onion pieces.

Tropical Thai Ham and Shrimp Kebabs

These kebabs can serve as an appetizer or as a main entrée – just vary the quantity.

½ cup	each: light mayonnaise and peanut butter	125 mL
½ cup	pineapple juice	125 mL
¼ cup	each: liquid honey and soy sauce	50 mL
2	cloves garlic, crushed	2
¼ tsp	cayenne pepper	1 mL
1 lb	sliced ham, ¾ inch (2 cm) thick	500 g
12	cleaned jumbo shrimp	12

1 In bowl, combine mayonnaise, peanut butter, pineapple juice, honey, soy sauce, garlic and cayenne. Stir well to blend; reserve half of the sauce for dipping. Pour remaining sauce into a resealable plastic bag or shallow nonreactive dish. Place ham in bag, turn to coat and refrigerate for 4 hours or overnight. Add shrimp during last hour of marinating.

2 Remove ham and shrimp from marinade; discard marinade. Thread ham and shrimp alternately onto metal or soaked wooden skewers. (The number of skewers depends on whether the kebabs will be used as an appetizer or a main course.)

3 Preheat grill on medium. Place kebabs on oiled grill rack. Close lid and cook (use Direct Grilling, page 7) for 8 minutes or until ham is golden brown and shrimp is opaque; turn frequently. Remove from skewers and serve with reserved dipping sauce.
Makes 12 appetizer or 4 main course servings.

Suggested Menu: Zucchini Fingers (page 156) and fluffy rice will complement the kebabs perfectly. If another grilled item is not too much, the Pineapple and Papaya Kebabs with Lime Rum Sauce (page 217) can be prepared ahead of time.

Middle Eastern Lamb Kebabs with Pine Nut Couscous

Yogurt is widely used in Middle Eastern cooking. Here, it makes a low-fat marinade that brings a taste of the Middle East to the lamb. Couscous, another staple of the Middle East, is the perfect accompaniment.

Yogurt Marinade

1 cup	plain yogurt	250 mL
2	cloves garlic, crushed	2
1 tbsp	finely minced onion	15 mL
1 tsp	granulated sugar	5 mL
1 tsp	dried oregano or 1 tbsp (15 mL) fresh	5 mL
½ tsp	salt	2 mL
½ tsp	dried thyme or 2 tsp (10 mL) fresh	2 mL
¼ tsp	freshly ground pepper	1 mL

Lamb

1 lb	lean boneless lamb (leg or shoulder)	500 g
	Pine Nut Couscous (see page 186)	
	Fresh parsley	
	Cherry tomatoes, halved	

1 *For marinade:* In bowl, combine yogurt, garlic, onion, sugar, oregano, thyme, salt and pepper.

2 Trim excess fat from lamb and discard. Cut lamb into 1-inch (2.5 cm) pieces and place in shallow nonreactive dish or resealable plastic bag. Pour marinade over lamb, cover and refrigerate for 2 to 6 hours.

3 Remove lamb from marinade; reserve marinade. Place marinade in small saucepan, bring to a boil, reduce heat and cook for 5 minutes; keep warm. Thread lamb onto 4 metal or soaked wooden skewers.

4 Preheat grill on medium. Place kebabs on oiled grill rack. Close lid and cook (use Direct Grilling, page 7) for about 10 minutes or until meat is cooked to desired stage of doneness; turn twice, brushing with warm marinade.

5 Place foil package of Pine Nut Couscous on grill rack beside kebabs. Grill for about 10 minutes or until heated through; turn frequently.

6 Open package and divide couscous between 4 warm dinner plates. Remove lamb from skewers onto couscous; garnish with parsley and cherry tomatoes.

Makes 4 servings.

Suggested Menu: Serve with Grilled Eggplant brushed with olive oil (see page 168) and a sprinkle of chopped fresh mint. Whole wheat pita breads and a crisp, fruity rosé wine complete this international menu.

Middle Eastern Lamb Kebabs with Pine Nut
Couscous, page 124

Venison Kebabs with Cranberry Gravy

Venison is the meat lover's health salvation. This red meat is lean and tender, high in protein, low in fat (about one-half the fat of most beef, lamb and pork cuts). It is delicious, either simply grilled or prepared with an elaborate sauce.

Venison and Marinade

2 tsp	olive oil	10 mL
1	shallot, finely chopped	1
2	cloves garlic, minced	2
1 cup	dry red wine	250 mL
1 tbsp	balsamic vinegar	15 mL
¼ tsp	freshly ground pepper	1 mL
1½ lb	loin of venison	750 g

Cranberry Gravy

½ cup	cranberry juice	125 mL
¼ cup	chopped dried cranberries	50 mL
1 tbsp	ketchup or chili sauce	15 mL
	Chopped fresh parsley	

1 In nonstick skillet, heat oil over medium-high heat. Cook shallot and garlic for about 4 minutes or until softened. Add wine, vinegar and pepper; allow to cool.

2 Cut venison into ¾-inch (2 cm) cubes and place in shallow nonreactive dish or resealable plastic bag. Pour cool marinade over meat; turn to coat and refrigerate for 12 hours or overnight.

3 Remove meat from marinade; strain marinade and reserve.

4 Preheat grill over medium-high. Thread meat onto 6 metal or soaked wooden skewers. Place kebabs on oiled grill rack. Close lid and cook (use Direct Grilling, page 7) for about 3 to 4 minutes per side for medium-rare or until browned on the outside but still pink in the center; turn once.

5 *For gravy:* Meanwhile, in small saucepan, combine cranberry juice, dried cranberries, ketchup and strained marinade. Bring to a boil, reduce heat and cook until liquid is partially reduced. If desired, thicken gravy with cornstarch and water.

6 Place skewers on warmed plates, and serve with Cranberry Gravy; sprinkle with parsley.
Makes 6 servings.

Suggested Menu: Serve with Grilled Sweet Potatoes (page 169) and Wild Rice, Raisin and Apple Casserole (page 189).

Tip: Venison is best served rare to medium-rare. If grilled to medium, it develops a livery taste.

Curried Tuna, Shrimp and Scallop Brochettes

The Orange Sesame Dipping Sauce is a cooling complement to curried multi-seafood kebabs.

Seafood

1 lb	tuna steak	500 g
8	jumbo shrimp	8
8	large scallops	8
¼ cup	dry sherry	50 mL
1 tbsp	sesame oil	15 mL
1 tsp	each: curry powder and grated lemon peel	5 mL
Dash	cayenne pepper	Dash

Orange Sesame Dipping Sauce

⅓ cup	each: chicken broth and orange juice	75 mL
2	green onions, thinly sliced	2
1 tbsp	rice vinegar	15 mL
1 tsp	sesame oil	5 mL

1 *For seafood:* Wipe tuna with paper toweling, remove skin and cut into 1-inch (2.5 cm) pieces. Remove shell and vein from shrimp. Wipe scallops. In resealable plastic bag, combine sherry, oil, curry powder, lemon peel and cayenne. Add tuna, shrimp and scallops; turn to coat. Refrigerate for 2 to 6 hours.

2 Remove fish from marinade; reserve marinade. Place marinade in small saucepan, bring to a boil, reduce heat and cook for 5 minutes; keep warm. Alternately thread seafood onto 4 metal or soaked wooden skewers.

3 Preheat grill on medium-high. Place kebabs on oiled grill rack. Close lid and cook (use Direct Grilling, page 7) for about 10 minutes or until tuna flakes easily with a fork and shrimp and scallops are opaque; turn once or twice, basting occasionally with warm marinade.

4 *For sauce:* In small bowl, combine chicken broth, orange juice, onions, vinegar and oil; mix well. Remove seafood from skewers to plates. Serve with a small bowl of dipping sauce.
Makes 4 servings.

Suggested Menu: Serve with Grilled Asparagus (page 168), Szechwan Vegetable Salad (page 177) and cooked rice.

Scallop and Shrimp Kebabs with Vegetables

These two favorite seafoods grilled with sweet peppers and mushrooms and brushed with Ginger Sherry Marinade make a succulent entrée.

Ginger Sherry Marinade

¼ cup	dry sherry	50 mL
1 tbsp	sesame oil	15 mL
1 tbsp	grated gingerroot	15 mL
2 tsp	light soy sauce	10 mL
1	large clove garlic, crushed	1

Seafood

16	sea scallops	16
12	jumbo shrimps	12
8	squares each: sweet red and green peppers	8
12	medium mushrooms	12

1 *For marinade:* In bowl, combine sherry, oil, gingerroot, soy sauce and garlic. Place scallops and shrimp in shallow nonreactive dish or resealable plastic bag. Pour marinade over, turn to coat; cover and refrigerate for 1 to 2 hours.

2 Blanch pepper cubes in boiling water for 1 minute; drain well.

3 Remove seafood from marinade; reserve marinade. Place marinade in small saucepan, bring to a boil, reduce heat and cook for 5 minutes; keep warm. Thread scallops, shrimp, pepper cubes and mushrooms alternately onto 4 metal or soaked wooden skewers.

4 Preheat grill on medium-high. Place kebabs on oiled grill rack. Close lid and cook (use Direct Grilling, page 7) for about 10 minutes or until shrimp and scallops are opaque; turn once or twice, basting occasionally with warm marinade. *Makes 4 servings.*

Suggested Menu: Serve with Grilled Zucchini or Yellow Squash (page 169), crusty rolls and cooked jasmine rice. The spicy sweet-tart fruit flavors of a medium-dry Riesling will complement the shrimp.

Skewered Swordfish and Vegetables

The thick, meaty texture of swordfish is ideal for kebabs. The use of bottled barbecue sauce in the marinade is a convenient way of introducing a variety of flavors.

1 lb	firm-fleshed fish (swordfish, salmon, tuna, halibut or haddock)	500 g

Marinade

½ cup	bottled barbecue sauce (flavor of your choice)	125 mL
2 tbsp	fruit juice (apple, orange, pineapple, mango)	25 mL
2 tbsp	canola oil	25 mL
1	sweet green pepper, cut into 2-inch (5 cm) pieces	1
1	yellow squash or zucchini, cut into 1-inch (2.5 cm) pieces	1
12	cherry tomatoes	12
8	small new potatoes, precooked	8

1 Cut fish into 1-inch (2.5 cm) cubes. Place in shallow nonreactive dish or resealable plastic bag.

2 *For marinade:* In small bowl, combine barbecue sauce, juice and oil. Pour over fish, turn to coat; refrigerate for at least 1 hour.

3 Remove fish from marinade; reserve marinade. Place marinade in small saucepan, bring to a boil, reduce heat and cook for 5 minutes; keep warm.

4 Preheat grill on medium-high. Thread fish, green pepper, squash, cherry tomatoes and potatoes alternately onto 4 metal or soaked wooden skewers. Place kebabs on oiled grill rack. Close lid and cook (use Direct Grilling, page 7) for about 10 minutes or until fish and vegetables are done; turn often, basting with warm marinade. Fish is cooked when it flakes easily with a fork and is opaque. *Makes 4 servings.*

Suggested Menu: Serve with a green salad tossed with Poppy Seed Vinaigrette (page 180) and try one of the grilled fruit recipes for dessert (see pages 214 to 217).

Variations:

Substitute meat, poultry or other types of seafood, and choose appropriate vegetables to create an almost endless variety of skewer treats. Here are some examples:

1 Lamb with mushrooms, cherry tomatoes and sweet yellow pepper and a bottled garlic sauce.

2 Shrimp or scallops with sweet red pepper, green onion chunks and artichoke quarters and a Cajun sauce.

3 Ham with pineapple or peaches, maraschino cherries and onion wedges and a sweet and sour sauce.

4 Chicken with snow peas, water chestnuts and sweet red pepper and an Oriental-flavored sauce.

Ground Chicken and Pepper Kebabs

Ground chicken (or turkey) is an economical, convenient alternative to more expensive chicken breasts. As with other recipes involving ground meats, these kebabs should be well cooked.

1½ lb	lean ground chicken or turkey	750 g
1 cup	quick rolled oats	250 mL
1	egg, lightly beaten	1
3 tbsp	milk	45 mL
1 tbsp	each: horseradish and Worcestershire sauce	15 mL
½ tsp	salt	2 mL
¼ tsp	freshly ground pepper	1 mL
24	pieces sweet green pepper (2 peppers)	24
16	cherry tomatoes	16
16	large mushrooms, trimmed	16
4	green onions, trimmed and cut into 2 pieces	4
1 cup	barbecue sauce (your choice)	250 mL

1 Combine chicken, oats, egg, milk, horseradish, Worcestershire sauce, salt and pepper. Lightly shape into 24 meatballs.

2 Thread 3 meatballs, 3 green pepper pieces, 2 cherry tomatoes, 2 mushrooms and 1 piece of green onion alternately onto 8 metal or soaked wooden skewers. Brush lightly with barbecue sauce.

3 Preheat grill on medium-high. Place kebabs on oiled grill rack. Close lid and cook (use Direct Grilling, page 7) for 8 to 12 minutes or until brown and chicken is no longer pink inside; turn frequently, brushing with extra sauce.
Makes 8 servings.

Suggested Menu: Slice 8 submarine buns lengthwise and toast on grill. Place contents of 1 skewer in each bun and serve. Possible condiments include mustard, Mexican Cranberry Salsa (page 18), more barbecue sauce and banana peppers.

Tip: Fresh ground chicken should be used within 2 days of purchase or frozen for longer keeping. There are two basic rules for the safe handling of chicken and turkey; keep it clean, and keep it cold until you cook it. Be sure to wash your hands before and after handling raw poultry.

Spicy Chicken Kebabs with Vegetables

These chicken kebabs can be as spicy as you wish. It's all in the length of time the chicken stays in the marinade.

Spicy Marinade

2 tbsp	each: soy sauce and molasses	25 mL
1 tbsp	red wine vinegar	15 mL
1 to 2 tsp	hot pepper sauce	5 to 10 mL
½ tsp	each: ground ginger and cloves	2 mL
⅛ tsp	each: salt, cayenne and freshly ground pepper	0.5 mL

Chicken and Vegetables

1 lb	boneless, skinless chicken breast	500 g
12	medium mushrooms	12
12	pieces sweet green pepper	12
1	large onion, cut into 12 wedges	1
	Green onion fans	

1 *For marinade:* In shallow nonreactive dish or resealable plastic bag, combine soy sauce, molasses, vinegar, pepper sauce, ginger, cloves, salt, cayenne and pepper; stir well. Add chicken, turn to coat. Refrigerate for 2 to 4 hours (depending on depth of flavor desired).

2 Remove chicken from marinade; discard marinade. Thread chicken and vegetables alternately onto 4 metal or soaked wooden skewers.

3 Preheat grill on medium-high. Place kebabs on oiled grill rack. Close lid and cook (use Direct Grilling, page 7) for 7 minutes per side or until chicken is no longer pink inside.

4 Remove chicken and vegetables from skewers to warm plates to serve. Garnish each with a green onion fan.

Makes 4 servings.

Suggested Menu: Look for a crisp, smooth white wine, such as a Sauvignon Blanc to serve with these chicken kebabs. Black beans and saffron-flavored rice pair well with the sunny and spicy flavors of this dish.

Tip: To make green onion fans, cut onion in thin slices from the stem almost, but not quite, to the green top; fan out on plate as a garnish.

Polynesian Chicken Mango Kebabs, page 133

Polynesian Chicken Mango Kebabs

Bold herbs and spices teamed with lime and coconut milk make a satisfying marinade for chicken. If you have time, let the chicken marinate overnight.

Lime-Coconut Marinade

½ cup	coconut milk	125 mL
2 tbsp	lime juice	25 mL
1 tsp	grated lime peel	5 mL
3	cloves garlic, minced	3
1	green onion, finely chopped	1
1 tsp	coriander seeds, crushed	5 mL
½ tsp	each: ground cumin and paprika	2 mL
¼ tsp	each: salt and freshly ground pepper	1 mL
⅛ tsp	hot pepper sauce	0.5 mL

Chicken and Mango

4	boneless, skinless chicken breast halves	4
1 tbsp	liquid honey	15 mL
1	large mango, peeled and cubed	1
	Toasted sesame seeds	

1 *For marinade:* In bowl, combine coconut milk, lime juice and peel, garlic, onion, coriander, cumin, paprika, salt, pepper and pepper sauce.

2 Cut chicken into 1-inch (2.5 cm) cubes. Place in shallow nonreactive dish or resealable plastic bag. Pour marinade over chicken, cover and refrigerate for 2 to 4 hours or overnight.

3 Remove chicken from marinade; reserve marinade. Place marinade in small saucepan, stir in honey and bring to a boil. Reduce heat and simmer for 5 minutes; keep warm.

4 Preheat grill on medium-high. Thread chicken cubes and mango alternately onto 4 metal or soaked wooden skewers. Place kebabs on oiled grill rack. Close lid and cook (use Direct Grilling, page 7) for about 10 minutes or until browned and chicken is no longer pink inside; turn three times, brushing with warm marinade. Remove chicken and mango from skewers and sprinkle with sesame seeds.

Makes 4 servings.

Suggested Menu: Fluffy rice and Grilled Asparagus (page 168) drizzled with Mint Vinaigrette make a refreshing accompaniment for this entrée.

Mint Vinaigrette: Combine 1 tbsp (15 mL) water, 1 tbsp (15 mL) olive oil, 2 tsp (10 mL) rice vinegar and 1 tsp (5 mL) minced fresh mint leaves.

Marinated Tofu, Melon and Green Onion Kebabs

Vegetarian foods can be bold-flavored and exciting, depending on the extras added and the marinade used. This vegetarian kebab is full of eastern flavors – gingerroot, soy and cilantro.

Mint Marinade

¼ cup	each: chopped fresh mint and cilantro	50 mL
¼ cup	each: light soy sauce and lime juice	50 mL
1 tbsp	brown sugar	15 mL
1 tbsp	finely chopped gingerroot	15 mL
2 tsp	canola oil	10 mL
1 tsp	curry powder	5 mL
¼ tsp	crushed chili peppers	1 mL
1	clove garlic, minced	1

Tofu, Melon and Onion

1	pkg (350 g) extra firm tofu, drained	1
3	green onions, cut diagonally in 2-inch (5 cm) pieces	3
12	cantaloupe cubes, about 1 inch (2.5 cm)	12
	Salt and freshly ground pepper to taste	

1 *For marinade:* In small bowl, combine mint, cilantro, soy sauce, lime juice, sugar, gingerroot, oil, curry powder, chili peppers and garlic; mix well.

2 Cut tofu into 2-inch (5 cm) cubes; you should have 16 cubes. Place in resealable plastic bag or shallow nonreactive dish. Pour marinade over, turn to coat, and refrigerate for several hours; turn tofu occasionally.

3 Drain tofu, reserve marinade. Thread tofu, onions and cantaloupe alternately onto 4 metal or soaked wooden skewers.

4 Preheat grill on medium-high. Place kebabs on oiled grill. Close lid and cook (use Direct Grilling, page 7) for about 10 minutes or until tofu is crisp and melon and onion are tender. Turn kebabs several times, basting with reserved marinade. Sprinkle lightly with salt and pepper and serve.
Makes 4 servings.

Suggested Menu: The obvious choice is to serve the kebabs on a bed of cooked rice or noodles, possibly with steamed snow peas and sweet red pepper strips.

Vegetable and Tofu Kebabs

This is a vegetarian meal for everyone. Thanks to tofu's ability to take on the flavors of the foods it accompanies – in this case the marinade – even dedicated meat eaters will be sure the tofu is chicken. A Sauvignon Blanc will go well with the flavors of these tofu kebabs.

Marinade

¼ cup	light soy sauce	50 mL
2	cloves garlic, minced	2
1 tbsp	minced gingerroot	15 mL
1 tsp	each: lemon juice and olive oil	5 mL
⅛ tsp	freshly ground pepper	0.5 mL

Tofu and Vegetables

1	pkg (350 g) extra firm tofu, drained	1
1	red onion, cut into wedges	1
16	pieces sweet red pepper	16
12	3-inch (7.5 cm) strips zucchini	12

1 *For marinade:* In small bowl, combine soy sauce, garlic, gingerroot, lemon juice, oil and pepper; mix well.

2 Cut tofu into 2-inch (5 cm) cubes; you should have 16 pieces. Place tofu in a resealable plastic bag or shallow nonreactive dish. Pour marinade over, turn to coat, and refrigerate for several hours; turn tofu occasionally.

3 Drain tofu; reserve marinade. Thread tofu, red onion, red pepper and zucchini alternately onto 4 metal or soaked wooden skewers.

4 Preheat grill on medium-high. Place kebabs on oiled grill rack. Close lid and cook (use Direct Grilling, page 7) for about 10 minutes or until tofu is crisp and vegetables are tender. Turn kebabs several times, basting with reserved marinade. *Makes 4 servings.*

Tip: For best results, use firm tofu; the silken variety is too soft to hold on the skewers.

Chicken on a Spit, page 149

CHAPTER 6

Spit Roasting

THE GOURMET WAY to roast is on a rotating spit exposed to an indirect medium-high heat source, with a drip pan on a cooking rack under the meat to catch the drippings and the grill lid closed. Because of the rotating motion, the meat is kept constantly bathed in its own juices, and there are no flare-ups because the drippings are caught in the pan. All sides cook evenly producing a juicy, moist, flavorful result. Spit roasting also requires less attention than other grilling methods. Many meats are ideal for spit roasting – whole chicken,

duck, Cornish hens, roasts of beef, veal, lamb and pork, and even meaty country-style pork ribs to name a few. The recipes in this section provide new perspectives to cooking traditional roasts.

Choose a compact, evenly shaped roast that is well tied with string, preferably boneless and with some fat covering to protect it.

Tie poultry with string or wire to keep the shape uniform all around. Wings and legs, once tied securely to the body, can be covered with pieces of foil to prevent overcooking.

INDIRECT GRILLING

Preheat grill on high, then reduce heat according to chart below. Remove roasts about 5°F (2°C) below desired degree of doneness. Let meat stand covered with foil for 15 minutes before serving.

Meat Cut	Temperature		Grilling Time		
	internal		grill	minutes per lb	minutes per kg
Roasts:					
Beef	rare 140°F (60°C)		medium-high	18 to 20	40 to 45
	medium 160°F (70°C)		medium-high	22 to 25	50 to 60
	well-done 170°F (75°C)		medium-high	30	75
Veal	medium 160°F (70°C)		medium-high	25	55
Lamb	medium 160°F (70°C)		medium-high	about 20	about 40
Pork:					
Roasts	160°F (70°C)		medium-high	20 to 30	45 to 75
Country-style ribs	160°F (70°C)		medium-low	20 to 30	45 to 75
Poultry:					
Whole turkey	170°F (75°C)		medium-high	30	75
Whole chicken	170°F (75°C)		medium-high	30	75
Cornish hens	180°F (80°C)		medium-high	30	75

Insert the pointed end of the spit rod lengthwise through the center of the meat or poultry. Test for balance by rotating the rod in your hands. (The rotisserie will not turn properly with an unbalanced load, placing undue strain on the rotisserie motor.) Insert holding forks at right angles to each other. Tighten the fork screws with pliers as they tend to loosen with prolonged turning. Insert a meat thermometer so the bulb is in the thickest part of the meat or in the thickest part of the breast for poultry. Make sure the thermometer does not touch the spit.

Preheat the grill on high. Turn off the burner under the position where the roast will rotate, but leave the remaining burner(s) on. Fill a shallow metal pan with liquid (such as water, beer, juice, wine or broth) and place it on the grill rack beneath where the roast will rotate. Place the spit with the roast on it in the rotisserie and start the rotisserie motor.

Close the lid and cook for the specified time (see chart). Lower the heat to medium-high after the surface of the meat has browned.

Never allow the liquid in the pan to evaporate completely. Juices from the cooking meat will drip into the liquid, producing a superb sauce or *au jus* gravy.

If you apply a basting sauce, add some liquid from the dripping pan for extra flavor. Most basting should be done toward the end of the roasting.

The process for spit roasting over charcoal is much the same; arrange the hot coals so they are not under the roast to allow room for the dripping pan.

Tips:

1 Remove meat from spit about 5°F (2°C) below desired degree of doneness. Meat will continue cooking, covered with foil, during the 10 to 15 minutes standing time.

2 To test poultry for doneness, cut into the thickest part of the meat near a bone; juices should run clear and meat should not be pink. It is always recommended that poultry be spit-roasted without a bread stuffing.

Chutney-Peppered Rotisserie of Beef

Chutney and pepper flavors permeate the roast through both the marinade and the rub.

Rub

1 tbsp	each: black and green peppercorns	15 mL
1 tsp	each: mustard seeds and celery seeds	5 mL
½ tsp	each: garlic powder and salt	2 mL

Beef

4 lb	boneless rolled rib or sirloin or tenderloin roast of beef	2 kg

Marinade

½ cup	pineapple juice	125 mL
⅓ cup	each: orange juice and steak sauce	75 mL
¼ cup	chutney (if coarse, cut with kitchen scissors)	50 mL
2 tbsp	Worcestershire sauce	25 mL
2 tsp	each: granulated sugar, seasoned salt and lemon pepper	10 mL

1 *For rub:* Crack peppercorns, mustard and celery seeds to a coarse meal: place in a plastic bag and crush with bottom of a heavy skillet, or place in a spice grinder and pulse. Set aside.

2 Trim excess fat from beef and discard. Place in resealable plastic bag and reserve.

3 *For marinade:* In small bowl, combine pineapple and orange juice, steak sauce, chutney, Worcestershire sauce, sugar, seasoned salt and lemon pepper. Pour over roast, turn to coat and refrigerate for 6 hours or overnight; turn bag occasionally.

4 Preheat grill on high. Remove roast from marinade; reserve marinade. Press rub over roast. Place roast on spit, be careful to balance meat and follow spit manufacturer's directions. Adjust heat to medium-high and cook (see Spit Roasting, page 137) for about 1½ hours (see chart on page 137).

5 Meanwhile, place marinade in small saucepan, bring to a boil, reduce heat and cook for 5 minutes; keep warm. Brush roast often with warm marinade. Remove from spit to carving board; cover loosely with foil for about 15 minutes before slicing.

Makes 6 to 8 servings.

Tip: Remove roast from spit about 5°F (2°C) below desired doneness. Meat will continue cooking, covered with foil, during the 15 minutes standing time.

Rotisserie Pork with Salsa Marinade

Escape summer heat and supper hour hassles. Spit-roast pork for tonight's dinner, and pre-plan leftovers for tomorrow. Thoughts turn to Mexico whenever salsa appears in a recipe. The level of spiciness in this one is your choice according to which salsa you use.

| 4 lb | boneless loin of pork (center cut) | 2 kg |

Salsa Marinade

2 tsp	olive oil	10 mL
1	small onion, finely chopped	1
½ cup	each: ketchup and salsa (mild, medium or hot)	125 mL
1 tbsp	dry mustard	15 mL
2 tsp	red wine vinegar	10 mL
½ tsp	dried oregano or 1 tbsp (15 mL) fresh	2 mL
¼ tsp	hot pepper sauce	1 mL

1 Trim excess fat from roast and discard. Place roast in resealable plastic bag.

2 *For marinade:* In nonstick skillet, heat oil on medium; cook onion for 5 minutes or until softened. Add ketchup, salsa, mustard, vinegar, oregano and pepper sauce. Bring to a boil, reduce heat and simmer for 10 minutes; cool slightly before pouring over roast. Close bag and refrigerate for at least 4 hours or overnight; turn bag occasionally. Remove roast from marinade. Place marinade in small saucepan, bring to a boil, reduce heat and cook for 5 minutes; keep warm.

3 Preheat grill on high. Place roast on spit; be careful to balance meat and follow spit manufacturer's directions. Adjust heat to medium-high and cook (see Spit Roasting, page 137) for about 2 hours or until meat thermometer registers 160°F (70°C); brush frequently with warm marinade. Remove meat from spit to carving board; cover loosely with foil for about 10 minutes before slicing.

Makes 8 servings.

Tonight's Suggested Menu: Serve with a green salad consisting of a variety of salad greens tossed with a Lime-Dijon Vinaigrette (page 172), (substitute lime juice for lemon juice), Mexican Corn Salad (page 190) and warm flour tortillas. It makes a great south-of-the-border meal.

Tomorrow's Suggested Menu: Serve cold slivered pork in a main course salad with lots of fresh greens, mandarin orange sections, sliced cucumber and diced sweet red pepper. Toss the salad with Poppy Seed Vinaigrette (page 180). It's an easy meal.

Rotisserie Pork with Salsa Marinade, left, page 140; and Rotisserie Country-style Ribs with Port Wine Marinade, right, page 142

Rotisserie Country-style Ribs with Port Wine Marinade

Spit roasting is the ideal way to grill ribs because they can be cooked slowly and evenly without scorching. The port marinade gives the ribs just the right blend of tanginess, heat and pungency that goes well with pork.

Port Wine Marinade

⅔ cup	port wine	150 mL
½ cup	orange juice	125 mL
1	piece gingerroot	1
	(2 inch/5 cm), minced	
2	cloves garlic, minced	2
1 tbsp	each: liquid honey and lime juice	15 mL
½ to 1 tsp	crushed chili peppers	2 to 5 mL

Spareribs

3 lb	country-style ribs	1.5 kg
	Orange slices	

1 In small saucepan, cook wine, orange juice, gingerroot, garlic, honey, lime juice and chili peppers until hot. Cool slightly and reserve.

2 Place ribs in shallow nonreactive dish large enough to allow ribs to lay flat in single layer. Pour marinade over ribs, turn to coat; cover and refrigerate for at least 4 hours or overnight. Remove ribs from marinade; reserve marinade. Place marinade in small saucepan, bring to a boil, reduce heat and cook for 5 minutes; keep warm.

3 Preheat grill on high. Lace ribs accordion style on spit rod; be careful to balance meat and follow spit manufacturer's directions. Adjust heat to medium-low and cook (see Spit Roasting, page 137) for about 1½ hours or until meat thermometer registers 160°F (70°C). Brush frequently with warm marinade.

4 Remove ribs from spit, cover loosely with foil for about 10 minutes before cutting into serving-size pieces. Serve with sliced oranges.
Makes 6 servings.

Suggested Menu: Serve with Grilled Corn on the Cob with Herb Butter (page 164), sliced tomatoes and potato salad. It makes a marvelous summertime meal.

Spit-Roasted Leg of Lamb

Suggested Menu: Start with Beet Borscht (page 24), then serve Szechwan Vegetable Salad (page 177) and brown rice with the lamb.
Tip: Lamb is at its most tender and delicious when cooked until the meat is well browned on the outside but still pink in the center.

The Soy Ginger Lemon Marinade and Baste lends a gentle taste of the Orient to the roasted lamb. This marinade can also be used for lamb chops.

4 to 5 lb	boneless leg of lamb	2 to 2.5 kg
¾ cup	Soy Ginger Lemon	175 mL
	Marinade and Baste (page 195)	
2	large lemons, each cut into 4 slices	2

1 Trim excess fat from lamb and discard. Place roast in resealable plastic bag. Pour marinade over lamb, reseal and refrigerate for at least 4 hours or overnight; turn bag occasionally.

2 Remove roast from marinade; reserve marinade. Preheat grill on high. Place roast on spit; be careful to balance meat and follow the spit manufacturer's directions. Adjust heat to medium-high and cook (see Spit Roasting, page 137) for about 1½ hours or until meat thermometer registers 160°F (70°C).

3 Meanwhile, place reserved marinade in small saucepan, bring to a boil, reduce heat and cook for 5 minutes. Brush roast occasionally with warm marinade. Place thick lemon slices on grill rack during last 10 minutes of grilling time.

4 Remove roast from spit to carving board; cover loosely with foil for about 10 minutes before slicing. Serve with grilled lemon slices.

Makes 6 to 8 servings.

Garlic Rotisserie Beef Tenderloin, page 145

Garlic Rotisserie Beef Tenderloin

Entertain with stylish simplicity! Spit-roasted beef tenderloin – who could ask for anything more divine, yet it's ever so easy on the chef.

Garlic Marinade

1	head Roasted Garlic (see page 15)	1
⅓ cup	dry red wine	75 mL
2 tbsp	extra virgin olive oil	25 mL
1½ tsp	dried oregano or	7 mL
	2 tbsp (25 mL) fresh	
½ tsp	freshly ground pepper	2 mL
1 lb	beef tenderloin	500 g
	(about 3 inches/7.5 cm thick)	
	Fresh oregano leaves	

1 *For marinade:* When garlic is roasted, squeeze out the pulp, place it in small bowl and mash with a fork. Stir in wine, oil, oregano and pepper.

2 Trim excess fat from beef and discard. Place beef in resealable plastic bag, pour wine mixture over and turn to coat. Close bag and refrigerate for 4 to 12 hours; turn bag occasionally.

3 Remove beef from marinade; reserve marinade. Place marinade in small saucepan, bring to a boil, reduce heat and cook for 5 minutes; keep warm.

4 Preheat grill on high. Place meat on spit; be careful to balance meat and follow spit manufacturer's directions. Adjust heat to medium-high and cook (see Spit Roasting, page 137) for about 30 minutes (see chart on page 137); brush often with warm marinade. Remove beef from spit to carving board; cover loosely with foil for 10 to 15 minutes before slicing.
Makes 3 to 4 servings.

Suggested Menu: Serve with Grilled Carrots and Grilled Fennel (page 168), crusty whole wheat rolls, and a robust red wine such as Cabernet Sauvignon. Warm Pear Salad with Stilton (page 181) would be an ideal salad course to follow the entrée.

Apple-stuffed Veal Roast with Mint Garlic Rub

Fresh from the garden, mint and rosemary, along with a juicy apple, contribute to the complex flavors in this recipe. The mint rub is suitable for both veal and lamb.

Mint Garlic Rub

⅓ cup	each: granulated sugar and garlic powder	75 mL
⅓ cup	chopped fresh mint or 2 tbsp (25 mL) dried	75 mL
1 tbsp	chopped fresh rosemary or 1 tsp (5 mL) dried	15 mL
¼ tsp	freshly ground pepper	1 mL
4 lb	boneless veal loin roast	2 kg

Apple Stuffing

1 tbsp	olive oil	15 mL
1 cup	sliced mushrooms	250 mL
1	large green apple, diced and peeled	1
1 tsp	lemon juice	5 mL
½ tsp	grated lemon peel	2 mL
	Salt and freshly ground pepper	

1 *For rub:* In plastic bag, combine sugar, garlic powder, mint, rosemary and pepper. Shake to blend. Place veal in bag; shake to coat thoroughly. Remove veal and set aside.

2 *For stuffing:* In nonstick skillet, heat oil on medium-high; cook mushrooms and apples for 10 minutes or until softened. Remove from heat, stir in lemon juice, peel, and salt and pepper to taste; set aside.

3 Cut a wide deep pocket in side of roast; stuff apple mixture into pocket. Tie roast at 1-inch (2.5 cm) intervals with heavy string.

4 Preheat grill on high. Place roast on spit; be careful to balance meat and follow spit manufacturer's directions. Adjust heat to medium-high and cook (see Spit Roasting, page 137) for about 1½ hours or until meat thermometer registers 160°F (70°C). Remove meat from spit to carving board; cover loosely with foil for about 10 minutes before slicing.

Makes 6 to 8 servings.

Suggested Menu: Serve with Caramelized Leeks and Onions (page 163) and a green vegetable. Flaming Blueberry Mango Crisp (page 214) is an easy dessert to finish this marvelous meal.

Apple-stuffed Veal Roast with Mint Garlic Rub, page 146

Rotisserie Cornish Hens with Provençal Stuffing

The Provence-style tomato, mushroom, and onion stuffing makes these juicy miniature chickens irresistible. Prior to the 19th century, tomatoes were regarded with suspicion by the residents of Provence, but once accepted, tomatoes had a revolutionary effect on the cooking of the region. Many of today's recipes from the south of France contain tomatoes.

2	Cornish hens,* thawed	2

Provençal Tomato Stuffing

2	cloves garlic, halved	2
2 tbsp	butter or margarine	25 mL
1	medium onion, chopped	1
1½ cups	sliced mushrooms	375 mL
2	large tomatoes, diced	2
3 tbsp	chopped fresh tarragon or 1 tbsp (15 mL) dried	45 mL
1 tbsp	chopped fresh parsley or 1 tsp (5 mL) dried	15 mL
2 tsp	chopped fresh thyme or ½ tsp (2 mL) dried	10 mL
½ tsp	each: salt and freshly ground pepper	2 mL
3 tbsp	dried bread crumbs	45 mL

1 Wash and dry hens.

2 *For stuffing:* Rub cut side of garlic over cavity and outer skin of each hen; crush garlic. In nonstick skillet, melt butter over medium heat. Add garlic and onion and cook for about 5 minutes or until tender. Add mushrooms and tomatoes. Cook for about 10 minutes or until slightly thickened; stir often. Add tarragon, parsley, thyme, salt and pepper. Taste and adjust seasoning; cool slightly; stir in bread crumbs. Spoon stuffing into cavity of each hen. Truss with skewers and kitchen cord.

3 Preheat grill on high. Place hens on spit; be careful to balance hens and follow spit manufacturer's directions. Adjust heat to medium-high and cook (see Spit Roasting, page 137) for about 1¼ hours or until juices run clear and meat thermometer registers 180°F (80°C). Remove hens from spit to carving board, cover loosely with foil for about 10 minutes before cutting in half to serve.

Makes 4 servings.

* The difference between a Cornish hen and a broiler chicken is mainly the size. The hens weigh less than 1½ pounds (750 g) and are an excellent size for 1 to 2 servings. The all-purpose broiler chicken weighs between 1½ and 4 pounds (750 g and 2 kg) and so serves 2 to 5.

Tip: Use this stuffing for small broiler chickens, or press a small amount into a pocket cut in thick pork or lamb chops.

Chicken on a Spit

Suggested Menu: Serve with Potatoes and Onions in a Pouch (page 155) and Shredded Zucchini, Carrot and Parsnip (page 167, grill space not required).

On returning from a visit to Sardinia, our daughter Martha told us of the most wonderful chicken she was served in a restaurant. It was roasted with lemons and black or pimento-stuffed green olives placed in the cavity. Since rotisserie poultry should never be stuffed with a bread mixture, it seemed like a good idea. I tried it, and was greatly pleased with the result. Vary the amount of lemon and olives according to the size of the bird.

6 to 8 lb	chicken	3 to 4 kg
2	large lemons, cut into chunks	2
1 cup	olives, black or green	250 mL
	Salt and freshly ground pepper	

1 Rinse bird and pat dry inside and out. Remove neck and giblets. Skewer neck skin to back. Tuck drumsticks under the band of skin across the tail. Twist wing tips under the back. Place lemons and olives in cavity; sprinkle bird lightly with salt and pepper. Truss bird with string or wire; cover wing tips and drumsticks with foil, if desired. Insert a meat thermometer into the center of the inside thigh muscle, being careful to not touch bone.

2 Preheat grill on high. Place bird on spit; be careful to balance meat and follow spit manufacturer's directions. Adjust heat to medium-high and cook (see Spit Roasting, page 137) for about 2½ hours or until meat thermometer registers 170°F (75°C). Remove bird from spit to carving board; cover loosely with foil for about 10 minutes before carving. Serve with a small amount of lemon-olive mixture.

Makes 6 to 8 servings.

Grilled Red and White Onions, page 156; and
Eggplant with Anchovy-Parsley Sauce, page 157

CHAPTER 7

Vibrant Vegetable Grilling

JUST ABOUT EVERYTHING tastes better on the grill. This is certainly true with vegetables. It seems these days that no cookout is complete without them. The bold flavors and colors of fresh produce are perfect for grilling. Vegetables provide a light approach to outdoor cooking, a fitting accent with the current concerns about healthy eating. As well, grilling vegetables simplifies outdoor meal preparation as the activity becomes part of outside entertaining; since the grill is on for the meat, why not add a few extras? Serve grilled vegetables either as side dishes or as appetizers.

Roasting intensifies the flavor of vegetables, making them delicious either hot or cold. The natural sugars in such vegetables as onions, garlic and sweet peppers caramelize when grilled, imparting a depth and richness that no amount of pan sautéing could ever achieve. Other vegetables, such as eggplant and exotic mushrooms like portobello, acquire the same woodsy smokiness as a good grilled steak.

In this chapter, you will find exciting vegetable combinations such as Caramelized Leeks and Onion (page 163) and new ways to grill vegetables, such as Herb-stuffed Mushrooms (page 158). In case you don't have any grill room left, there are also recipes that can be prepared on the kitchen stove. Sweet Potatoes, Carrots, Turnip and Prunes (page 158) is a good example and a perfect companion to your grilled dinner.

Methods vary, but almost any vegetable can be cooked on the grill. Here are a few general guidelines. See pages 168–9 for detailed instructions for specific vegetables.

- When grilling vegetables, lay them perpendicular to the spaces in the grill rack so they don't fall through into the fire. You can also use grill baskets, but I like to place vegetables directly on the grill to get those great grill marks.
- Slice or cut large vegetables into chunks so they will grill to tenderness in a reasonable time along with other smaller vegetables that may be cooking at the same time.
- Foil pouches keep smaller vegetables from slipping through the grill rack, and also insulate delicate produce from direct heat. The steaming process in the pouches allows the seasonings to mingle and intensify.
- To prevent vegetables from sticking to the grill rack, marinate them in an oil-based mixture or brush them with oil (not butter, which burns at a relatively low temperature).

- To ensure even, thorough cooking, watch the coals or heat source carefully and turn the vegetables regularly.
- Some vegetables, such as broccoli, asparagus, cauliflower and potatoes, require blanching or precooking to prevent them burning on the outside before softening within.
- Natural wrappers such as corn husks keep grilling vegetables moist and tender.
- Unless specified otherwise, grill vegetables by the Direct Grilling method (page 7) at medium-high heat with the lid closed.
- Finally, since vegetables tend to absorb off-flavors more quickly than meat or poultry, the grill rack must be as clean as possible.

DIRECT GRILLING

Artichoke Kebabs with Thyme

Grill bottled or canned artichokes on skewers for a vibrant vegetable accompaniment to many grilled meats. This way, all the "fuss and muss" of cooking raw artichokes is done for you.

2	cans (14 oz/398 mL) artichoke hearts, drained	2
2 tbsp	each: lemon juice and olive oil	25 mL
1 tbsp	minced fresh thyme or 1 tsp (5 mL) dried	15 mL
	Salt and freshly ground pepper	
	Fresh thyme sprigs	
18	cherry tomatoes (optional)	18

1 Cut artichokes in half and place in a bowl. In a second bowl, combine lemon juice, oil, thyme and salt and pepper to taste. Pour over artichokes; toss well, cover and refrigerate for several hours to develop the flavors.

2 Drain artichokes; reserve marinade. Thread artichoke halves (alternating with tomatoes, if using) on metal or soaked wooden skewers; leave a small space between each piece.

3 Preheat grill on medium. Place kebabs on oiled grill rack. Close lid and cook (use Direct Grilling, page 7) for 12 minutes or until vegetables are lightly browned; turn and brush often with reserved marinade.

Makes 6 servings.

Variation: If you choose to grill whole artichokes, I find it best to cook them beforehand (see directions on page 176). Then, lightly oil the artichoke and cook on preheated oiled grill rack (use Direct Grilling, page 7) until leaves have started to brown; turn frequently. (See photograph on page 30 of a whole artichoke grilled and served with Moroccan Lamb Chops, recipe on page 57.)

Artichoke Kebabs with Thyme,
page 152

Kebab of Vegetables

Spit cooking vegetables is a way to enjoy many different vegetables at one meal.

1	large potato, cut into bite-size pieces	1
2	medium carrots, cut into bite-size pieces	2
1	medium onion, cut into wedges	1
1	medium zucchini, cut into bite-size pieces	1
1 cup	whole mushrooms	250 mL

Rum Sauce

3 tbsp	rum or 1 tsp (5 mL) rum extract	45 mL
2 tbsp	melted butter or margarine	25 mL
2	cloves garlic, crushed	2
¼ tsp	each: paprika and ground nutmeg	1 mL
⅛ tsp	each: salt and freshly ground pepper	0.5 mL

1 In saucepan, partially cook potatoes, carrots and onion for about 10 minutes or until barely tender; drain well. Arrange vegetables alternately on soaked wooden skewers.

2 *For sauce:* In small bowl, combine rum, butter, garlic, paprika and nutmeg. Brush vegetables with sauce and sprinkle with salt and pepper.

3 Preheat grill on medium-high. Place kebabs on oiled grill; close lid and cook (use Direct Grilling, page 7) for about 20 minutes or until crisp and golden brown; turn several times.
Makes 4 servings.

Tip: Soak wooden skewers in water for at least 30 minutes before adding food to prevent them from scorching.

Minted Peas with Lettuce

Mint adds a refreshing taste to this combination of peas and lettuce. For many, peas cooked in the French style with lettuce, is the very best way. The lettuce replaces the need for added liquid.

1 tbsp	butter or margarine	15 mL
2 cups	shredded iceberg lettuce	500 mL
1	pkg (300 g) frozen green peas or 3 cups 750 mL fresh	(750 mL)
2 cups	trimmed snow peas	500 mL
2	green onions, thinly sliced	2
1½ tsp	chicken bouillon powder	7 mL
2 tbsp	chopped fresh mint or 1½ tsp (7 mL) dried	25 mL
	Salt and freshly ground pepper	

1 Preheat grill on medium. In an aluminum foil pan, melt butter over medium heat, either on the grill or on the stove. Place lettuce in pan and top with peas, snow peas and onions. Sprinkle with bouillon powder and mint and lightly with salt and pepper; cover tightly with foil.

2 Place pan on grill rack; close lid and cook (use Direct Grilling, page 7) for about 8 minutes or until peas are just cooked and lettuce wilted.
Makes 4 to 6 servings.

Variation: Diced carrots and mushrooms can be added. Sauté the mushrooms in butter, then proceed as above.

Creamed Spinach

Bacon, onion and garlic work magic with ordinary spinach.

1	pkg (300 g) chopped frozen spinach	1
2	slices back bacon, finely chopped	2
½ cup	finely chopped onion	125 mL
1	clove garlic, minced	1
2 tbsp	all-purpose flour	25 mL
¼ tsp	each: salt and lemon pepper	1 mL
1 cup	milk	250 mL

1 Cook spinach according to package directions; drain well.

2 In medium saucepan, cook bacon, onion and garlic for 5 minutes or until onion is softened. Add flour, salt and lemon pepper; cook briefly. Gradually whisk in milk. Cook, stirring constantly, until thickened and smooth. Add spinach, mix well and heat to serving temperature.

Makes 4 servings.

Suggested Menu: Serve on a bed of cooked lentils with Rock Cornish Hens with Sherry-Peach Glaze (page 80).

Potatoes and Onions in a Pouch

Potatoes and Onions in a Pouch

Grilling potatoes and onions together in a foil package gives us an interesting two-vegetable accompaniment for beef or poultry dishes. Spanish or any other sweet onion can be substituted.

1	large Vidalia onion, peeled and thickly sliced	1
2	medium white or sweet potatoes, peeled and thickly sliced	2
2	cloves garlic, minced	2
	Salt and freshly ground pepper	
2 tbsp	melted butter or margarine	25 mL
	Sliced green onion	

1 Place overlapping slices of onion and potato on large sheet of heavy-duty foil. Sprinkle lightly with salt and pepper; drizzle with melted butter. Fold foil edges together to form tight seal.

2 Preheat grill on medium. Place foil package on grill rack; close lid and cook (use Direct Grilling, page 7) for about 25 minutes, or until vegetables are tender and starting to turn golden brown; turn often.

3 Open package, sprinkle with green onions and serve.

Makes 3 to 4 servings.

Variation: Sliced carrots are a colorful addition to the potatoes and onions. For a change, you can also add sliced mushrooms – either button or one of the exotic varieties such as shiitake, portobello or oyster.

Zucchini Fingers

Similar to French-fried zucchini, these fingers are easier to make and just as tasty. They're lower in fat too!

½ cup	unseasoned dried bread crumbs	125 mL
3 tbsp	grated Parmesan cheese	45 mL
2	medium zucchini,	2
	cut in 1- x 4-inch (2.5 x 10 cm) strips	
½ cup	bottled creamy herb	125 mL
	salad dressing	
	Fresh parsley sprigs	

1 In small bowl, combine bread crumbs with cheese. Dip zucchini strips into salad dressing, then coat with bread crumb mixture.

2 Preheat grill on medium. Place zucchini on oiled grill rack. Close lid and cook (use Direct Grilling, page 7) for about 10 minutes per side or until crisp and golden.

Makes 4 servings.

Variation: Coat zucchini fingers beforehand and refrigerate until ready to grill. Yellow squash, thickly sliced onions and eggplant slices can also be grilled this way.

Grilled Red and White Onions

The aromatic pine flavors of rosemary and the sweet pungency of balsamic vinegar blend with the humble onion to create a rather exotic vegetable – excellent with grilled meats and poultry.

2 tbsp	balsamic vinegar	25 mL
2 tsp	chopped fresh rosemary	10 mL
	or ½ tsp (2 mL) dried	
2	large red onions	2
2	large Vidalia or Spanish onions	2
1 tbsp	olive oil	15 mL
½ cup	chopped fresh parsley	125 mL
	Salt and freshly ground pepper	

1 In small saucepan, heat vinegar and rosemary over low heat until warm (do not boil). Remove pan from heat, cover and let mixture stand for 20 minutes.

2 Peel onions and slice crosswise into ¾-inch (2 cm) thick slices.

3 Preheat grill on medium-high. Brush both sides of onions lightly with oil. Place onions in single layer on oiled grill rack, keeping slices intact. Cook onions in batches on uncovered grill (use Direct Grilling, page 7) for about 5 minutes on each side, or until softened and grill marks appear. Transfer onions when tender to large bowl; separate into rings.

4 Toss onions with vinegar mixture, parsley and salt and pepper to taste. Serve warm or at room temperature.

Makes 6 servings.

Suggested Menu: Serve with Eggplant with Anchovy-Parsley Sauce (page 157) and a great grilled steak.

Variation: Brush sliced onions with bottled Dijon Vinaigrette. Grill for about 10 minutes or until tender and grill marks appear, and garnish with chopped fresh mint.

DIRECT GRILLING

Eggplant with Anchovy-Parsley Sauce

Thin lengthwise slices of eggplant are grilled, rolled and served with a fabulous anchovy sauce

2	large eggplants	2
	Salt	
2 tbsp	olive oil, divided	25 mL

Anchovy-Parsley Sauce

¼ cup	finely chopped onion	50 mL
6	large cloves garlic, diced	6
½ cup	red wine	125 mL
2 tbsp	each: anchovy paste and drained, washed capers	25 mL
¼ cup	chopped fresh parsley	50 mL
¼ tsp	freshly ground pepper	1 mL

1 Trim eggplants; slice lengthwise into ½-inch (1 cm) thick strips. Lightly sprinkle with salt, let stand for 30 minutes. Remove resulting moisture with paper toweling.

2 Preheat grill on medium-high. Place eggplant on oiled grill rack and brush lightly with olive oil. Close lid and cook (use Direct Grilling, page 7) for several minutes per side or until golden brown. Remove and roll each slice into a cylinder; keep warm.

3 *For sauce:* Meanwhile, in nonstick skillet, heat remaining oil on medium heat. Cook onion and garlic for 1 minute; add wine, anchovy paste and capers. Cook until heated and slightly thickened. Stir in parsley and pepper.

4 Serve several slices of eggplant on each plate with a small amount of sauce.

Makes 4 servings.

Sweet Potato, Carrots, Turnip and Prunes

What could be more delectable than caramelized vegetables – sweet potatoes, carrots, turnips and chopped onion – flavored with orange. This recipe is a "gourmet" choice to cook, and so very easy.

2	medium sweet potatoes, peeled and thickly sliced	2
2	large carrots, sliced lengthwise	2
2	small white turnips, sliced	2
¼ cup	finely chopped onion	50 mL

Orange Marinade

2	oranges: juice and long shreds of zest	2
3 tbsp	each: liquid honey and dark rum	45 mL
1 tsp	dried thyme or 1 tbsp (15 mL) chopped fresh	5 mL
	Salt and freshly ground pepper	
12	pitted prunes	12

1 In large saucepan, bring water to a boil. Cook sweet potatoes, carrots, turnip and onion just until tender; drain well and place in large bowl.

2 In small dish, combine orange juice and zest, honey, rum and thyme. Pour over vegetables and toss to coat.

3 Preheat grill on medium-high. Place vegetables on oiled grill rack or in grill basket; sprinkle with salt and pepper. Close lid and cook (use Direct Grilling, page 7) for about 12 minutes or until vegetables are starting to become golden; brush occasionally with orange mixture and turn once. Top with prunes when vegetables are turned.
Makes 6 servings.

Suggested Menu: Chicken on a Spit (page 149) is an excellent choice to serve with these vegetables.

Herb-stuffed Mushrooms on Skewers

Herbes de Provençe enhance the flavor of grilled mushrooms in this unique stuffed treatment of mushrooms.

¼ cup	dry white wine or sherry	50 mL
1 tbsp	chicken bouillon granules	15 mL
24	large mushrooms	24
¼ cup	finely chopped onion	50 mL
2 tbsp	olive oil, divided	25 mL
⅓ cup	fine dried bread crumbs	75 mL
½ to 1 tsp	*herbes de Provençe**	2 to 5 mL
	Fresh parsley sprigs	

*See page 56

1 In microwaveable container, heat wine and bouillon on high (100%) until bouillon dissolves.

2 Remove mushroom stems; chop finely. In non-stick skillet, sauté stems and onion in 1 tbsp (15 mL) oil. Remove from heat; add wine mixture, bread crumbs and herbs; mix well.

3 Fit two mushroom caps together with some stuffing between them. Place 2 or 3 pairs on short soaked wooden or metal skewers.

4 Preheat grill on medium. Place kebabs on oiled grill rack; close lid and cook (use Direct Grilling, page 7) for 3 to 5 minutes, brushing with remaining olive oil.

Makes 12 double mushrooms, 4 to 6 side servings.

Suggested Menu: Serve these mushrooms with any grilled beef, pork, poultry, venison or fish.

Tip: Assemble beforehand, refrigerate, then grill just before serving.

DIRECT GRILLING

Grilled Tarragon Shiitake Mushrooms

The size, meaty flesh and full bodied flavor of shiitake mushrooms make them ideal for grilling. Add the sesame taste of tahini for mushroom magic!

Tahini Baste

2 tbsp	each: water and tahini*	25 mL
1 tbsp	each: lemon juice and soy sauce	15 mL
1 tbsp	chopped fresh gingerroot	15 mL
2 tsp	granulated sugar	10 mL
1	clove garlic, crushed	1
Pinch	crushed red pepper flakes	Pinch
8	large shiitake mushrooms	8
3 tbsp	dry sherry	45 mL
1 tsp	sesame oil	5 mL
	Fresh tarragon	

1 *For baste:* In bowl, combine water, tahini, lemon juice, soy sauce, gingerroot, sugar, garlic and pepper flakes; reserve.

2 Clean mushrooms (do not peel) and pat dry. In medium bowl, toss mushrooms with sherry and sesame oil. Cover and let stand for 30 minutes.

3 Preheat grill on medium. Place mushrooms on lightly oiled grill rack; close lid and cook (use Direct Grilling, page 7) for about 10 minutes or until golden brown; turn and brush often with reserved baste. Garnish with tarragon and serve.

Makes 4 servings.

*Tahini, a thick paste made of ground sesame seeds, is frequently used in Middle Eastern cooking. It can be purchased in specialty food and health food stores.

Suggested Menu: Serve with Steak Pinwheels with Mushroom and Asparagus (page 51) and fluffy basmati rice. The steak pinwheels are also stuffed with shiitake mushrooms.

Corn-stuffed Rainbow Peppers

These pepper halves can be made beforehand, refrigerated and then grilled with the meat course. Since sweet peppers welcome almost any savory stuffing, rice or even couscous can be used instead of corn for a great alternative.

2	medium red, yellow, green and/or orange sweet peppers	2
	Canola oil	
1	small onion, finely chopped	1
2 tbsp	butter or margarine	25 mL
1 cup	fresh or frozen corn kernels	250 mL
½ cup	shredded Monterey Jack cheese	125 mL
1 tbsp	each: finely chopped fresh	15 mL
	parsley, chives and basil or 1 tsp (5 mL) dried	
	Salt and freshly ground pepper	
	Fresh parsley, chives or basil	

1 Remove stem end from peppers, halve lengthwise and remove seeds. Lightly brush peppers with oil; set aside.

2 In small skillet, sauté onion in butter for 5 minutes. Remove to bowl; stir in corn, cheese, herbs and salt and pepper to taste. Divide mixture between pepper halves.

3 Preheat grill on medium. Place pepper halves, filling side up, on oiled grill rack. Close lid and cook (use Direct Grilling, page 7) for about 12 minutes or until peppers are softened and cheese is melted. Serve warm or at room temperature with a garnish of fresh herbs.

Makes 4 servings, ½ pepper per serving.

Grilled Mediterranean Vegetables

Reminiscent of Spain, Italy or southern France, this recipe is ideal for a North American backyard summer dinner. Grilling the vegetables in a grill basket saves the trouble of turning each piece individually. However, all the vegetables are large enough to be cooked directly on the grill rack. The result is a perfectly cooked assortment of the garden's best.

⅓ cup	extra virgin olive oil	75 mL
1	clove garlic, minced	1
1 tbsp	minced fresh oregano or 1 tsp (5 mL) dried	15 mL

Vegetables

1	medium eggplant, sliced diagonally, ½ inch (1 cm) thick	1
1	large zucchini, sliced diagonally, ½ inch (1 cm) thick	1
1	large sweet red pepper, cut lengthwise into 1-inch (2.5 cm) strips	1
6	large mushrooms	6
3	Belgian endives, sliced lengthwise	3
	Salt and freshly ground pepper	
2 tsp	balsamic vinegar	10 mL

1 In small dish, combine oil, garlic and oregano. Lightly brush all vegetables with some of the mixture. Sprinkle lightly with salt and pepper.

2 Preheat grill on medium-high. Place vegetables either in a grill basket or directly on oiled grill rack. Close lid and cook (use Direct Grilling, page 7) for about 12 minutes or until tender; turn often, brushing with oil if needed.

3 Transfer vegetables to a warm serving platter; drizzle with balsamic vinegar and serve immediately.

Makes 6 servings.

Braised Red Cabbage

This pungent, colorful vegetable dish goes well with pork. When the grill is busy, it's nice to have a recipe for the stove top.

4 cups	coarsely shredded red cabbage	1 L
⅔ cup	water	150 mL
⅓ cup	red wine vinegar	75 mL
3 tbsp	red currant or apple jelly	45 mL
¼ tsp	each: ground cinnamon, salt and freshly ground pepper	1 mL
⅛ tsp	each: ground allspice and cloves	0.5 mL

In large saucepan, combine cabbage, water, vinegar, jelly and seasonings. Cover and bring to a boil over high heat; reduce heat to low and cook gently for 30 minutes or until cabbage is crisp-tender. Stir occasionally. Taste and adjust seasonings, if required.

Makes 4 servings.

Roasted Beets with Creamy Orange Sauce

Beets develop a much mellower flavor when roasted than when boiled. Try this recipe in the oven when the weather is cold and on the grill in grilling season. These roasted beets are wonderful with Pungent Pork Tenderloin Medallions (page 62).

8	medium beets, peeled and sliced	8
1 tbsp	olive oil	15 mL
2 tsp	red wine vinegar	10 mL
	Salt and freshly ground pepper	
⅓ cup	light sour cream	75 mL
	Zest and juice of 1 orange	

1 Place beet slices in overlapping layers on a large square of heavy aluminum foil. Drizzle with oil and vinegar; sprinkle with salt and pepper to taste.

2 Preheat grill on medium-high. Place foil package on grill rack and cook (use Indirect Grilling, page 7) for about 1 hour or until beets are tender; turn occasionally. Open package and turn beets into serving bowl.

3 In small bowl, combine sour cream, orange juice and zest. Serve with roasted beets.

Makes 6 servings.

Tip: If one foil package is too bulky, divide beets into 2 or more packages. The smaller packages will also cook faster.

Tomato-Basil Bruschetta

Traditional bruschetta are slices of garlic bread roasted over an open fire and served warm. Today we make a number of variations, but they are still based on a simple, basic theme.

6	thick slices Italian bread	6
2	cloves garlic, halved	2
1	large onion, sliced and separated into rings	1
1 tbsp	olive oil	15 mL
1 tsp	granulated sugar	5 mL
1 tbsp	herb or Dijon mustard	15 mL
2	medium tomatoes, each cut into 6 slices	2
⅓ cup	chopped fresh basil	75 mL
2	green onions, sliced	2
	Salt and freshly ground pepper	
½ cup	grated Parmesan cheese	125 mL
	Fresh basil leaves	

1 Cut each bread slice crosswise in half. Rub one side with cut garlic cloves; mince garlic and reserve. Toast garlic side of bread on preheated grill rack or under the broiler.

2 In heavy nonstick skillet, cook garlic and onion in hot oil for about 5 minutes or until tender. Add sugar, reduce heat and cook for 5 minutes or until onion has started to caramelize. Stir in mustard. Spoon some of onion onto each half bread slice. Place 1 tomato slice over onion, sprinkle with basil, green onions, salt, pepper and cheese. Allow to stand at room temperature for up to 1 hour.

3 Preheat grill on medium. Place bread slices on oiled grill rack; cook, uncovered, (use Direct Grilling, page 7) for about 2 minutes or until bottom of bread has toasted and tomato is warmed. Garnish with extra basil leaves and serve.
Makes 12 slices.

For the most authentic flavor, use Parmigiano-Reggiano cheese from Italy. Buy it by the piece and grate just before using.

Tomato-Basil Bruschetta

Caramelized Leeks and Onions

Although this recipe is low in calories, the melted Brie and onion combination creates a rich-tasting consistency.

2 tbsp	olive oil, divided	25 mL
4 cups	thinly sliced Vidalia onions (2 onions)	1 L
3 cups	thinly sliced leeks, white part only (3 to 4 leeks)*	750 mL
½ tsp	dried thyme or 2 tsp (10 mL) fresh	2 mL
½ tsp	each: salt and freshly ground pepper	2 mL
⅓ cup	red wine	75 mL
¼ cup	beef broth	50 mL
2 tbsp	diced Brie cheese	25 mL
	Chopped fresh parsley	

1 Preheat grill on medium. Place large heavy skillet with oil on grill rack; heat until hot. Add onions and leeks. Cover skillet and cook (use Direct Grilling, page 7) for about 30 minutes or until vegetables are golden; stir often. Season with salt and pepper and thyme.

2 Add wine and broth; cook, uncovered, for 5 minutes or until liquid has almost evaporated. Remove onion mixture to a bowl; stir in Brie and serve when cheese is melted. Sprinkle with parsley. *Makes 4 servings.*

Suggested Menu: Serve with Chutney-Peppered Rotisserie of Beef (page 139) or any of the other grilled beef recipes. This onion-leek mixture is also perfect served on thick slices of crusty French or Italian bread for a lunch time sandwich.

*To clean leeks: Trim root ends and outer leaves and cut off all but about 1 inch (2.5 cm) of the dark green portion. Starting at the stem end, with a sharp knife, make a lengthwise incision to within 1 inch (2.5 cm) of root end. Make a second incision at right angles to the first one. Wash leeks thoroughly, shaking to loosen any dirt. Pat dry, then slice as required.

Lemon Mashed Potatoes

Lemon adds a flavor magic to mashed potatoes that complements fish, poultry and veal dishes.

4 cups	cubed, peeled baking potatoes	1 L
	(4 medium potatoes)	
½ cup	light sour cream	125 mL
1 tbsp	lemon juice	15 mL
1 tsp	granulated sugar	5 mL
½ tsp	each: grated lemon peel	2 mL
	and salt	
¼ tsp	white pepper	1 mL
	Snipped fresh chives	

In large saucepan, cook potatoes in boiling water until tender; drain. Return potatoes to saucepan, add sour cream, juice, sugar, peel, salt and pepper. Beat at medium speed with an electric mixer until smooth. Serve garnished with chives.
Makes 4 servings.

Suggested Menu: Serve with Apricot-glazed Veal Cutlets (page 67).

Grilled Corn on the Cob with Herb Butter

It's summer, and the eating is great! Succulent corn every night of the week. That's what many people want. Place foil-wrapped corn alongside when grilling other foods.

8	fresh cobs of corn, husked and	8
	silk removed	
2 tbsp	finely chopped fresh herbs	25 mL
	– tarragon, thyme, basil, cilantro or chives	
⅛ tsp	salt and freshly ground pepper	0.5 mL
¼ cup	melted butter or margarine	50 mL

1 Place each cob of corn on a piece of heavy-duty foil. In small bowl, combine fresh herbs, salt, pepper and melted butter. Brush lightly over each cob. Wrap corn securely in foil.
2 Preheat grill on medium. Place corn on grill rack; close lid and cook (use Direct Grilling, page 7) for about 20 minutes or until corn is tender; turn often.
Makes 8 servings, 1 cob each, or 4 servings, 2 cobs each.

Tip: Since steam builds up inside the foil packages, they will be very hot. Take care when opening.

Grilled Corn on the Cob with Herb Butter, page 164

Basil Ratatouille Kebabs

The flavors are similar to those of the traditional ratatouille of Provence, but this recipe takes some liberties by grilling the vegetables rather than cooking them in a skillet. Bon appétit!

1	small eggplant, halved lengthwise, peeled and cut into ½-inch (1 cm) slices	1
1	medium yellow squash, cut into thick slices	1
1	medium sweet red pepper, cut into square pieces	1
1	small onion, cut into 4 wedges	1
¼ cup	loosely packed fresh basil leaves, chopped	50 mL
2 tbsp	lemon juice	25 mL
2 tsp	olive oil	10 mL
¼ tsp	each: salt and freshly ground pepper	1 mL
2	medium tomatoes, quartered	2

1 In large resealable bag, place eggplant, squash, red pepper, onion, basil, lemon juice, oil, salt and pepper. Seal bag, shake contents to coat vegetables, and allow to marinate for about 1 hour. Remove vegetables from bag; reserve marinade. Thread vegetables alternately with tomatoes on metal or soaked wooden skewers.

2 Preheat grill on medium-high. Place kebabs on oiled grill rack. Close lid and cook (use Direct Grilling, page 7) for 7 minutes per side, basting occasionally with reserved marinade.

Makes 4 servings.

Double Cheese-topped Potatoes

Chèvre and Stilton or Gorgonzola cheeses top grilled potatoes in this easy-to-do recipe.

6	small baking potatoes	6
1 tbsp	olive oil	15 mL
	Salt and freshly ground pepper	
1	roll (140 g) creamy chèvre cheese (about ½ cup/125 mL)	1
½ cup	crumbled Stilton or Gorgonzola cheese	125 mL
	Fresh parsley sprigs	

1 Cut each potato in half lengthwise. Brush cut side with olive oil; sprinkle lightly with salt and pepper.

2 Preheat grill on medium. Place potatoes, cut side down on oiled grill rack; close lid and cook (use Indirect Grilling, page 7) for about 45 minutes or until potatoes are tender; turn once.

3 Meanwhile, stir cheeses together until almost smooth. Turn potatoes, cut side up, during last 5 minutes; top with a small amount of cheese mixture; close lid and cook briefly until cheese has started to melt. Remove from grill, garnish with parsley and serve.

Makes 6 servings.

Tip: Extra cheese mixture left? Keep it to spread on crackers at appetizer time.

Grilled Basil Tomatoes

2 *Herb Tomatoes:* Sprinkle finely minced fresh or dried herbs on tomatoes before grilling.

3 *Honey-Mustard Tomatoes:* Combine 1 tbsp (15 mL) each of olive oil and lemon juice and 1 tsp (5 mL) each of liquid honey and grainy mustard; brush over halved tomatoes before grilling.

When summer's vast multitude of "the star of the garden" appears, we find as many ways as possible to eat them. This recipe is a favorite. Serve it as a vegetable side dish or as a quick appetizer while guests or family are waiting for slower-cooking grilled meat dishes.

4	large ripe tomatoes	4
2 tbsp	chopped fresh basil or 2 tsp (10 mL) dried	25 mL
1	small clove garlic, minced	1
1 to 2 tsp	olive oil	5 to 10 mL
1 tsp	lemon juice	5 mL
	Salt and freshly ground pepper	
1 cup	plain (4% M.F.) or Greek-style yogurt (optional)	250 mL

1 Cut ½ inch (1 cm) off stem end of tomatoes and remove core. Sprinkle with basil, garlic, oil, lemon juice, and salt and pepper to taste.

2 Preheat grill on high. Place tomatoes on oiled grill rack. Close lid and cook (use Direct Grilling, page 7) for about 10 minutes or until tender and warm throughout.

3 Serve with yogurt, if using.

Makes 4 servings.

Variations:

1 *Pesto Tomatoes:* Remove cores from tomatoes; cut in half crosswise. Using a spoon, remove a small amount of pulp. Spoon 1 tsp (5 mL) of Broccoli Pesto (page 12) into cavity. Grill as above.

Shredded Zucchini, Carrot and Parsnip

This agreeable combination of vegetable flavors is a change from any one of them served alone, and their colors are so attractive on the plate. The cooking method is particularly healthy since all the liquid and water-soluble vitamins are retained.

⅔ cup	chicken broth	150 mL
2 cups	shredded zucchini	500 mL
2 cups	shredded carrot	500 mL
1 cup	shredded parsnip	250 mL
½ tsp	each: dried basil and oregano or 2 tsp (10 mL) fresh	2 mL
¼ tsp	freshly ground pepper	1 mL
2 tbsp	chopped fresh parsley	25 mL

In large nonstick saucepan over medium-high heat, bring broth to a boil. Add vegetables and seasonings. Cover and cook for 10 minutes or until vegetables are just tender, stirring occasionally. Sprinkle with parsley and serve.

Makes 6 servings.

Grilling Vegetables

Use a grill basket to keep vegetables from falling through the grill. In most cases, as specified in the following recipes, I prefer to parboil vegetables before grilling. This shortens the grilling time and helps to ensure more even cooking. You'll also find it easier to cook vegetables on medium-high; use Direct Grilling (page 7) with the grill lid closed.

Herb and Oil Bastes for Vegetables

You'll find it handy to prepare seasoned mixtures ahead of time and keep them ready to brush on vegetables at the grill.

Oil and Vinegar Baste: In small bowl, combine ⅓ cup (75 mL) extra virgin olive oil and 2 tbsp (25 mL) balsamic, red or white vinegar; add 2 tbsp (25 mL) of finely chopped fresh herbs – a combination of several herbs, such as oregano, rosemary, basil, tarragon and thyme or a single herb. You can also replace fresh herbs with 2 tsp (10 mL) dried herbs. Store in tightly sealed container in the refrigerator for up to 5 days.

Oil and Garlic Herb Baste: In a plastic bag, combine 1 tsp (5 mL) canola oil, 1 clove garlic, crushed, ½ tsp (2 mL) paprika and ¼ tsp (1 mL) each of salt and dried oregano or basil. Add vegetables to the bag and toss before grilling. This mixture is best for small sliced or cubed vegetables.

Pesto Baste: In small bowl, combine 2 tbsp (25 mL) Broccoli Pesto (page 8) with 1 to 2 tbsp (15 to 25 mL) olive oil and freshly ground pepper.

Vegetables

Grilled Asparagus: Snap off and discard tough stems of 1 bunch of asparagus; wash and pat dry. Microwave on high (100%) for 3 minutes. Brush lightly with one of the bastes. Grill for about 4 minutes or until tender and lightly charred; turn once. Sometimes it is nice to tie several stalks together before grilling, using cooked green onion tops. I also like to sprinkle grilled asparagus with grated Parmesan cheese.

Grilled Carrots: Cut 5 medium carrots in half lengthwise; parboil or microwave for about 3 minutes. Brush with one of the bastes; grill for about 5 minutes or until tender and browned; turn occasionally.

Grilled Corn in the Husk: Pull back husks and remove silk. Replace husks, tie at top with heavy twine or string. Soak in cold water for 1 hour. Remove from water; place on preheated oiled grill rack. Grill for about 20 minutes or until kernels are tender; turn frequently during grilling and brush with water occasionally.

Grilled Eggplant Slices: Remove stem and blossom end from 1 medium eggplant and cut lengthwise into thin slices; do not precook. Brush slices lightly with 4 tsp (20 mL) olive oil or a mixture of 1 tbsp (15 mL) olive oil and 1 tsp (5 mL) sesame oil. Grill for about 8 minutes or until flesh is tender; turn once, and season lightly with salt and pepper after turning.

Grilled Fennel: Snip off feathery leaves and remove stems; parboil whole bulb for about 8 minutes. Cut fennel lengthwise into 6 to 8 wedges. Brush lightly with one of the bastes. Grill for about 8 minutes; turn once.

Grilled Leeks: Cut off green tops; trim bulb roots and remove 1 or 2 layers of white skin. Parboil for about 8 minutes, then halve lengthwise. Wash well and brush lightly with olive oil.

Grill for about 8 minutes or until leeks are tender and golden brown.

Grilled Mushrooms: Clean mushrooms and pat dry; do not peel or precook. Brush lightly with one of the bastes. Grill for about 10 minutes or until golden brown; turn occasionally.

Caramelized Onions: Place heavy skillet on grill rack for short time to preheat. Add 2 tbsp (25 mL) olive oil and heat for 3 minutes. Add 1 thickly sliced red or yellow onion. Sauté for about 12 minutes or until soft and caramelized; turn frequently.

Grilled Squash: Pierce the skin of acorn or pepper squash with a fork. Wrap securely with foil and grill for about 1 hour; turn once. Remove from grill, open foil carefully; cut squash in half and discard seeds.

Grilled Sweet Peppers: You can either cut peppers in half and remove seeds or grill them whole; do not precook. Grill peppers for about 20 minutes or until skins are charred all over; turn often. Place peppers in paper bag until cool. Peel away black skin, brush with one of the bastes, and serve.

Grilled New Potatoes or Grilled Sweet Potatoes: Cut larger potatoes in half; parboil for 10 minutes or until almost tender. Remove from pan; peel sweet potatoes, if using. Cut potatoes into slices and brush with one of the bastes. Grill for about 12 minutes or until tender and golden brown; turn once. You can also grill sliced potatoes from the raw stage without parboiling; allow about 35 minutes grilling time.

Grilled White Turnip: Parboil peeled slices of turnip in boiling water for 5 minutes or until barely tender. Grill for about 12 minutes or until tender; turn often.

Grilled Zucchini and Yellow Squash: Remove ends and cut lengthwise in quarters; do not precook. Brush lightly with one of the herb and oil bastes. Grill for about 6 minutes or until zucchini is tender; turn once. You can also cut the zucchini or yellow squash diagonally into ½-inch (1 cm) thick slices.

Sauces for Grilled Vegetables

Here are a few sauce ideas for grilled vegetables. These are more appropriate when the vegetable is lightly brushed with unflavored oil.

Yogurt Cucumber Sauce: In bowl, combine ⅔ cup (150 mL) finely chopped seedless cucumber, ½ cup (125 mL) plain yogurt, and 2 tbsp (25 mL) chopped fresh mint, basil, chives or oregano. Season to taste with salt and freshly ground pepper. If desired, stir in a small crushed garlic clove. Makes 1 cup (250 mL). This sauce is excellent with asparagus, tomatoes and carrots.

Chèvre Sauce: In small saucepan, combine ½ cup (125 mL) chèvre cheese with 2 tbsp (25 mL) sour cream; heat until cheese is almost melted. Stir in 1 chopped green onion and 1 small tomato, diced. Makes ½ cup (125 mL). This sauce is excellent with carrots, onions, leeks and zucchini.

Mint Yogurt: Drain 1 cup (250 mL) plain yogurt for several hours. Stir thickened yogurt (sometimes called yogurt cheese) into chopped fresh mint and grated orange or lemon peel. Makes about ½ cup (125 mL). Enjoy this sauce with carrots, asparagus, sweet peppers and fennel.

CHAPTER 8

All Those Extras

SMOKY-SWEET SALADS, pasta possibilities, and greens galore—this chapter is full of wonderful extras to complement the book's many grilled entrées. Some are hot, some are cold, all are delicious!

You'll love the elegant salad of lightly grilled asparagus topped with a luscious sour cream-mayonnaise dressing (page 174). Grilled red onions combined with Belgian endive and mixed salad greens, and dressed with olive oil and pungently sweet balsamic vinegar (page 174) will, I trust, become as popular in your home as it is in mine. Not all of the recipes in this chapter are grilled; a number can be made ahead to simplify final meal assembly. In fact, it's nice for the chef to have a few stove-top and refrigerator dishes ready to arrive at the table.

Two truly summer salads, Mexican Corn Salad (page 190) and Grilled Rosemary Potato Salad (page 191) and a marvelous Summertime Pasta (page 179) bursting with luscious garden-ripe tomatoes provide a starchy element so enjoyable with grilled meat, poultry or fish.

As an extra bonus, I've added two of my favorite homemade salad dressings—a Creamy Buttermilk Dressing and Poppy Seed Vinaigrette (page 180). You would be hard pressed to purchase better!

Black Olive, Rice and Spinach Salad

Rice with bits of red peppers and green onions on a bed of spinach, garnished with black olives, makes a handsome salad. A generous splash of fresh lemon juice gives it a fresh and vibrant taste.

Lemon-Dijon Vinaigrette

3 tbsp	lemon juice	45 mL
1 tbsp	Dijon mustard	15 mL
1 tsp	each: lemon zest and garlic powder	5 mL
¼ cup	extra virgin olive oil	50 mL

Salad

1½ cups	cooked white or brown rice (about ½ cup/125 mL) raw	375 mL
½ cup	diced sweet red pepper	125 mL
2	green onions, thinly sliced	2
1	bunch fresh spinach, trimmed and torn into bite-size pieces	1
½ cup	kalamata olives, pitted	125 mL
	Paprika, salt and freshly ground pepper	

1 *For vinaigrette:* In large bowl, whisk together lemon juice, mustard, zest, garlic powder and olive oil until thick and smooth.

2 *For salad:* Stir rice, red pepper and onions into vinaigrette; cover and refrigerate until ready to serve.

3 At serving time, slice 1 cup (250 mL) packed spinach into long shreds and stir into rice mixture. Arrange remaining spinach on large serving platter. Top with rice mixture and olives, sprinkle with paprika, salt and pepper and serve.
Makes 6 servings.

Suggested Menu: Serve with grilled chicken, Chicken on a Spit (page 149), or grilled pork or beef. Tip: You can pit olives with a cherry pitter. Just position the olive as you would a cherry and squeeze. Out pops the pit, leaving the olive ready to serve whole or to slice.

Black Olive, Rice and Spinach Salad, top, page 172; and
Asparagus Salad with Creamy Dressing, bottom, page 174

Asparagus Salad with Creamy Dressing

Grill extra asparagus when they are plentiful to use in this appetizing salad.

1 bunch	Grilled Asparagus (page 168) chilled – about 16 to 24 spears	1

Creamy Dressing

2 tbsp	each: light mayonnaise and sour cream	25 mL
2 tsp	lemon juice	10 mL
1 tsp	anchovy paste	5 mL
1/8 tsp	each: dry mustard, salt, freshly ground pepper, garlic powder and hot pepper sauce	0.5 mL
	Snipped fresh chives	

1 Arrange asparagus on an oval serving dish.

2 *For dressing:* In small bowl, combine mayonnaise, sour cream, lemon juice, anchovy paste, mustard, salt, pepper, garlic powder and hot sauce; stir well. Drizzle dressing over asparagus and sprinkle with chives. Cover and chill until serving time.

Makes 4 servings.

Endive Salad with Grilled Red Onions

Onions are cooked on the grill and then combined with chilled salad greens to toss with a splendid balsamic vinaigrette.

Onions

3	large red onions, thickly sliced in rounds	3
1 tbsp	extra virgin olive oil	15 mL

Salad

3	large Belgian endive, cut crosswise in 1/2-inch (1 cm) slices	3
2 cups	mixed salad greens or mesclun	500 mL
1	bunch arugula, torn	1
1	bunch watercress, stems removed	1

Vinaigrette

1 tsp	cumin seeds	5 mL
1/4 cup	extra virgin olive oil	50 mL
3 tbsp	balsamic vinegar	45 mL
1 tsp	liquid honey	5 mL
	Salt and freshly ground pepper	

1 *For onions:* In bowl, toss onions with oil. Remove to shallow pan. Preheat grill on medium. Place pan on grill rack. Close lid and cook (use Direct Grilling, page 7) for about 15 minutes or until browned and crisp; stir occasionally. Remove and keep warm.

2 *For salad:* In large bowl, toss endive with greens, arugula and watercress. Cover and chill until serving time.

3 *For vinaigrette:* In nonstick skillet, toast cumin seeds over medium-high heat until browned. In bowl, whisk oil, vinegar, honey, salt and pepper to taste; add cumin seeds. Toss vinaigrette with salad greens. Serve salad onto individual plates, topping each with warm grilled onions.

Makes 8 servings.

Tossed Greens with Warmed Chèvre

The warm creamy tartness of chèvre and the memorable pungency of basil distinguish this European-style salad.

Basil Pesto Vinaigrette and Salad

2 tbsp	red wine vinegar	25 mL
2 tbsp	chopped fresh basil leaves	25 mL
	or 2 tsp (10 mL) dried	
⅛ tsp	each: dry mustard, salt	0.5 mL
	and freshly ground pepper	
⅓ cup	extra virgin olive oil	75 mL
6 cups	assorted salad greens	1.5 L
	or mesclun	

Toast and cheese

6	thin slices French baguette,	6
	lightly brushed with olive oil and toasted	
6	thick slices chèvre cheese (125 g pkg)	6
	Chopped fresh parsley or tarragon	

1 *For vinaigrette:* In small bowl, whisk together vinegar, basil, mustard, salt and pepper. Slowly whisk in oil until dressing is creamy and thick. Set aside.

2 *For salad:* In large salad bowl, arrange greens, cover and refrigerate.

3 *For toast:* Preheat grill on medium. Place toasted bread on baking sheet; top each slice with cheese. Heat toasts on grill rack or in a 300°F (150°C) oven until cheese is softened and just beginning to melt.

4 Toss salad greens with prepared vinaigrette. Divide onto 6 serving plates. Top each with toasted bread and melted cheese. Sprinkle with parsley and serve.

Makes 6 servings.

Artichoke Salad

Artichokes, peppers, tomatoes and an olive oil vinaigrette make an irresistibly easy salad to accompany a grilled meal. Olive oil, one of the world's most ancient foods, is enjoying a renaissance. People living in the countries on the Mediterranean sea have long known its wonderful flavor and health benefits, and we are now recognizing these same benefits in our North American cuisine.

2	cans (14 oz/398 mL) artichoke hearts or 4 medium artichokes*	2

Olive Oil Herb Vinaigrette

1 cup	packed fresh parsley leaves	250 mL
½ cup	thinly sliced green onions or chives	125 mL
¼ cup	extra virgin olive oil	50 mL
2 tbsp	red wine vinegar	25 mL
1 tbsp	Dijon mustard	15 mL
4 tsp	lemon juice	20 mL
	Salt and freshly ground pepper	
	Red leaf lettuce	
½	sweet yellow pepper, cubed	½
1	large tomato, sliced	1

1 Drain artichoke hearts and cut into quarters. (If using fresh artichokes, see below.)

2 *For vinaigrette:* In food processor or blender container, process parsley and onions until finely chopped. Add oil, vinegar, mustard and lemon juice. Process until all ingredients are smooth. Season to taste with salt and pepper.

3 Arrange lettuce on serving plate; place artichoke hearts on lettuce. Add yellow pepper and tomato. Drizzle some of the vinaigrette over everything. Chill until serving time or serve at room temperature if desired.

Makes 6 servings and ¾ cup (175 mL) vinaigrette.

Tip: Store extra vinaigrette in refrigerator to serve at a later time with a green salad.

*Fresh artichokes: Bring a large saucepan with water to a boil. Remove and discard tough lower layers of leaves from artichokes until pale inner leaves are reached. Slice one-third off the top. Using scissors, snip off the sharp, thorny end of the remaining leaves. Cut stem to about 1 inch (2.5 cm).

Drop artichokes into boiling water to cover. Add 2 tsp (10 mL) olive oil, 4 tsp (20 mL) red wine vinegar, 2 large cloves garlic, 1 bay leaf and 10 peppercorns. Bring to a boil, cover and cook gently for about 20 minutes or until tender and a leaf will pull away easily. (Depending on the season and the size, artichokes may require as long as 40 minutes of cooking to become tender.) Place artichokes upside down to drain.

When artichokes are cool enough to handle easily, slice vertically. With a spoon, scoop out the inedible fuzzy *choke*. Allow to cool, then cut into quarters to use in salad.

Szechwan Vegetable Salad

This exotic salad with an Oriental influence requires only a quick steaming of the broccoli and snow peas. Calorie counters will love this salad.

Vinaigrette

1	large clove garlic, crushed	1
2 tbsp	white wine vinegar	25 mL
1 tbsp	each: canola and sesame oil	15 mL
2 tsp	soy sauce	10 mL
1	piece gingerroot (1 inch/2.5 cm), minced	1
1 tsp	granulated sugar	5 mL
¼ to ½ tsp	hot red chili peppers	1 to 2 mL
⅛ tsp	hot pepper sauce	0.5 mL

Vegetables

1 cup	snow peas, trimmed	250 mL
1 cup	broccoli florets	250 mL
6	medium mushrooms, thinly sliced	6
1 cup	bean sprouts	250 mL
2	green onions, white part only cut in thin strips	2

1 *For vinaigrette:* In small bowl, combine garlic, vinegar, oils, soy sauce, gingerroot, sugar, chili peppers, hot sauce and 2 tbsp (25 mL) water. Stir well and reserve.

2 *For vegetables:* Place snow peas in steamer basket over boiling water. Cover and cook for about 3 minutes or until just tender; drain and chill. Repeat for broccoli.

3 Arrange mushroom slices in circle on large shallow serving platter. Top with broccoli and bean sprouts. Tuck snow peas in around outer part of circle. Chill until serving time.

4 Drizzle with reserved dressing and top with onion strips.

Makes 6 servings.

Suggested Menu: This salad is an excellent accompaniment for grilled fish, chicken breasts or lamb served with fluffy rice.

Szechwan Vegetable Salad

Spring Greens with Strawberries

This attractive and yet simple salad with strawberries can be combined with any variety of greens. I like the peppery taste of arugula and mesclun in combination with the sweetness of the berries. Dressing the berries a short time before tossing gives the salad a lovely strawberry vinaigrette flavor.

Dressing

3 tbsp	each: white wine vinegar and water	45 mL
1 tbsp	each: liquid honey and extra virgin olive oil	15 mL
2 tsp	chopped fresh mint	10 mL
½ tsp	salt	2 mL
⅛ tsp	white pepper	0.5 mL

Salad

3 cups	sliced strawberries	750 mL
6 cups	mesclun or mixed greens including spinach, arugula, leaf lettuce, watercress and radicchio	1.5 L
2 tbsp	toasted pine nuts*	25 mL

1 *For dressing:* In small bowl, whisk together vinegar, water, honey, oil, mint, salt and pepper until well blended; set aside.

2 *For salad:* In large bowl, combine strawberries and ¼ cup (50 mL) dressing. Cover and refrigerate until serving time.

3 In salad bowl, toss mixed greens with marinated strawberries and remaining dressing. Sprinkle with pine nuts and serve.
Makes 6 servings.

*Place pine nuts in shallow pan; bake in low oven for 3 to 5 minutes or until toasted.

Insalata Caprese

Insalata Caprese is served widely in Italy either as an antipasto course or at lunch as a single course. It is frequently found on buffets. Serve with crusty rolls or thickly sliced Italian bread and iced tea or a dry white Italian wine such as a Soave.

3	firm but not overripe tomatoes	3
1	pkg (300 g) buffalo mozzarella or bocconcini cheese	1
	Extra virgin olive oil	
	Salt, freshly ground pepper and oregano, to taste	
6	basil leaves	6
12	pitted green or black olives	12

1 Wash and slice tomatoes evenly. Slice mozzarella into evenly thick slices.
2 Drizzle the bottom of a shallow serving dish with some oil; sprinkle with salt, pepper and oregano. Alternately arrange tomato and cheese slices. Sprinkle again with salt, pepper, oregano and oil. Garnish with basil leaves and olives.
Makes 6 servings.

Whole Wheat Linguine with Arugula and Romano

Arugula, briefly sautéed to tame its peppery bite, is tossed with cooked pasta and grated cheese to create this exciting pasta dish.

1	pkg (1 lb/454 g) whole wheat linguine	1
3 tbsp	olive oil, divided	45 mL
3	large cloves garlic, minced	3
¼ tsp	hot red chili pepper	1 mL
8 cups	torn arugula	2 L
¼ cup	grated Romano cheese	50 mL
	Salt and freshly ground pepper to taste	

1 In large saucepan, cook linguine in boiling water for 9 minutes or until *al dente* (tender but still firm). Drain well and return to saucepan to keep warm.

2 Meanwhile, heat 2 tbsp (25 mL) oil in large nonstick skillet. Add garlic and chili pepper; sauté for about 15 seconds or until fragrant. Add arugula; sauté for about 2 minutes or until wilted.

3 Add arugula, cheese and remaining oil to the pasta; toss to combine. Season to taste with salt and pepper.

Makes 4 servings.

Suggested Menus: This pasta makes a wonderful side dish for many of the grilled meats, fish or poultry. Add a green salad to round off a great meal.

Summertime Pasta

Delicious warm, this dish can also be prepared ahead and served at room temperature. It's so easy to make with only three main ingredients-pasta, luscious field-ripe tomatoes and fresh basil. You'll be finding your own additions according to what is in the refrigerator.

2 cups	cubed mozzarella cheese	500 mL
6	medium field tomatoes, diced	6
3	cloves garlic, minced	3
¼ cup	extra virgin olive oil	50 mL
1 cup	loosely packed fresh basil, coarsely chopped	250 mL
	Salt and freshly ground pepper	
½ to 1 tsp	hot red chili peppers	2 to 5 mL
1	pkg (1 lb/454 g) rigatoni or penne rigate	1

1 In large bowl, toss cheese, tomatoes, garlic, oil, basil, and salt, pepper and chili peppers (to taste). Let stand for about 30 minutes.

2 In large saucepan, cook pasta in boiling water for 12 minutes or until *al dente* (tender but still firm); drain well. Add pasta to cheese mixture and toss. Serve hot or at room temperature.

Makes 4 to 6 servings.

Suggested Menu: Serve with Italian bread to sop up the delicious leftover juices. Most grilled meats will welcome this pasta dish as an accompaniment.

Creamy Buttermilk Dressing

This is our choice whenever a light, creamy dressing is needed. It also makes a good dip.

⅔ cup	light mayonnaise	150 mL
½ cup	buttermilk	125 mL
1 tbsp	cider vinegar	15 mL
2 tsp	liquid honey	10 mL
1 tsp	each: lemon juice and Dijon mustard	5 mL
¼ tsp	each: salt, paprika and freshly ground pepper	1 mL

In small bowl, whisk together mayonnaise, buttermilk, vinegar, honey, lemon juice, mustard, salt, paprika and pepper until dressing becomes quite thick. Transfer to a tightly sealed container and refrigerate for up to 1 week.
Makes about 1 cup (250 mL).

Poppy Seed Vinaigrette

You can choose either an apricot or an orange flavor for this poppy seed vinaigrette. Both are superb.

½ cup	orange juice or apricot nectar	125 mL
¼ cup	lemon juice	50 mL
3 tbsp	finely chopped onion	45 mL
3 tbsp	poppy seeds	45 mL
1 tbsp	granulated sugar	15 mL
½ tsp	each: dry mustard and salt	2 mL
⅓ cup	canola oil	75 mL

In blender or food processor, process juices, onion, poppy seeds, sugar, mustard and salt until blended. Slowly add oil while processor is running. Transfer to a tightly sealed container and refrigerate for several hours before using. Keeps refrigerated for about 1 week. Whisk at serving time.
Makes about 1 cup (250 mL).

Warm Pear Salad with Stilton

Grilled pears and Stilton tossed with assorted greens make a unique salad. You can prepare it year-round by substituting a stove-top skillet for the outdoor grill. Apples can be used instead of pears.

2	ripe, but firm Bartlett pears	2
½	medium red onion, peeled and thinly sliced into rings	½
5 tsp	olive oil, divided	25 mL
1 tsp	liquid honey	5 mL
½ tsp	each: dry mustard and salt	2 mL
⅛ tsp	freshly ground pepper	0.5 mL
2	Belgian endive, cut crosswise in 1-inch (2.5 cm) slices	2
1	bunch watercress, tough stems removed	1
½ cup	crumbled Stilton cheese	125 mL
2 tsp	red wine or sherry vinegar	10 mL
1 tsp	Worcestershire sauce	5 mL
	Salt and freshly ground pepper	

1 Cut pears lengthwise into quarters, core and cut each quarter into 1-inch (2.5 cm) chunks; place in small bowl. Add onions.

2 In another bowl, combine 4 tsp (20 mL) oil, honey, mustard, salt and pepper. Pour over pears and onions and toss well; set aside.

3 Preheat grill on medium-high. Remove pears and onions from honey mixture; reserve liquid. Place pears and onions on oiled grill rack or in grill basket. Close lid and cook (use Direct Grilling, page 7) for 10 minutes or until pears and onions are softened and golden brown; brush occasionally with reserved liquid.

4 In large salad bowl, place endive, watercress, cheese, remaining oil, vinegar and Worcestershire sauce. Toss in warm pears and onions. Season to taste with salt and pepper and serve warm.
Makes 4 servings.

Grilled Pepper Gazpacho Salad

Bring the wonderful flavors and colors of Gazpacho soup to a salad. The roasted peppers add their own sweet smoky signature.

3	medium sweet red peppers	3
3	large tomatoes, peeled and chopped	3
¾ cup	chopped seedless cucumber	175 mL
2 tbsp	finely chopped onion	25 mL
1	small clove garlic, minced	1
3 tbsp	extra virgin olive oil	45 mL
2 tbsp	red wine vinegar	25 mL
1 tbsp	chopped fresh basil leaves	15 mL
1 tbsp	finely chopped jalapeño pepper	15 mL
	Salt and freshly ground pepper	
	Leaf lettuce	

1 Preheat grill on medium-high. Place whole red peppers on lightly oiled grill rack. Close lid and cook, (use Direct Grilling, page 7) for about 20 minutes or until peppers are streaked with brown and tender when pierced; turn frequently. Place peppers in paper bag to cool for about 15 minutes. Peel away the blackened skin; remove and discard stems and seeds. Slice into thin julienne pieces.
2 Meanwhile, in large bowl, combine tomatoes, cucumber, onion and garlic. Whisk together oil, vinegar, basil, hot pepper, and salt and pepper to taste. Pour over tomato mixture. Add roasted pepper slices and stir gently to combine.
3 Chill briefly and serve on lettuce.
Makes 6 servings.

Watercress and Bean Sprout Salad

This salad is simple to prepare, and the crunchy texture is a change from tossed greens. A light version of a Roquefort dressing adds a special flavor statement.

Buttermilk Roquefort Dressing

⅓ cup	buttermilk	75 mL
2 tbsp	crumbled Roquefort cheese	25 mL
1 tsp	red wine vinegar	5 mL
½ tsp	each: Dijon mustard and	2 mL
	Worcestershire sauce	
	Salt and freshly ground pepper	
8 cups	bean sprouts	2 L
1	bunch watercress, trimmed of	1
	coarse stems	
½ cup	thinly sliced radish (optional)	125 mL

1 *For dressing:* In food processor or blender, process buttermilk, cheese, vinegar, mustard and Worcestershire sauce until smooth; season to taste with salt and pepper.

2 In large salad bowl, toss bean sprouts, watercress and radish, if using. Drizzle with dressing and toss.

Makes 6 servings and about ⅓ cup (75 mL) dressing.

Suggested Menu: This salad is a delicious accompaniment to Orange-Spiced Pork Chops (page 67) and either Grilled Sweet Potatoes (page 169) or Grilled Rosemary Potato Salad (page 191).

Tip: Dressing can be made 3 days ahead and stored in a tightly sealed container in the refrigerator. Stilton or blue cheese can replace Roquefort.

* Croutons: If you have stale bread, cube it and dry in the oven to make your own low-fat croutons. Store in an airtight container. Alternatively stir together 1 tbsp (15 mL) olive oil and 2 crushed garlic cloves, and brush over both sides of 3 thick slices of Italian bread. Place bread on preheated grill rack, close lid and toast, turning once, until bread is crisp and browned. Allow to cool, then cut into cubes.

Panzanella Salad

This most famous of Italian salads is usually associated with Tuscany. Summer field tomatoes provide great eye appeal and wonderful flavors. This salad is best served at room temperature.

4	medium tomatoes, cubed	4
1 cup	diced cucumber	250 mL
2	cloves garlic, crushed	2
½ cup	chopped red onion	125 mL
2	green onions, sliced	2
⅓ cup	extra virgin olive oil	75 mL
¼ cup	chopped fresh basil	50 mL
2 tbsp	red wine vinegar	25 mL
¼ cup	grated Parmesan cheese	50 mL
¼ tsp	each: salt and freshly ground pepper	1 mL
1 cup	bread croutons*	250 mL
1 cup	kalamata olives, pitted and sliced	250 mL

1 In large salad bowl, gently stir together tomatoes, cucumber, garlic, onions, oil, basil, vinegar, cheese, salt and pepper. Cover and let stand at room temperature for up to 2 hours.

2 Sprinkle with croutons and olives and serve.
Makes 6 to 8 servings.

Variation: For a lighter salad to serve more people, toss mixture with one head of torn romaine lettuce.

Multi-Vegetable Tortellini Salad

Tortellini provides an interesting variation in a pasta salad. For even more variety, there is the choice of meat- or cheese-filled tortellini. Serve this pasta salad as an accompaniment to a simple grilled meal of chicken, pork chops or steak.

Zesty Italian Vinaigrette

1 tbsp	anchovy paste	15 mL
1	large clove garlic, crushed	1
3 tbsp	red wine vinegar	45 mL
⅓ cup	grated Parmesan cheese, divided	75 mL
1 tbsp	lemon juice	15 mL
⅓ cup	each: chicken broth and	75 mL
	extra virgin olive oil	
	Salt and freshly ground pepper	

Salad

1	pkg (454 g) frozen tortellini	1
2 cups	broccoli florets, blanched	500 mL
12	cherry tomatoes, halved	12
3	green onions, sliced	3
½	each: medium sweet green and	½
	red pepper, thinly sliced	
½ cup	each: chopped fresh parsley	125 mL
	and basil	
	Shredded lettuce, optional	

1 *For vinaigrette:* In food processor or blender container, process anchovy paste, garlic and vinegar until mixed. Add ¼ cup (50 mL) cheese and lemon juice; process until blended. With machine running, slowly add broth and oil until blended. Season to taste with salt and pepper. Remove to airtight container and refrigerate.

2 In large saucepan, cook tortellini in boiling water for 12 minutes or until *al dente* (tender but still firm). Drain well and cool.

3 *For salad:* In large salad bowl, place tortellini, broccoli, tomatoes, onions and green and red pepper. Sprinkle with remaining cheese, parsley and basil. Add ½ cup (125 mL) vinaigrette and toss gently. Cover and refrigerate until ready to serve.

4 Serve salad on shredded lettuce, if using.

Makes 6 servings and ¾ cup (175 mL) vinaigrette.

Tip: Store extra dressing refrigerated for up to 1 week; shake before using.

Orzo Spinach Pilaf

Orzo, a rice shaped pasta, is an interesting replacement for rice in this spinach pilaf.

1	bag (300 g) spinach, trimmed and washed	1
	or 1 pkg (300 g) frozen chopped spinach, thawed	
	Salt and freshly ground pepper	
2 cups	orzo	500 mL
1 tbsp	olive oil	15 mL
3	cloves garlic, thinly sliced	3
½ cup	finely chopped onion	125 mL
1 cup	sliced mushrooms	250 mL
1	medium zucchini, diagonally sliced into 12 pieces	1
1	medium sweet red pepper, seeded and cut into large dice	1
	Freshly grated Parmesan cheese	

1 In large saucepan, cook spinach with water that remains on leaves after washing, until wilted but bright green; or, cook frozen spinach according to package directions; drain well. Season to taste with salt and pepper.

2 In food processor or blender, purée spinach until almost smooth. Spoon ½ cup (125 mL) spinach purée into large bowl; reserve remaining purée for another use.*

3 In large saucepan, cook orzo in boiling water for about 10 minutes or until *al dente* (tender but still firm). Drain well and stir into spinach.

4 Meanwhile, in large nonstick skillet, heat oil on medium-high. Add garlic and onion; cook for 5 minutes. Add mushrooms, zucchini and red pepper; cook, stirring often, for 10 minutes or until vegetables are tender. Stir into orzo-spinach mixture and toss to combine.

5 Serve sprinkled with Parmesan cheese.
Makes 6 servings.

*One package of spinach provides enough purée to double this recipe or to make it again.

Suggested Menu: Serve with Grouper with Gazpacho Sauce (page 101).
Variation: Toss orzo pasta with olive oil and some chopped sun-dried tomatoes for an excellent side dish with grilled chicken or beef.

Pine Nut Couscous

Couscous comes to us from Morocco, Tunisia and Algeria. It is made from 100% natural durum wheat semolina. Easy as instant rice to prepare, and versatile either hot or cold, it's a wonderful alternative to rice, potatoes and pastas.

2	green onions, sliced	2
2	cloves garlic, minced	2
1 tbsp	olive oil	15 mL
1 cup	boiling water	250 mL
1 tsp	instant chicken bouillon granules (1 small pouch)	5 mL
1 cup	dry couscous	250 mL

| ¼ tsp | freshly ground pepper | 1 mL |
| ¼ cup | toasted pine nuts | 50 mL |

In medium saucepan, sauté onions and garlic in oil for 5 minutes. Add boiling water and bouillon granules; return to boil. Remove from heat; stir in couscous, cover and let stand for 5 minutes. Season to taste with pepper and fluff with a fork. Sprinkle with pine nuts and serve.

Makes 4 servings.

Suggested Menu: Middle Eastern Lamb Kebabs with Pine Nut Couscous (page 124) make excellent dining, and Cucumber Raita (page 44) adds a special touch.

Tip: To heat couscous when other foods are being grilled, place prepared couscous on a large piece of heavy-duty foil; do not add nuts when cooking couscous on the grill. Close foil to make a secure package. Place foil package on grill rack for 8 to 10 minutes on medium-high; turn frequently. Open package and sprinkle with pine nuts before serving.

Variation: Turn this recipe into a marvelous salad by replacing the pine nuts with halved grapes and tossing cold couscous with a small amount of mayonnaise.

Caribbean-style Rice

Inspiration for this recipe comes from visits to Grenada, the spice island. We never tire of the fragrant and spicy mixtures of foods typical of the island's cuisine.

1 tbsp	canola oil	15 mL
½ cup	finely chopped onion	125 mL
1 cup	uncooked long grain converted brown or white rice	250 mL
½ tsp	each: ground cinnamon and cloves	2 mL
¼ tsp	each: ground nutmeg and salt	1 mL
1 cup	chicken broth	250 mL
½ cup	each: orange juice and water	125 mL
2 tbsp	lime juice	25 mL
	Salt and freshly ground pepper	
½ cup	each: finely chopped fresh parsley and raisins	125 mL
¼ cup	peanuts	50 mL

1   In large saucepan, heat oil on medium-high; cook onion for 5 minutes. Add rice, cinnamon, cloves, nutmeg and salt. Cook for 4 minutes or until rice becomes golden (but not brown). Add broth, orange juice, water, lime juice, salt and pepper. Bring to a boil, reduce heat, cover and cook for 20 minutes or until rice is tender and liquid absorbed.

2   Stir in parsley and raisins, top with peanuts and serve.

Makes 4 servings.

Suggested Menu: Simple grilled chicken breasts or pork chops and vegetables are appropriate to serve with this deliciously spicy rice dish.

Bulgur Tabbouleh

Tabbouleh is a salad of Middle Eastern origin made with bulgur wheat, chopped tomatoes, onions, and parsley or mint. This version is served at room temperature and will be a great addition to any Mediterranean or grilled menu.

1 cup	bulgur wheat	250 mL
¾ cup	lightly packed fresh parsley	175 mL
	or mint, or a combination, chopped	
1	large tomato, chopped	1
3	green onions, sliced	3

Vinaigrette

3 to 4 tbsp	red wine vinegar	45 to 60 mL
	or lemon juice	
2 tbsp	extra virgin olive oil	25 mL
¼ tsp	each: salt and freshly ground	1 mL
	pepper	

1 In bowl, pour 3 cups (750 mL) boiling water over bulgur; allow to stand for 10 minutes. Drain and cool. (The fully cooked grains are chewy but never crunchy). Stir in parsley, tomato and onions.
2 For vinaigrette: Whisk together 3 tbsp (45 mL) vinegar, oil, pepper and salt. Pour over bulgur; stir lightly. Cover and let stand for 4 hours at room temperature to allow flavors to blend. Taste and add extra vinegar if needed.
Makes 6 servings.

Suggested Menu: Tabbouleh is ideal served with another Mediterranean-type recipe such as Moroccan Lamb Chops (page 57).

Variation: You can replace the bulgur with 1/2 cup (125 mL) uncooked converted long grain brown rice. Cook the rice in 3/4 cup (175 mL) boiling water, covered, for 5 minutes; drain. Combine all ingredients and proceed as above.

Wild Rice Crêpes

Wild rice is known for its luxurious nutty flavor and chewy texture; added to a crêpe, it provides the crowning touch to an elegant dinner.

2	eggs	2
1 cup	all-purpose flour	250 mL
1 tsp	granulated sugar	5 mL
⅛ tsp	each: salt, freshly ground	0.5 mL
	pepper, ground nutmeg	
1 cup	milk	250 mL
¾ cup	cooked wild rice	175 mL
	(¼ cup/50 mL raw)	
1 tbsp	chopped fresh parsley	15 mL
1 tbsp	butter or margarine	15 mL

1 In food processor or blender, place eggs, flour, sugar, salt, pepper and nutmeg. With motor running, slowly add milk; process until smooth. Pour batter into a bowl and stir in cooked wild rice and parsley; cover and refrigerate for 2 hours.

2 Heat an 8-inch (20 cm) nonstick crêpe pan or small skillet over medium-high heat; add butter to melt. Pour butter into crêpe batter and mix well. Pour about ¼ cup (50 mL) batter into pan, tilting to spread thinly. Cook for about 45 seconds or until surface is no longer shiny and bottom is golden. Flip crêpe; brown second side for 30 seconds. Repeat with remaining batter.

3 Place crêpes in single layer in a large pan, cover and keep warm in low oven until ready to use.

Makes 4 servings, 3 crêpes per serving.

Suggested Menu: Serve with Duck Breasts with Mango Orange Sauce (page 85), multigrain rolls, a spinach salad and a light-bodied red wine such as a Pinot Noir.

Wild Rice, Raisin and Apple Casserole

The unique nutty flavor of wild rice makes this casserole the perfectly elegant accompaniment to Venison Kebabs with Cranberry Gravy (see picture and recipe on page 126) or any grilled poultry.

¾ cup	uncooked wild rice (2¼ cups/550 mL cooked)	175 mL
2	bay leaves	2
3 tbsp	butter or margarine	45 mL
½ cup	each: chopped celery and onion	125 mL
2	medium unpeeled tart apples, cored and chopped	2
½ cup	golden raisins	125 mL
1 tsp	each: dried sage, dried thyme and salt	5 mL
¼ tsp	freshly ground pepper	1 mL

1 Wash wild rice thoroughly under cold running water. In medium saucepan, bring 4 cups (1 L) water to a boil. Add wild rice and bay leaves, reduce heat, cover and cook gently for 45 minutes or until rice is tender; drain and discard bay leaves.

2 In large nonstick skillet, melt butter on medium-high; cook celery and onion for 5 minutes or until softened; stir into rice. Add apples, raisins, sage, thyme, salt and pepper. Heat to serving temperature.

Makes 6 servings.

Tip: Wild rice varies; check for doneness after 45 minutes, but allow up to 1 hour for cooking time.

Warm Spinach and Radicchio Salad

No lettuce! Cooked greens! This is certainly a different approach to a salad, and the first taste signals that it has more than novelty going for it!

1 tbsp	extra virgin olive oil	15 mL
1	clove garlic, minced	1
1½ cups	chopped spinach	375 mL
1 cup	chopped arugula	250 mL
1 cup	sliced radicchio	250 mL
1 tbsp	chopped Italian or regular parsley	15 mL
	Salt and freshly ground pepper	

In large nonstick skillet, warm oil over medium heat. Sauté garlic for 30 seconds; add spinach, arugula and radicchio and cook just until wilted, stirring often. Add parsley and season to taste with salt and pepper. Toss well and serve.
Makes 4 servings.

Suggested Menu: This warm salad makes a wonderful bed for Quails with Lemon Marinade (page 82). Round out the menu with brown rice or wild rice. You might even try a combination of the two; since wild rice takes slightly longer to cook, add it to the water in the pan first, and give it a head start of about five minutes.

Mexican Corn Salad

Fresh, colorful and simple, this salad is the essence of summer. It is best made a few hours ahead of time. Plan burgers, steak or chicken on the grill to keep the rest of dinner preparation simple.

8	ears of corn, husked and blanched* or 1 pkg (1 kg) frozen corn niblets	8
2	large firm field tomatoes, cubed	2
½	each: small sweet green and red pepper, diced	½
½	ripe avocado, diced	½
3	green onions, sliced	3
2	medium cloves garlic, minced	2

Dressing

⅓ cup	cider vinegar	75 mL
¼ cup	extra virgin olive oil	50 mL
1½ tsp	ground cumin	7 mL
½ tsp	each: chili powder, salt and freshly ground pepper	2 mL
¼ cup	chopped fresh cilantro	50 mL

1 With sharp knife, cut kernels from cobs to make 4 cups (1 L). In large saucepan, cook corn, covered, over medium heat in lightly salted water for 10 minutes or until tender or cook frozen corn according to package directions. Drain and cool slightly.

2 Gently stir in tomatoes, green and red pepper, avocado, onions and garlic.

3 *For dressing:* Whisk together vinegar, oil and seasonings. Pour over corn mixture. Stir in cilantro; toss to combine. Cover and refrigerate for several hours to allow flavors to develop. *Makes 6 servings.*

> **Tip:** * The best way to remove corn from the cob when you want whole kernels is with a very sharp knife. First, dip the ear in boiling water for a minute or two, then hold it under cold running water to "set" the milk so it does not spurt when you are cutting off the kernels. Hold the ear, tip end up in a bowl. Cut down the ear, removing a few rows at a time. You will get about 1/2 cup (125 mL) kernels from each ear of corn.

DIRECT GRILLING

Grilled Rosemary Potato Salad

This simple summer salad with rosemary overtones is a perfect accompaniment to grilled pork chops, steaks, chicken, ribs or lamb.

12	small new potatoes, unpeeled and halved	12

Rosemary Oil

2 tbsp	extra virgin olive oil	25 mL
4 tsp	minced fresh rosemary or 1¼ tsp (6 mL) dried	20 mL
2	cloves garlic, minced (optional)	2

Dressing

3 tbsp	light mayonnaise	45 mL
2 tbsp	white wine	25 mL
1 tbsp	white wine vinegar	15 mL
1 tsp	Dijon mustard	5 mL
	Salt and freshly ground pepper	
2	green onions, sliced	2
½ cup	sliced celery	125 mL
¼ cup	chopped fresh parsley	50 mL

1 In saucepan of boiling water, cook potatoes until barely tender; drain.

2 *For oil:* In small bowl, combine oil, rosemary and garlic; set aside.

3 *For dressing:* In second bowl, combine mayonnaise, wine, vinegar, mustard, salt and pepper to taste, onions, celery and parsley; stir well and set aside.

4 Preheat grill on medium-high. Drizzle rosemary oil on potatoes; toss well. Place potatoes on grill rack, cut side down. Close lid and cook (use Direct Grilling, page 7) for about 10 minutes or until tender and golden brown; turn frequently. To serve, transfer potatoes to bowl with dressing; toss and serve warm.
Makes 6 servings.

Basil and Mustard Dipping Sauce, top right, page 199;
Pineapple, Soy and Honey Dipping Sauce, left, page 199;
and Yogurt-Dill Marinade and Dipping Sauce, bottom right, page 199.

CHAPTER 9
Marinades, Rubs,
Pastes, Bastes and Sauces

THESE ARE MIXTURES WE add to meats, poultry, fish and sometimes vegetables before, during and after the grilling process to enhance their flavors. Much of the art of grilling lies in these additions. Their skillful use will make the foods from your grill sing!

Marinades

Marinades are seasoned liquids in which poultry, fish, meat and sometimes vegetables are placed before cooking to enhance the flavor of the food and also to tenderize less tender cuts of meat. These mixtures include herbs, spices, sometimes oil, and an acidic liquid, such as vinegar, citrus juice, wine or yogurt. During the marinating process, the flavor of the marinade permeates the food, and the acidic ingredient penetrates and tenderizes the meat fibers. Marinades are also brushed on food during the grilling process. Mastering marinades is a grill chef's elixir.

Intensity of the flavor developed and extent of tenderizing depends on the length of marinating time. As a general rule, vegetables and fish require minimal time – about 20 minutes. Poultry is best marinated for 2 hours in strong-flavored marinades

and for up to 4 hours in milder ones. Beef, pork, lamb and turkey can marinate from 2 to 24 hours.

Marinating Tips:
- A heavy self-sealing plastic bag is the most tidy choice for marinating. Turn the bag occasionally to distribute the marinade evenly.
- Always marinate meats, poultry and fish in the refrigerator.
- If you use leftover marinade as a sauce or brush on grilling food, be sure to boil it for 5 minutes to kill any harmful bacteria left from marinating raw food.
- Marinades should never be reused.

Rubs

Rubs are blends of herbs and spices that are sprinkled on or rubbed into meats before cooking to flavor the surface. These dry mixtures provide a short-cut to achieving robust flavors in larger cuts of meat such as whole beef brisket roasts, pork and lamb shoulders and legs, whole chickens and turkeys. Chutney-Peppered Rotisserie of Beef (page 139) and Salt-Free Rub (page 198) are examples of rubs.

Pastes

Pastes are similar to rubs but these mixtures include a liquid, such as honey, juice, oil or vinegar, which gives them a different consistency. Mustard Beef Paste (page 198) is an example of a paste.

Bastes

Bastes are similar to marinades, but they are applied during the cooking process, usually toward the end of grilling. Maple Cranberry Chicken Quarters (page 75) is a good example of a baste.

Sauces

Sauces are liquid seasonings applied to food either towards the end of the grilling or during eating. Since red tomato and sweet sauces tend to scorch, use them only during the final 10 to 15 minutes of cooking, or serve them alongside cooked meat.

Classic Tomato Barbecue Sauce, left, and Tomato-Herb Sauce

Classic Tomato Barbecue Sauce

Many people prefer less sweet barbecue sauces like this one. In addition to personal taste considerations, a less sweet sauce is not as likely to char during grilling and allows a more versatile selection of accompanying foods.

2	large onions, chopped	2
1	sweet red pepper, seeded and chopped	1
3	cloves garlic, crushed	3
2 tbsp	canola oil	25 mL
4 tsp	chili powder	20 mL
1 tsp	each: hot pepper sauce, prepared mustard and Worcestershire sauce	5 mL
1	can (7½ oz/213 mL) tomato sauce	1
½ cup	chili sauce	125 mL
3 tbsp	red wine vinegar	45 mL
1 tbsp	granulated sugar	15 mL

1 In large heavy saucepan, cook onion, red pepper and garlic in hot oil over medium-high heat for 5 minutes or until softened; stir often. Stir in chili powder, pepper sauce, mustard, Worcestershire sauce, tomato and chili sauce, vinegar and sugar. Bring to a boil, reduce heat, cover and cook gently for 20 minutes or until sauce has thickened. Stir often, especially as the sauce begins to thicken.
2 Store sauce in tightly sealed container in the refrigerator for up to 2 weeks. For longer storage, freeze or process in a boiling water canner-2 cup (500 mL) mason jars for 35 minutes.
Makes 2 cups (500 mL).

Tomato-Herb Sauce

The fresh tomato and herb flavors go well with grilled beef or veal. You can also use this sauce with pasta, or brush it on grilling chicken or fish. Serve either cold or warm.

1 tbsp	olive oil	15 mL
1 to 2	large cloves garlic, minced	1 to 2
4	large ripe tomatoes, peeled and diced	4
2 tbsp	each: finely chopped fresh oregano, basil and thyme or 1½ tsp (7 mL) dried	25 mL
½ tsp	each: salt and freshly ground pepper	2 mL
2 tbsp	chopped fresh Italian parsley	25 mL

In large saucepan, heat oil over medium heat. Add garlic; sauté for 1 minute. Add tomatoes, oregano, basil, thyme, salt and pepper. Bring to a boil, reduce heat and cook gently for 30 minutes or until sauce is thickened. Stir in parsley, cool and refrigerate.

Makes 1½ cups (375 mL).

Soy Ginger Lemon Marinade and Baste

Soy Ginger Lemon Marinade and Baste

This simple marinade with Oriental overtones is perfect with meat or poultry. It is used as a marinade for Spit-Roasted Leg of Lamb (page 143).

½ cup	each: lemon juice and soy sauce	125 mL
¼ cup	canola or olive oil	50 mL
1	piece gingerroot (2 inch/5 cm), grated	1
2 tbsp	ketchup	25 mL
4	cloves garlic, crushed	4
¼ tsp	freshly ground pepper	1 mL

1 In small bowl, combine lemon juice, soy sauce, oil, gingerroot, ketchup, garlic and pepper. Shake well. Store in tightly sealed jar in the refrigerator.

2 When ready to use, place meat, poultry or fish in shallow nonreactive dish or resealable plastic bag. Pour about ½ cup (125 mL) marinade over meat. Turn to coat, cover and refrigerate for up to 2 hours or overnight (depending on the meat being used and depth of flavor desired); turn meat occasionally.

3 Remove meat from marinade; reserve marinade. Place marinade in small saucepan, bring to a boil, reduce heat and cook for 5 minutes; keep warm. Grill meat as desired, basting often with warm marinade.

Makes about 1½ cups (375 mL), sufficient for about three uses (depending on the amount of meat being marinated).

Balsamic Marinade with Herbs

This marinade adds lots of zip to any meat it meets, especially the less tender cuts.

¼ cup	balsamic vinegar	50 mL
1	green onion, finely chopped	1
2 tbsp	finely chopped fresh parsley	25 mL
1 tbsp	minced fresh tarragon or 1 tsp (5 mL) dried	15 mL
1 tbsp	each: Dijon mustard, water and olive oil	15 mL
	Salt and freshly ground pepper	

In small bowl, whisk together vinegar, onion, parsley, tarragon, mustard, water, oil, and salt and pepper to taste.
Makes about ½ cup (125 mL).

Citrus Marinade

The fresh lemon and orange flavors of this easy-to-make marinade lend themselves to both shrimp and chicken.

2	large cloves garlic, thinly sliced	2
3 tbsp	olive oil	45 mL
3 tbsp	each: lemon and orange juice	45 mL
2 tbsp	dark brown sugar	25 mL
4 tsp	balsamic vinegar	20 mL
1 tsp	each: lemon and orange zest	5 mL
	Freshly ground pepper	

1 In small skillet, cook garlic in oil for 5 minutes or until it just starts to turn brown. Remove from heat and discard garlic; cool.

2 Add lemon and orange juice, sugar, vinegar and zests. Stir to blend. Add pepper to taste.
Makes about ⅔ cup (150 mL).

Balsamic Marinade with Herbs

Grilled Red Pepper Sauce

The smoky, pungent grilled pepper flavor of this sauce goes so well with so many foods. Make large quantities when peppers are in season and freeze for future use. You can also make the sauce with green, orange or yellow peppers.

6	sweet red peppers, grilled (see page 169) and seeded	6
2	cloves garlic, minced	2
1 tbsp	balsamic or herb vinegar	15 mL
¼ to ½ tsp	hot pepper sauce	1 to 2 mL
¼ cup	chopped fresh cilantro or Italian parsley	50 mL
	Salt and freshly ground pepper	

In food processor, process peppers, garlic and vinegar until almost smooth. Remove to bowl, stir in pepper sauce, cilantro, and salt and pepper to taste. Store in refrigerator for up to 3 days or freeze for longer storage.
Makes 1½ cups (375 mL)

Horseradish Sauce

Serve this zesty sauce with grilled beef dishes. Whisk in a small amount of plain yogurt or light mayonnaise to turn it into a creamy dressing for a beef salad.

¼ cup	each: canola oil and red wine vinegar	50 mL
2 tsp	Dijon mustard	10 mL
1 to 2 tsp	prepared horseradish	5 to 10 mL
½ tsp	salt	2 mL
¼ tsp	each: freshly ground pepper and ground thyme	1 mL

In bowl, whisk together oil, vinegar, mustard, horseradish, salt, pepper and thyme. Cover and refrigerate for up to one week; whisk before using.
Makes about ½ cup (125 mL).

Salt-free Rub

Here's a rub for meat or poultry. The rub helps develop that crisp crust essential to true barbecue.

½ cup	granulated sugar	125 mL
2 tbsp	chili powder	25 mL
2 tsp	each: dried parsley, garlic powder and onion powder	10 mL
1 tsp	each: celery seed and paprika	5 mL
1 tsp	freshly ground pepper	5 mL
½ tsp	each: dried basil, marjoram, sage, cumin, dry mustard and dill seed	2 mL

In bowl, combine sugar, chili powder, parsley, garlic and onion powder, celery seed, paprika, pepper, basil, marjoram, sage, cumin, mustard and dill seed; mix well. Store in tightly sealed container.
Makes about ¾ cup (175 mL).

Tip: Use about 1/4 cup (50 mL) of the mixture for every 1 to 2 lb (500 g to 1 kg) of meat. Press the mixture over the meat surface before grilling to help develop the crust.

Mustard Beef Paste

Give your beef roast a marvelous all-over flavor boost with this mustard rub.

2 tbsp	grainy Dijon mustard	25 mL
2 tsp	horseradish	10 mL
2 tsp	dried basil	10 mL
1 tsp	olive oil	5 mL
½ tsp	each: freshly ground pepper, cayenne and chili powder	2 mL

1 In small bowl, combine mustard, horseradish, basil, oil, pepper, cayenne and chili powder; mix well.
2 Pat this mixture over all surfaces of a beef roast before placing on the grill or spit.
Makes about ¼ cup (50 mL), sufficient for a 4 lb (2 kg) roast.

Poultry Rub

Applied before grilling, this rub adds spice to chicken, duck, geese, turkeys, Cornish hens and quail.

1 tbsp	each: granulated sugar and salt	15 mL
2 tsp	lemon pepper	10 mL
1½ tsp	ground allspice	7 mL
1 tsp	each: grated orange, lime and lemon peel	5 mL
½ tsp	paprika	2 mL
¼ tsp	cayenne pepper	1 mL

In small bowl, combine sugar, salt, lemon pepper, allspice, orange, lime and lemon peel, paprika and cayenne; stir well.
Makes about 3 tbsp (45 mL).

Pineapple, Soy and Honey Dipping Sauce

This is a favorite for dipping seafood kebabs and chicken nuggets and for drizzling over cooked rice.

¼ cup	pineapple juice	50 mL
3 tbsp	sherry vinegar	45 mL
2 tbsp	soy sauce	25 mL
4 tsp	liquid honey	20 mL
1 tbsp	each: olive oil, water and chopped gingerroot	15 mL
1	large clove garlic, crushed	1
	Salt and freshly ground pepper	

In small bowl, whisk together juice, vinegar, soy sauce, honey, oil, water, gingerroot, garlic, and salt and pepper to taste. Heat before serving.
Makes about ⅔ cup (150 mL).

Basil and Mustard Dipping Sauce

Use as a dip for raw vegetables, or as a sauce for cooked vegetables or plain grilled fish.

½ cup	light sour cream	125 mL
2 tbsp	finely chopped green onion or chives	25 mL
2 tbsp	chopped fresh basil	25 mL
1 tsp	Dijon mustard	5 mL
⅛ tsp	freshly ground pepper	0.5 mL

In small bowl, stir together sour cream, onion, basil, mustard and pepper. Cover and refrigerate for up to 3 days.
Makes ⅔ cup (150 mL).

Yogurt-Dill Marinade and Dipping Sauce

The tangy flavor of yogurt in this marinade is very effective with lamb, chicken and fish.

¾ cup	plain yogurt	175 mL
1 tbsp	liquid honey	15 mL
1 tbsp	white wine vinegar	15 mL
	Salt and freshly ground pepper	
1 tbsp	chopped fresh dill or 1 tsp (5 mL) dried	15 mL
2 tsp	finely chopped onion	10 mL

In small bowl, whisk together yogurt, honey, vinegar, and salt and pepper to taste. Stir in dill and onion. Cover and refrigerate for up to 1 week.
Makes about 1 cup (250 mL).

Light No-fail Hollandaise Sauce

Serve this low-fat, low-calorie, speedy-to-make version of a classic sauce with grilled vegetables.

½ cup	light sour cream or plain yogurt	125 mL
2 tbsp	light mayonnaise	25 mL
1 tsp	lemon juice	5 mL
½ tsp	each: dried tarragon and chervil	2 mL
	Lemon zest (optional)	

1 In small saucepan, combine sour cream, mayonnaise, lemon juice and seasonings. Cook, stirring occasionally, over low heat or until warm. Alternatively, microwave in glass dish on low (30%) for 2 minutes or until warm; stir once.

2 Spoon sauce over grilled vegetables. Garnish with lemon zest if desired.

Makes about ⅔ cup (150 mL), sufficient for 4 servings.

Variations:

1 *Mustard Sauce:* Add 1 tbsp (15 mL) Dijon mustard to the cooked sauce.

2 *Choron Sauce:* Add 2 tsp (10 mL) tomato paste to sauce ingredients before cooking.

Light Bearnaise Sauce

While it is particularly good with grilled beef, this marvelous sauce also does amazing things for fish and vegetables. It is quick and easy to prepare with the help of a microwave oven.

1 cup	plain yogurt	250 mL
2 tsp	all-purpose flour	10 mL
1	egg white	1
2 tsp	white wine vinegar	10 mL
1 tsp	Dijon mustard	5 mL
1 tbsp	each: chopped fresh parsley and tarragon	15 mL
1	green onion, finely chopped	1
⅛ tsp	each: garlic powder and white pepper	0.5 mL

In small microwaveable bowl, whisk together yogurt, flour, egg white, vinegar and mustard. Microwave at medium-high (70%) for 2 to 3 minutes or until sauce is thickened and bubbly; stir several times. Stir in parsley, tarragon, onion, garlic powder and pepper.

Makes 1¼ cups (300 mL).

Sesame-Orange Dipping Sauce

Serve this dipping sauce with meat, chicken or fish kebabs. The plainer the meat and fish flavors, the more appropriate the sauce. It is also wonderful drizzled over cooked rice.

⅓ cup	chicken broth	75 mL
¼ cup	orange juice	50 mL
1 tbsp	each: rice vinegar and soy sauce	50 mL
2 tsp	finely chopped gingerroot	10 mL
1 tsp	sesame oil	5 mL
¼ cup	thinly sliced green onions (optional)	50 mL

In small bowl, combine broth, juice, vinegar, soy, gingerroot and oil; stir well. Add green onions, if using, just before serving.
Makes ¾ cup (175 mL), about 6 servings.

Sesame-Orange Dipping Sauce

Blond Barbecue Sauce

Use this perky sauce to brush-on during grilling and serve it with the grilled food afterwards. It is especially good with lighter meats, such as veal, chicken and fish, as well as most grilled vegetables.

⅓ cup	lemon juice	75 mL
3 tbsp	Dijon mustard	45 mL
2 tbsp	each: light mayonnaise and barbecue sauce	25 mL
½ tsp	garlic powder or 1 clove garlic, minced	2 mL
½ tsp	grated lemon peel	2 mL
¼ tsp	hot pepper sauce	1 mL

In bowl, combine lemon juice, mustard, mayonnaise, barbecue sauce, garlic powder, lemon peel and pepper sauce; stir to blend. Store in sealed container for up to 3 days.
Makes ⅔ cup (150 mL).

Serving Suggestion: Serve this sauce with such grilled vegetables as carrots, broccoli, asparagus, leeks, onion slices and fennel; (see pages 168–9) for grilling instructions.

Fresh Tomato Vinaigrette

This fresh-tasting vinaigrette is best with hearty greens, such as romaine lettuce or spinach. It is also excellent for marinating chicken, veal and beef and can be used as a baste for fish and chicken.

3	plum tomatoes, quartered	3
1½ tbsp	extra virgin olive oil	22 mL
1 tbsp	sherry wine vinegar	15 mL
1 tsp	Dijon mustard	5 mL
1 tbsp	chopped fresh oregano or marjoram	15 mL
	Salt and freshly ground pepper	

1 In food processor, purée tomatoes until smooth. Press through a sieve to remove seeds; discard seeds.

2 In small bowl, whisk together tomato pulp, oil, vinegar and mustard. Stir in oregano, salt and pepper to taste.

Makes about 1 cup (250 mL).

Red Pepper and Basil Mayonnaise

The subtle smoky pungency of the roasted red peppers goes well with fish. It keeps the fish moist but adds fewer calories than if the fish were fried in oil.

½ cup	drained bottled roasted red peppers	125 mL
⅓ cup	light mayonnaise	75 mL
4 tsp	Dijon mustard	20 mL
1	clove garlic, crushed	1
1 tsp	lemon juice	5 mL
	Salt and freshly ground pepper	
½ cup	chopped fresh basil	125 mL

1 In blender or food processor, process red peppers, mayonnaise, mustard, garlic, lemon juice, and salt and pepper to taste. Spread 2 tbsp (25 mL) on one side of 4 fish fillets or steaks and grill.

2 Add ½ cup (125 mL) basil to remaining mixture and serve as a sauce with the grilled fish.

Makes about ¾ cup (175 mL).

Fresh Relishes

Here are three fresh relishes to accompany grilled foods. Each is so easy to make, why not make all three.

Confetti Refrigerator Relish

This relish is like a side-dish salad, except it can be stored in the refrigerator for up to 2 weeks. It goes well with a grilled backyard supper, nicely complementing fish and hamburgers.

1 pint	cherry tomatoes, stemmed and halved	500 mL
½	each: medium sweet green and yellow pepper, diced	½
1 cup	finely chopped red onion	250 mL
⅓ cup	cider vinegar	75 mL
¼ cup	water	50 mL
1 tbsp	each: granulated sugar and olive oil	15 mL
1 tsp	each: celery seeds, mustard seeds and pickling salt	5 mL
⅛ tsp	each: freshly ground pepper and hot pepper sauce	0.5 mL

1 In medium bowl, combine tomatoes, green and yellow peppers and onion.
2 In small saucepan, bring vinegar, water, sugar, oil and seasonings to a boil for 1 minute. Pour over vegetables; stir to blend. Allow the relish to cool. Refrigerate for at least 3 hours before serving.
Makes about 4 cups (1 L).

Pickled Cucumber

Serve this tangy, fresh-tasting cucumber relish with grilled fish or chicken.

In food processor with thin slicing blade, slice 1 medium unpeeled seedless cucumber. Toss slices with 1 tbsp (15 mL) cider vinegar, 1½ tsp (7 mL) granulated sugar, a pinch of crushed hot pepper flakes and salt to taste. Cover and marinate for up to 2 hours.
Makes about 2 cups (500 mL).

Pickled Onions

This is a great accompaniment for grilled meats.

Cut 1 medium red or white onion into thin wedges. In small saucepan, combine onion, ½ cup (125 mL) cider vinegar, 1 tsp (5 mL) pickling spices and ½ tsp (2 mL) coarse salt. Cook for 2 minutes, remove from heat and chill until ready to serve.
Makes 1 cup (250 mL).

Chicken Breast with Creamy
Tarragon Sauce, page 206

CHAPTER 10

Indoor Grilling

ANY FOOD COOKED OUTDOORS by Direct Grilling (page 7) on a charcoal or gas-fired grill can be cooked indoors on the grill option now available on many kitchen ranges. Gas-fired or electric, these indoor grills are wonderful for frustrated apartment dwelling grill chefs. They are also great when it's raining cats and dogs or when the outdoor grill is covered with a mountain of snow.

There are a number of important differences between outdoor grilling and indoor grilling. You have to live with any smoke your grill ventilation system can't handle, and flare-ups are a more dangerous fire hazard indoors than outdoors. Cleanup after indoor grilling is more demanding because you live more intimately with your kitchen stove than with your outdoor grill. These concerns can be addressed by taking greater care to remove fat from food before grilling, by eliminating excess amounts of sweet sauces and bastes, and by only applying these mixtures during the last 10–15 minutes of grilling.

Here are a few more tips for successful indoor grilling:

- Check manufacturer's instructions to make sure your grill can be used inside. Never use propane or charcoal grills indoors.
- Adequate ventilation is the key to indoor grilling. Be sure the ventilation system is powerful enough to exhaust grilling fumes outdoors.
- Choose meat that is at least ¾ inch (2 cm) thick as it cooks better than thinner cuts. Remove excess fat and discard. Score edges of any remaining fat, being careful to not cut the meat.
- Choose foods which require shorter cooking time to keep smoke to a minimum.
- Brush grill grates lightly with oil prior to pre-heating.
- *Always* preheat the grill on high for 5 minutes.
- Suggested cooking times and control settings for electric grills are approximate because of voltage variations.
- An aluminum foil tent or cover for foods on the grill rack will speed up cooking and help to keep the cooked top side of foods warm after turning. Never use foil inside the grill area.
- Apply sauces and bastes only during the last 10–15 minutes of cooking time. When basting meats or applying sauces, remember that excessive amounts will end up inside the grill.
- Never leave the grill unattended during its operation. Keep a fire extinguisher within reach.

Chicken Breast with Creamy Tarragon Sauce

Suggested Menu: Serve with Grilled Asparagus (see page 168), Grilled Tarragon Shiitake Mushrooms (page 159), crusty rolls and cooked rice.

Dijon mustard and tarragon add excitement to grilled chicken breasts.

| 4 | boneless, skinless chicken breast halves | 4 |
| | Salt and white pepper | |

Sauce

¼ cup	each: light sour cream and light mayonnaise	50 mL
1 tbsp	Dijon mustard	15 mL
2 tsp	dried tarragon leaves or 2 tbsp (25 mL) fresh	10 mL
1	green onion, finely chopped	1
	Fresh tarragon	

1 Remove excess fat from chicken and discard. Preheat indoor grill on high for 5 minutes. Place chicken on lightly oiled grill rack. Sprinkle with salt and pepper; cook for about 10 minutes or until chicken is no longer pink inside; turn once. Cover with foil for 5 minutes before serving.

2 *For sauce:* In a small bowl, conbine sour cream, mayonnaise, mustard, tarragon and green onion. Serve a spoonful of sauce with cooked chicken and garnish with tarragon.

Makes 4 servings.

Southwestern Chicken Drumsticks

The rub and the basting sauce bring flavors of the southwest to our indoor grill. Any meaty chicken pieces can be used in place of drumsticks.

Spice Rub

1	clove garlic, minced	1
2 tbsp	packed brown sugar	25 mL
½ tsp	each: lemon peel and dry mustard	2 mL
¼ tsp	each: salt, cayenne and freshly ground pepper	1 mL
6	chicken drumsticks	6

Beer Basting Sauce

¼ cup	flat beer or apple juice	50 mL
1 tbsp	each: brown sugar and lemon juice	15 mL
½ tsp	each: dry mustard, salt and freshly ground pepper	2 mL

1 *For rub:* In small bowl, combine garlic, sugar, peel, mustard, salt, cayenne and pepper. Mash together with back of spoon. Rub mixture into chicken pieces. Place chicken in single layer in a shallow nonreactive dish, cover and refrigerate for 6 hours or overnight.

2 *For sauce:* In saucepan, combine beer, sugar, lemon juice, mustard, salt and pepper. Bring to a boil, reduce heat and simmer for 5 minutes; keep warm.

3 Preheat indoor grill on high for 5 minutes. Place chicken on oiled grill rack. Reduce heat to medium, cover with foil and cook for 30 minutes. Lift foil and brush occasionally with Basting Sauce. Cover and continue grilling or until meat is no longer pink near the bone.

Makes 6 servings.

Vermouth-basted Fish Fillets

Use this baste with almost any fish fillet. We have enjoyed it with whitefish, rainbow trout, perch, sole and snapper.

2 tbsp	dry vermouth	25 mL
1 tbsp	olive oil	15 mL
Pinch	salt and freshly ground pepper	Pinch
½ lb	fish fillets	250 g
2	lemon slices	2

1 In small bowl, combine vermouth, oil, salt and pepper.

2 Preheat indoor grill on high for 5 minutes. Place fish, skin side down, on lightly oiled grill rack, brush with vermouth mixture. Cover loosely with a tent of foil; cook for about 8 minutes or until fish is opaque and flakes easily. Serve with lemon slices.

Makes 2 servings.

Suggested Menu: Serve with Pine Nut Couscous (page 186) and a green vegetable.

Gingered Steak

Great flavors develop in any meat marinated in this extra-zesty ginger marinade.

| 2 lb | round or flank steak | 1 kg |

Marinade

½ cup	finely minced onion	125 mL
3 tbsp	lemon juice	45 mL
2 tbsp	finely minced gingerroot	25 mL
2	cloves garlic, crushed	2
1 tsp	each: ground cumin and crushed green peppercorns	5 mL
½ tsp	brown sugar	2 mL
4 drops	hot pepper sauce	4 drops
1 tsp	canola oil	5 mL

1 Trim excess fat from steak and discard. Place steak in resealable plastic bag or shallow nonreactive dish.

2 *For marinade:* In food processor, purée onion, lemon juice, gingerroot, garlic, cumin, peppercorns, sugar, pepper sauce and oil until smooth. Pour over steak and coat evenly. Refrigerate for several hours or overnight; turn steak occasionally.

3 Remove steak from marinade; reserve marinade. Place marinade in small saucepan, bring to a boil, reduce heat and cook for 5 minutes; keep warm.

4 Preheat indoor grill on high for 5 minutes. Place steak on oiled grill rack. Cook to desired degree of doneness; brush occasionally during cooking with warm marinade; turn once.
Makes 4 to 6 servings.

Suggested Menu: Grill Potatoes and Onions in a Pouch (page 155) along with the meat around the outer edges of the grill rack. Add a large tossed green salad dressed with Fresh Tomato Vinaigrette (page 202) and a full-bodied red wine.

Lamb Dill Kebabs with Vegetables

Kebabs are as easily prepared on the indoor grill as outdoors. The vegetables are best precooked for a few minutes and then finished on the skewers with the meat. For more information about kebabs, see Kebab Grilling (page 117).

| 1 lb | lean boneless lamb (shoulder or leg) | 500 g |

Lemon-Dill Marinade

2 tbsp	each: olive oil and lemon juice	25 mL
1 tsp	dried dill or 1 tbsp (15 mL) fresh	5 mL
¼ tsp	freshly ground pepper	1 mL
3	potatoes, quartered	3
1	red onion, cut into 8 wedges	1
12	chunks of zucchini	12
	Lemon wedges	

1 Trim excess fat from lamb and discard. Cut into 1-inch (2.5 cm) cubes and place in resealable plastic bag. Combine oil, lemon juice, dill and pepper. Pour one-half of the mixture over lamb, turn to coat, and refrigerate for 2 to 6 hours. Reserve remaining oil-lemon mixture for basting.

2 In boiling water, cook potatoes for about 10 minutes or until almost tender; drain and reserve. Repeat with onion wedges.

3 Remove lamb from marinade; discard marinade. Thread lamb on metal or soaked wooden skewers alternately with potatoes, onion and zucchini.

4 Preheat indoor grill for 5 minutes on high. Place skewers on oiled grill rack and cook for about 12 minutes or until meat is cooked to desired stage of doneness. Turn skewers twice and brush with reserved oil-lemon mixture. Remove lamb and vegetables from skewers and serve with lemon wedges.

Makes 4 servings.

Sherried Veal Loin Chops

The sherry, garlic and thyme flavors of the marinade blend harmoniously with delicate veal.

Sherry Marinade

½ cup	dry sherry	125 mL
2	cloves garlic, crushed	2
1 tbsp	olive oil	15 mL
½ tsp	dried thyme	2 mL
¼ tsp	freshly ground pepper	1 mL

Veal

4	veal loin chops, ¾ inch (4 cm) thick	4

1 *For marinade:* Combine sherry, garlic, oil and seasonings. Place veal in resealable plastic bag or shallow nonreactive dish. Pour marinade over veal, turn to coat; refrigerate for several hours or overnight.

2 Remove veal from marinade; reserve marinade. Place marinade in small saucepan, bring to a boil, reduce heat and cook for 5 minutes; keep warm.

3 Preheat indoor grill on high for 5 minutes. Place veal on lightly oiled grill rack. Cook for about 6 minutes per side depending on degree of doneness desired; baste occasionally with warm marinade.

Makes 4 servings.

Pork Tenderloin with Red Pepper Coulis

The coulis provides a pepper red background to the cumin and garlic flavored tenderloin. Both the coulis and the rub can be used with other cuts of pork and beef.

Red Pepper Coulis

2	sweet red peppers, grilled (see page 169)	2
1 tsp	olive oil	5 mL
	Salt and freshly ground pepper	
	Hot pepper sauce	

Meat and Rub

1 lb	pork tenderloin	500 g
½ tsp	each: salt, brown sugar, paprika and freshly ground pepper	2 mL
¼ tsp	each: ground cumin, onion powder and garlic powder	1 mL
⅛ tsp	cayenne pepper	0.5 mL
	Fresh parsley	

1 *For coulis:* Cut roasted peppers in half and remove seeds. In blender or food processor, purée peppers, oil and just enough water to allow peppers to form a smooth paste. Remove and season to taste with salt, pepper and hot sauce. Set aside; reheat at serving time.

2 *For rub:* Trim excess fat from pork and discard. Score pork crosswise and place in shallow nonreactive pan. In small bowl, stir together salt, sugar, paprika, pepper, cumin, onion and garlic powder and cayenne. Press mixture over all pork surfaces. Cover and refrigerate for 30 minutes or longer.

3 Preheat indoor grill on high for 5 minutes. Place pork on oiled grill rack and cook for about 15 minutes; turn once. Remove meat from grill, cover with foil and let stand for 5 minutes before slicing.

4 On each dinner plate, place a small amount of warm coulis. Slice pork crosswise and fan slices over coulis; garnish with parsley and serve.

Makes 3 to 4 servings and about 1 cup (250 mL) of Red Pepper Coulis.

Lemon Broccoli with Garlic Oil

Cauliflower can be combined with or substituted for broccoli. Both are great served with fish or chicken.

2	medium cloves garlic, minced	2
¼ cup	olive oil	50 mL
1½ lb	broccoli, cut into spears	750 g
8	lemon slices	8
	Salt and freshly ground pepper	

1 In small bowl, combine garlic and oil.

2 In large saucepan, bring a large amount of water to a boil. Add broccoli and blanch for 2 minutes or until bright green and almost tender. Drain and refresh broccoli in cold water to stop cooking. Pat dry.

3 Preheat indoor grill on high. Brush broccoli with some of the garlic oil. Place on oiled grill rack; cook for about 10 minutes or until broccoli is tender and lightly tinged with brown; turn occasionally and brush with oil. During last 2 minutes, add lemon slices to grill; brush with oil and cook until warm. Season to taste with salt and pepper. Serve lemon slices with broccoli.

Makes 4 servings.

Stuffed Sweet Potatoes

Orange, ginger and nutmeg flavor these stuffed sweet potatoes.

6	medium sweet potatoes	6
½ cup	orange juice	125 mL
3 tbsp	butter or margarine	45 mL
1 tsp	each: grated orange zest and salt	5 mL
½ tsp	each: ground ginger and nutmeg	2 mL
Pinch	freshly ground pepper	Pinch
½ cup	chopped pecans	125 mL

1 In medium saucepan, parboil potatoes in boiling water until almost tender. When cool enough to handle, cut each potato in half; carefully remove pulp from shell. Mash pulp and combine with orange juice, butter, orange zest, salt, ginger, nutmeg and pepper. Stuff potato shells with mixture, divide pecans over the top.

2 Preheat indoor grill on high for 5 minutes. Place potatoes on oiled grill rack; turn heat to medium. Cover loosely with foil and cook for about 15 minutes or until potatoes are hot.

Makes 6 servings.

Tip: A cover of aluminum foil resembles the closing of the outdoor grill lid and helps to cook the food faster. In the case of the indoor grill, it also helps to keep the top of the food warm while the bottom is in direct contact with the hot grill.

Grilled Fruit Kebabs, page 215

CHAPTER 11

Sweet Endings

SINCE THE ENTRÉE IS finished and the fire is still glowing, why not grill a sweet ending finale? This chapter offers some delicious choices. For something simpler, a slice of lightly grilled fresh fruit makes a wonderful dessert. Generally fruit cooks best over the last coals of the fire or at medium-low on a gas-fired grill.

Here are a few suggestions for simple grilled desserts:

Strawberries: Warm large strawberries slowly, turning a few times, until slightly soft. They are wonderful over ice cream – like a fresh strawberry sauce!

Thread strawberries on soaked wooden skewers; shake icing sugar over fruit. Place skewers on preheated grill sprayed with nonstick cooking spray. Close lid and cook for 2 minutes per side or until heated. Serve with angel or pound cake, drizzled with your favorite liqueur.

Bananas: Underripe bananas are best. Remove peel from one side and place, skin side down, on the grill. Cook for 5 minutes, sprinkle with a teaspoon of brown sugar, cook 5 minutes longer, then sprinkle the bananas lightly with rum as you serve them.

Apples: Peel a firm apple, such as a Granny Smith, and cut into thick horizontal slices. Sprinkle with lemon juice and granulated sugar, grill for about 5 minutes, and dust with cinnamon just before serving.

Grilled Cheese: Brush a Camembert cheese lightly with oil and grill for 3 minutes on each side. Serve at the end of a meal with fresh fruit.

In our home, the decision to grill dessert depends on how dirty the grill racks have become. Frequently we cook the entrée on one grill rack and leave the other rack clean for another course. Often I cook a conventional meal in the kitchen and then grill a sensually warm dessert. Mind you, this is easiest with a gas grill. Who would want to start up a charcoal grill just for dessert?

Flaming Blueberry Mango Crisp

Flaming adds a dramatic touch to this wildly delicious dessert.

Topping

¾ cup	dried crumbled macaroon cookies	175 mL
¼ cup	ground almonds	50 mL
2 tbsp	finely chopped candied orange peel	25 mL
2 tbsp	melted butter or margarine	25 mL

Fruit

2	large mangoes, peeled and cut into thick slices	2
1 cup	blueberries	250 mL
¼ cup	granulated sugar	50 mL
2 tbsp	each: orange liqueur and rum	25 mL

1 *For topping:* In bowl, combine macaroons, almonds, orange peel and melted butter; mix well.
2 *Fruit:* In shallow foil baking pan, arrange mango slices and blueberries; sprinkle with sugar and topping mixture.
3 Preheat grill on high. Place baking pan on grill rack. Close lid and cook (use Direct Grilling, page 7) for about 8 minutes or until fruit is warmed throughout. Heat liqueur and rum and ignite. Drizzle, flaming, over the fruit.
Makes 6 servings.

Variation: Peaches, nectarines, pears or apricots may also be used. Another variation is to substitute granola cereal for the macaroons and add 1/4 cup (50 mL) flaked coconut.

Strawberry Brochettes

Here is a lovely fruit to grill in the early summer when they are plump, juicy and full of flavor.

2 cups	firm whole strawberries	500 mL
¼ cup	brown sugar	50 mL
¼ cup	Grand Marnier liqueur	50 mL
	Sweetened whipped cream	

1 Wash and hull strawberries; dip while still moist into sugar. Thread onto 6 small metal or soaked wooden skewers. Place each skewer on double thickness of foil. Drizzle liqueur over fruit; seal edges of foil securely.
2 Preheat grill on high. Place packages on grill rack; close lid and cook (use Direct Grilling, page 7) for about 4 minutes or until fruit is warm. Remove from grill and serve in the packages. Pass a bowl of sweetened whipped cream.
Makes 6 servings.

Grilled Fruit Kebabs

Choose any combination of fresh fruits in season to grill on individual bamboo skewers, one for each guest. In season, strawberries are a marvelous replacement for apricots or plums.

½	fresh pineapple, peeled and cut into small wedges	½
2	bananas, peeled and cut into 4 pieces	2
6	apricots, halved and pitted	6
6	plums, halved and pitted	6
3	pears, cut into large pieces	3
2	oranges	2
½	lemon	½
¾ cup	granulated sugar	175 mL
¼ cup	dark rum	50 mL
1 tsp	ground nutmeg	5 mL

1 Place prepared fruit in large bowl. Remove zest from oranges and lemon and squeeze juice. Combine zest, juice, sugar and rum; stir into fruit mixture. Allow fruit and liquid to blend at room temperature for at least 30 minutes.

2 Drain fruit; reserve liquid. Thread fruit alternately on soaked wooden skewers. Preheat grill on medium; spray with nonstick coating. Place kebabs on grill rack; cook, uncovered, (use Direct Grilling, page 7) for about 10 minutes; brush occasionally with drained liquid. Turn skewers frequently.
Makes 10 to 12 servings.

Serving Suggestion: Serve with assorted flavors of ice cream.

Grilled Fruit and Maple Pizza

Gourmet flatbreads, so readily available in the stores, make excellent pizza bases. Here we use them to carry a grilled maple fruit topping.

⅓ cup	softened butter or margarine	75 mL
¼ cup	pure maple syrup	50 mL
½ tsp	ground cinnamon	2 mL
1	round plain Italian-style regular or thin flatbread (14 oz/400 g)	1
1	pear, cored and sliced	1
1	red-skinned apple, cored and sliced	1
1 cup	halved grapes or sliced peaches	250 mL
1 cup	halved strawberries	250 mL
	Fresh mint leaves	

1 Cream together butter, maple syrup and cinnamon until smooth. Pour onto pizza shell and spread almost to the edge. Spray flat baking pan with nonstick coating. Place shell on pan and arrange fruit in an attractive design covering the base of the shell.

2 Preheat grill on medium. Place baking pan on grill rack; close lid and cook (use Direct Grilling, page 7) for 10 minutes or until fruit is almost tender and butter mixture is melted. Remove to cutting board and cut into wedges to serve.
Makes 6 to 8 servings.

Serving Suggestion: Top with lemon gelato or vanilla ice cream.

Decadent Chocolate Fondue Sauce

Many people believe that chocolate is the perfect finish for a meal. Satisfy your yearning with this luscious chocolate sauce over cake, ice cream, frozen yogurt or as a fondue for dipping fresh fruit.

½ cup	chocolate chips	125 mL
¼ cup	butter or margarine	50 mL
½ cup	corn syrup	125 mL
½ cup	granulated sugar	125 mL
1	can (385 mL) low-fat evaporated milk	1
4 tsp	cornstarch	20 mL
2 tsp	vanilla or rum extract	10 mL

In small saucepan, melt chocolate chips and butter over medium-low heat. Stir in corn syrup and sugar. Gradually stir in milk and cornstarch. Cook gently over low heat for 5 minutes or until bubbly and smooth; stir frequently. Remove from heat, stir in vanilla. Cool before storing in covered container in refrigerator. Serve either cold or warm.
Makes 2 cups (500 mL).

Banana Boats: Another use for this sauce is with grilled bananas. Open banana peel to form a pocket, drizzle with sauce and add a few marshmallows. Seal bananas in foil pouches and grill for about 10 minutes. Yummy!

Tip: If you are eating outdoors, you can prepare this sauce at the grill just before dessert.

For a Mexican flavor, stir in some ground cinnamon.

Soused Dessert Kebabs with Caramel Sauce

Wonderful things happen to day-old pound cake and fruit kebabs at the grill. Add a drizzle of a favorite spirit at serving time along with a dab of caramel sauce and we have a new dessert dimension.

Caramel Sauce

1 cup	caramel candies	250 mL
¼ cup	butter or margarine	50 mL
½ cup	packed brown sugar	125 mL
½ cup	evaporated milk	125 mL
1 tsp	vanilla extract	5 mL

Fruits and Cake

1	medium banana	1
1	pear	1
12	strawberries	12
12	small mango wedges	12
½	pound cake, cubed	½
	Brandy, rum, or liqueur (optional)	

1 *For sauce:* In heavy saucepan, over low heat, melt caramel candies and butter. Stir in sugar and milk. Simmer until smooth and thickened; stir frequently. Remove from heat, stir in vanilla and reserve.

2 *For fruits and cake:* Cut banana into 12 pieces. Core and slice pear into 12 wedges. Stem strawberries. On 6 long metal or soaked wooden skewers, alternately thread banana, pear, strawberries, mango and cake cubes.

3 Preheat grill on medium; spray with nonstick coating. Place kebabs on grill rack. Close lid and cook (use Direct Grilling, page 7) for about 5 minutes or until cake is toasted and fruit is warm; turn once.

4 Remove fruit and cake from skewers to 6 serving plates, drizzle lightly with brandy, if using, and then with prepared caramel sauce.

Makes 6 servings.

Tip: Store any remaining caramel sauce tightly covered in the refrigerator. Of course, this sauce is wonderful on ice cream.

DIRECT GRILLING

Pineapple and Papaya Kebabs with Lime Rum Sauce

This tropical fruit mixture, served alone or with frozen yogurt or ice cream, adds a sprightly ending to a grilled meal.

2	medium papayas, peeled, seeded and cubed	2
2 cups	cubed fresh pineapple	500 mL
	Juice of 2 limes	
½ cup	water	125 mL
¼ cup	dark rum	50 mL
2 tsp	vanilla extract	10 mL
1 tsp	ground cinnamon	5 mL
¼ tsp	ground cloves	1 mL
½ cup	packed brown sugar	125 mL

1 Place fruit in a resealable plastic bag or shallow nonreactive dish. Combine lime juice, water, rum, vanilla, cinnamon and cloves. Pour over fruit, reseal bag and refrigerate for several hours. Remove fruit from marinade; reserve marinade. In a saucepan, bring marinade and brown sugar to a boil; reduce heat and simmer for about 10 minutes or until sugar is dissolved and sauce is golden. Remove from heat and cool.

2 Thread fruit on soaked wooden skewers. Preheat grill on medium heat; spray with nonstick coating. Place kebabs on grill rack; close lid and cook (use Direct Grilling, page 7) until golden brown; baste occasionally with sauce. Serve kebabs with remaining sauce.

Makes 6 servings.

Grilled Fresh Pineapple: Now that you are in the swing of grilling your desserts, it's time to try grilling a whole pineapple. Cut off crown and remove skin from pineapple. Place fruit on metal barbecue spit. Follow manufacturer's directions, taking care that the fruit is well secured by the prongs at each end of the spit. Make a basting sauce of equal parts lime juice, orange juice, rum and liquid honey. During grilling, brush the fruit often with the sauce. Sprinkle generously with nutmeg. To serve, slice the fruit crosswise into 1/2-inch (1 cm) thick slices and accompany with plain cake and ice cream, frozen yogurt or gelato. What a delicious ending for a meal!

Ginger Ricotta Cream for Grilled Fruit

Keep a container of this creamy ricotta in the refrigerator during the fruit growing season, and use it for a fast dessert with whatever fruit is on hand.

1	pkg (475 g) smooth ricotta cheese	1
¼ cup	icing sugar	50 mL
3 tbsp	finely chopped crystallized ginger	45 mL
1 tsp	each: grated lemon peel and vanilla extract	5 mL
	Fresh fruit: halved, cored pears, peaches, apples or nectarines	
2 tbsp	melted butter or margarine	25 mL
2 tbsp	lemon juice	25 mL
1 tbsp	liquid honey	15 mL
	Fresh mint sprigs	

1 In large bowl, cream together ricotta cheese and sugar until smooth. Stir in ginger, lemon peel and vanilla. Store in tightly sealed container in refrigerator for up to 2 weeks.

2 *Prepare fruit:* In medium bowl, combine butter, lemon juice and honey. Toss with fruit to coat; let stand at room temperature for 30 minutes or up to 3 hours.

3 Preheat grill on medium-high; spray rack with nonstick coating. Place fruit, skin side down, on rack. Close lid and cook (use Direct Grilling, page 7) for 10 minutes or until skin starts to turn golden brown. Turn and cook for 5 minutes or until tender. Place fruit on individual dessert plates; serve with a spoonful of ricotta mixture and garnish with a mint sprig.

Makes about 2 cups (500 mL) sauce, sufficient for 8 to 10 desserts.

Warm Sabayon Sauce

Sabayon is a rich French custard dessert frequently served as a sauce. In Italy it is called *zabaglione*.

6	egg yolks	6
⅓ cup	granulated sugar	75 mL
⅔ cup	sweet white wine*	150 mL

In a double boiler or heavy saucepan, beat egg yolks and sugar with an electric mixer until thick and light colored. Beat in wine. Place over simmering water; cook, beating constantly until thick and fluffy. Pour into a pitcher or over fresh fruit in serving bowls.

Makes about 1½ cups (375 mL).

* For an Italian *zabaglione*, use Marsala, Madeira or sherry

Tip: Leftover sauce is best kept refrigerated.

Decadent Chocolate Fondue Sauce, top left, page 216;
Warm Sabayon Sauce, bottom left, page 218

Author's Acknowledgements

All Fired Up! contains a grilling repertoire far beyond the summer backyard cookout. Writing it was a broadening experience that could never have happened without the help of many organizations and individuals to whom I owe my sincerest thanks.

First and foremost I wish to acknowledge and thank my husband John. With his two grills, a new rather deluxe model purchased for the project and the family's "old faithful," he was the key player in all grilling activities. When he was not grilling he used his considerable writing and editing skills to complete the manuscript.

I wish to thank the following organizations for information that proved to be of invaluable help.

Canadian Department of Fisheries and Oceans
University of California at Berkeley Wellness Letters
New England Journal of Medicine
Beef Information Centre
Ontario Pork Producers Marketing Board
Ontario Chicken Marketing Board
Ontario Sheep Marketing Agency
Diversified Laboratories for Canadian Turkey Marketing Agency, 1994.

I also wish to thank the following individuals:

Denise Schon for inviting me to undertake this book. I have enjoyed working with Denise again and with Anna Barron.

Book designer, Linda Gustafson, and copy editor and indexer, Ruth Pincoe, for transforming my manuscript into this handsome finished book.

Marian Hebb and associate Monique Van Remortel who always make the legalities go so smoothly.

Our son and daughter-in-law, Andrew Howard and Rachael Smith, who exercised their marketing expertise to suggest the title of the book.

Dietitian friend Linda Bumstead of the Bruce-Grey Owen Sound Health Unit for providing me with the most current information from The Canadian Cancer Society on carcinogens in grilled foods. This information was an important consideration in selecting grilling techniques.

Neighbours Lorna and John Towler who arranged for yet another grill for recipe testing. Manufactured in Europe by their friend Mike Linghorne, this marvelous and very versatile appliance gave us the opportunity to cook and test on yet another style of grill.

All the tasters who offered their helpful comments as they ate their way through many grilled meals during the spring and summer of 1997.

Index